THE BUTCHER SHOP GIRL

A MEMOIR FOR
MISFITS & MAVERICKS

Carmen Kissel-Verrier

 FriesenPress

Suite 300 - 990 Fort St
Victoria, BC, V8V 3K2
Canada

www.friesenpress.com

ISBN
978-1-5255-8821-1 (Hardcover)
978-1-5255-8820-4 (Paperback)
978-1-5255-8822-8 (eBook)

1. BIOGRAPHY & AUTOBIOGRAPHY, PERSONAL MEMOIRS

Distributed to the trade by The Ingram Book Company

For Tyler and Paytyne

For Elizabeth and Anita

How lucky for me, to have had you both, at your best.
Both prairie mothers from another time—soft as wild crocus petals in early
spring with spines strong as Canadian steel.

Thank you for being the exact definition of unconditional love.

AUTHOR NOTE

"Do not regard yourself as a victim for long. Easier said than done—agreed. Sit with your shame. Make friends with your regret. Then let them go. These two comrades are chains around your wrists that will steal from your brighter tomorrow.

I've yet to find much use for shame or regret.
Prickly and paralyzing, you'd do well to ditch them both, forever."

— CKV

DISCLAIMER

Memories of twenty-plus years past tend to compete—one on top of the others—for attention.

Maybe that's just pain and embarrassment trying to hide behind ego?

When you twist open the rusty jar lid of your brain's time capsule, some thoughts are as best as you can remember, while other scenes remain so clear—as if they were just a blink ago.

This is a work of creative non-fiction. All of the events in this memoir are true to the best of the author's memory. Some names have been changed to protect the identity of certain parties. The author in no way represents any company, corporation, or brand, mentioned herein. The views expressed in this memoir are solely those of the author. The author retells content as recalled and understands any discomfort subsequently created.

Some names are pseudonyms (in no particular order): Ryan, Jolene, Carl, Annika, Françoise, Shay, Tannis, Alexa, Sandy B. Mine, Mack, Best Entertainment, Twilight, Annie Munroe, Joey Amoure, Jared, John, Jim, Orland, Bear, Randy.

AUTHOR NOTED APPRECIATION

Thank you to the fabulous publishing team at FriesenPress! All of you were supportive of this memoir and worked very hard to bring it to readers. A very special note of gratitude for the incredibly talented *Janine Alyson Young* for sensitive and respectful editorial authority and guidance. Thank you to the lovely *Diane Cameron,* who expertly assists vulnerable "first-timers." I hope you know how truly wonderful you are.

A very special recognition goes to *Brenda Lee Kissel.* Thank you for always being "in my corner." For everyone in my immediate family and in my gigantic extended families—thank you for your cheers of support! We are a powerful tribe filled with survivors. **Sean**, you've encouraged me to "keep going" on every wild idea that I've had for twenty years. Thank you to infinity—I love you so much. **Kelly**, you cheer the loudest for me, even when I've fallen flat on my face. You have no idea how much I appreciate our thirty years of friendship, thank you.

CONTENTS

ESCAPING BOLIVIA 1

HILL AND VALLEY RANCH, EST. 1950 26

DIVORCE, CONGLOMERATES, AND DARGIS LAND & CATTLE . . . 39

LIFE AT HOME 60

BOOM AND BUST 74

BACK ON THE FARM 90

YOUNG ANARCHIST 112

ADULTING 123

FRIENDS IN LOW PLACES 147

INTO THE CLUBHOUSE 170

SOUTHPAW TOUR 188

AFTER BOLIVIA 210

CROSSING BORDERS 233

CURTAIN CALL 251

THE
BUTCHER
SHOP
GIRL

1

ESCAPING BOLIVIA

*"A man attaches himself to a woman—
not to enjoy her, but to enjoy himself."*
—Simone De Beauvoir

HEAT GRIPPED SANTA CRUZ, BOLIVIA, with a sultry heaviness, even in the early hours. I looked at the room where I'd stayed for the past week, half my things still scattered across the floor, and knew I had no choice but to go.

"Come with me, Jacey. We have to get out of here now."

She looked at me, confused and exhausted from a full night of performances, and said, "I just don't understand why they would do this. They already have my passport."

"I know, but they don't have mine. Elena is trying to keep us here. She needs my passport to do that. All of this is wrong and about to get worse, Jacey. We should be *free* to leave anytime that we want! Look, do you remember that guy that I met in the club the other night? He told me where to get help, and I'm out of here, and *you* need to come with me."

"I'm not going," she said, bewildered. "It's all just too much."

"Fine, I'm not begging you," I said. "I'll go without you and I'm going right now."

We'd only met the week before on the plane, and I felt bad leaving her alone, but not bad enough to stay. I heaved the heavy wooden window shutter up and crept out the window and accessed the roof. I quietly teetered across the roofline pitch. I couldn't exit from the guest room door as I suspected that we were being watched. The sounds of traffic and the chaotic city reverberated through the night, but I moved as quietly as possible toward the fifteen-foot-high wall surrounding the compound. This same wall they'd told me would keep me safe was now like a prison holding me in. Shards of glass embedded in the top were like razor wire. My pink hard-shell suitcase, which I'd packed haphazardly in my rush, bumped against my legs as I crossed the roof to the wall. I lifted it up above my head and tossed it over, a silence followed by the thump of the case hitting the ground on the other side. I looked over my shoulder, then up at the wall, where the glass shards promised to cut me apart if my hand slipped or made a wrong move. Then I jumped up and grabbed the top of the wall. Using all my adrenaline and strength, I shimmied up and over. When my feet hit the dusty ground on the other side, I picked up my suitcase, and ran as fast as I could in the direction where the most lights were on. Blood dripped from my palms down to my fingertips.

At the corner, I hailed a passing cab. When he stopped, I got in and slammed the door and remembered to breathe perhaps for the first time since climbing out the window. My suitcase handle was bloody. I frantically hunched down in the cab, checking over my shoulder for anyone coming out of the compound.

"Can you take me to the US consular agency?" I told the expectant cab driver.

"No Englais," he said.

I dug through my purse and desperately produced the paper Tom had given me hours before. There was an address scribbled on it, and as soon as I gave it to the cab driver, he nodded and pulled away. A wave of relief came over me, but I was still so worried that the embassy wouldn't help me or that no one would be there. I yanked the long sleeve of my camel-coloured shirt from my arms and balled the extra fabric into my palms to stop the bleeding. A quick glance confirmed that there were only a few surface cuts that should stop bleeding soon. The car moved through the streets, and I watched the city pass through the windows—the goat farms, the walled-in compounds, the sidewalk markets, and the dark storefronts. This had been my first taste of the developing world, and even after a week, it overwhelmed me. It was almost as disorienting as the events that had led me to this hurried escape.

§

I first heard about these international trips in the dressing rooms, where the muffled sounds from the stage underscored shop talk. We'd be changing costumes or getting ready for a show, and girls would talk about going abroad for club openings and coming home with enough cash to buy a Lexus. Working the circuit in Western Canada as an exotic entertainer meant my coworkers on any given night were a rotating cast of girls from all over the country. Some clubs paid more or attracted a wealthier clientele, making them more desirable to work. And we all learned how to get ahead and make more money in the business by talking to the other girls. They'd say things like, "I was in Berlin for two weeks at this club opening. I was making so much money I wanted to extend my contract." The Canadian circuit offered big money, but the bigger money existed in high-end club openings abroad. And I wanted in.

Getting booked for these contracts meant getting in with the other big agency in Canada, Best Entertainment in Vancouver. A port city, Vancouver offered the international bridge to the rest of the world. And club owners from the farthest reaches of the world can't get enough Western World girls. Our skin, our hair, our brash attitudes. In the late 1990s Canadian exotic entertainers came highly desired because we tried hard and came ready with highly coordinated choreography and costumes. And because we took it all off with explosive, energetic sets filled with vibrant variety.

Dancing was easy for me because of years spent as a classically trained ballerina. The formal study of ballet is extremely disciplined. The epitome of top-class designation in dance. I ended up showcasing the complete opposite of that as an exotic entertainer. I always felt that the contradiction of my classically trained years as a ballerina really gave me the skills to crush it as *this kind* of entertainer. A "head start" apprenticeship, if you will. As long as I could look to the left and look to the right and not see anyone I knew from back at home, I could lose myself in the work on the stage, using all my talents and flexibility skills.

Enticed by these lucrative international opportunities, I sent my promo kit—headshot, body shot, and resume—to Best Entertainment and got a meeting. I had never worked for them before. But in their eyes, I wasn't perfect. My face and reputation as an entertainer preceded me, which was probably why they agreed to meet with me. But my breasts weren't as big as they typically liked. Mine were perky, 34 B-cups, nicely shaped. Good enough for a shot, they said, but not perfect. They said they'd try me out on a club opening in Santa Cruz, Bolivia. And if I did well there, they'd consider me for other, higher-scale events.

When you're nineteen, there's a lot you don't know. I was tough, but I didn't know anything, especially having never left Canada. But to me, fresh off the farm, Santa Cruz sounded like an oceanfront paradise. They upsold it as an opportunity for me to see how they operated. I didn't realize until after I signed the contract that Santa Cruz is completely landlocked and poverty-ridden. And I never considered the danger I might be putting myself in. With organized crime groups running our booking agencies, it wouldn't be hard to guess that criminal club owners might be in contact with other organized crime groups for their entertainment needs. But I never thought to worry about that. I took the six-week contract. Even if it wasn't the most lucrative job in the world, it would be an experience. And I was definitely looking for those.

§

A few weeks later, I was on a plane to Bolivia with two other girls on the same contract. One was the feature entertainer, Heather, who was over-the-top gorgeous with extra-large fake breasts. She was probably twenty-seven or twenty-eight years old, which was like being forty in this business. And she was the main blonde bombshell event. Then there was a girl named Jacey from Boise, Idaho. I'd never worked with an American girl before, and Jacey came off a bit odd. She looked like a beatnik wearing all hemp clothing, a fact she quickly pointed out to me, and drank from a silver cup that dangled off her hiker-style backpack. Jacey couldn't stop talking about the salt flats of Bolivia and maybe getting the chance to venture outside of the city to find good hiking. I rolled my eyes and assumed she was born and raised in a concrete city. Nature nuts are always from the city. Farm kids hop on a four-wheeler every day.

Girls in our business were very competitive if they didn't know each other; they didn't become instant friends on the plane and gab all the way there. They were borderline cutthroat. We were travelling with a handler from the agency, who was with us to make sure we got there safely and to manage us while we settled in. Eddie, the agent accompanying us, had the same used-car salesman feel as my agent, Carl, in Edmonton. He was polite, and very upbeat, and told us how much we were going to *love* this new club and its sexy owner, Elena, whom he'd met in Los Angeles at one of the Best Entertainment satellite agencies. These agents loved to make it seem like they were in it for us, there to protect us and make us happy, when really all they cared about was fulfilling the contract and getting that big remaining deposit money—balance due.

As the plane took off, I was excited. Eddie was excited. Even stone-cold Heather cracked a smile. Still, I was concerned with the club details and listened intently to what Eddie had to say about the club and ownership group; that's where the gold was. I was going to make a lot of money and I couldn't wait to get to my honeypot.

Money is the only thing a girl truly needs to survive on her own. Definitely not men, maybe not even family, but *money*. At nineteen, so far I knew that much about life. I was used to making big money.

I also knew how to make and multiply money too. My family started up businesses for breakfast. I wasn't worried about money. Still, I needed it to dodge away from home and to afford to stay away for an indefinite amount of time.

I struggled to make authentic connections with people. If they were left bolstered after an experience with me, that was a ruse for them, with typically little benefit for me. And I was tired of it in my regular off-work life. Working as much as I could allowed me to tune out and focus on easier necessary elements of my life, like shoring up capital to survive. My job required bursts of gregariousness and came with lots of moments filled with solitude. I liked those the best.

Bolivia was completely mercenary to me, otherwise nowhere near my top-ten list of destinations. Just another job and another way to make more money with a hit of adventure. Up until now my job hadn't required global travel. It could have been Timbuktu and I'd have taken the job if it looked remotely fiscally promising.

We flew from Vancouver to Panama. Along the long, intercontinental flight I smoked Player's Light cigarettes and watched the world pass through the window. In Panama, we stepped onto the tarmac to grab our final flight to Santa Cruz, Bolivia. It was dark and sticky-humid and hot. We next boarded a twin prop vessel with seating for fifty. It was a jalopy plane that instantly felt unsafe. Joining in on everyone else's nonchalance, we loaded up single-file through the very rear of this vessel, literally from the anus of this plane, not a side door. It looked like a cargo entrance. Once plateaued on the center aisle, we walked past chickens in cages, and two extra fat pigs also in cages, squealing and grunting. I began to pick at my fingernails anxiously with my thumbnail, trying to look relaxed as we found our seats closer to the cockpit. It was a short flight, and all the prerecorded flight information was Spanish, and no one demonstrated the seatbelts routine or indicated where the emergency exits were. Anxiety, my old friend, crept up with that familiar skin-prickling effect of cortisol rushing onto my capillaries. I became very scared of this bizarre plane and the upcoming flight experience. I popped my head up and counted from my row . . . how many rows I would be away from the door if we crashed and I needed to find an exit in the dark. Four—I was four rows away from the nearest exit.

Sometimes as a kid I was secretly OCD. This is the undesired bane of existence for any Virgo child. I lifted my feet slightly over train tracks and wouldn't step on a sidewalk crack and blew ten whisper kisses at every graveyard passed on the open road. I bit my fingernails down to the quick, and picked all the skin around my nails off until they bled and became very sore. It was worse when I was little and disappeared when I started getting acrylic nails. But this kind of panic called for something to help calm me down. Before this flight would take off, I created a secret flying ritual. Rituals help people with OCD. Your brain tells you that if you do this "one thing or sequence of things" every time you need to get through something scary—that you'll be fine. It provides this weird sense of justification that allows you to calm down and trust your own weird process, whether it be turning a door handle three times to the left before you open the door, or washing your hands a certain way. I looked around and all I saw was the seat pocket airline magazine in front of me. I pulled it out and looked out the window for anything stuck in the ground that would "ground" me. It couldn't be something built on top of the ground, but inside the ground, something that was structural or supporting something with ground strength. I saw a four-foot-tall parking blockade post; that would do. And I kept my eyes on it as I blindly felt to the last page of the magazine, fixated on the concrete post with my eyes. I felt for the second-last page and opened it, then the third-last page and opened it, while never looking at the magazine. I promised to myself to not look at the magazine pages to cement my new weird safety ritual. I then placed the closed magazine in the seat pocket and pulled on the elastic pocket three definite times, one, two, three. I then closed my eyes and I said one Lord's prayer and one Hail Mary in my head. I then asked God to protect my brother at home, and to watch over me until I landed safely back in Canada in six more weeks.

When we arrived in Bolivia, the club owner, Elena, had a car waiting for us at the shabby airport. All of us piled our suitcases filled with props and costumes into the rundown van. We stuffed into the van with little room for shoulders and legs. The sights overwhelmed me—the streets were crowded and chaotic and loud. This was my first time seeing anything like South America at all. When you're born and raised where I was born and raised, there's zoning: the business section of a town and the residential section of town. In Santa Cruz, there was no zoning. There was a goat farm right downtown next to an auto repair shop. I was shocked. I'd never seen anything like it. All was a mashup of themes and lifestyles competing for relevance. And seeing it rush past through the window of the car made me wonder for the first time what I'd really gotten myself into. With all of my girlfriends' stories ringing in my ears about how great going abroad was for them, I decided not to be so negative or scared. At the same time, I never put together that Berlin was probably a lot different than Santa Cruz.

After this eye-opening drive, we arrived at the club owner's compound. It sat in the middle of this crazy, no-zoning city, and was fortified by a fifteen-feet-high cement wall, encrusted along the top with shards of green and white glass. Big spikey chunks of glass, broken up from used soda bottles.

"What are these walls about?" I said to Eddie. He was a short man with a slight build and a weasel-like presence. He made me feel like my gut was being fooled, but otherwise gave no indication of insincerity.

"Well," he said, "it's South America, honey. We've got trash on the outside and paradise on the inside of these walls." Anytime any of us expressed doubt about what we were doing, he just talked up Elena. "She's absolutely wonderful. You'll love it here. Her staff is going to wait on you hand and foot. You'll have your own rooms and bathrooms."

He was right. The chaos and clutter of Santa Cruz fell silent when we entered Elena's luxury compound. Inside the walls were gardens and a beautiful Spanish Colonial mansion with a bright white stucco facade and clay roof tiles the colour of tanned leather. Our accommodation was an adjacent guesthouse that had five bedrooms, each with a private bathroom and balcony. There was a courtyard in the center, and the buildings were old, but I was sure it was very luxurious especially by Bolivian standards.

Breezing down a semi-circular suspended staircase, Elena welcomed us to Bolivia and her home with arms open wide. Draped in gold at the wrists and fingers tipped with a French manicure, she was a stunning Latina who had bright hazel eyes and a smile that revealed all her perfect teeth. Hers was the kind of beauty and perfection that money buys, from her bleached highlights to her enhanced breasts. She was very fit and her toned shoulders peaked out of her glamorous asymmetrical neckline top.

Elena explained how critical we were to the success of her new club. She'd done a lot to promote the opening and drum up excitement. There had never been an adult club like this in Santa Cruz, and she'd started an initiative to bring this kind of business to the city.

"I made promises to people that the whole city would benefit from bringing this business to Santa Cruz," she said in near-perfect English. "And I have promised the most beautiful and talented American entertainers. I need this to work, and I'm counting on you."

Standing there in the courtyard, surrounded by a lush garden and pillared house and flanked by her staff of housekeepers, Elena's presence commanded attention. She may have been only in her twenties, but she dripped money. Weary from a full day of travel and shock at seeing the developing world for the first time, my relief that we were staying in a nice place outweighed any concerns I had when, casually and as if it were all part of arriving and settling in, Elena said, "Let me have your passports, for safekeeping."

"Okay." Jacey dug into her bag and handed hers over. "Here you go."

"Hell, no," Heather, the feature entertainer, said. "My passport stays with me, always."

Elena blinked but didn't falter and turned to me.

Grabbing a clue from Heather, I said, "That's okay. I think I'll hang on to mine."

§

The next night, opening night at the club, I tucked my passport in my bag before leaving Elena's compound. It may have had only one stamp, but something told me I should keep it on me at all times. A car carried Heather, Jacey, and me to the club, where we became part of the flurry of activity preparing for the first night. Outside, the venue was tall, dark, and nondescript. Inside, the purply-red velvet fabric covered the walls and rope lights trimmed the aisles, bar, and stage. The floor sloped downward from the back of the room toward the stage, like a theater, and we had a dressing room in the back with easy access to the stage. While Eddie, our handler, and the club manager worked out how everything would work for the opening night show, I looked around for somewhere to stash my passport while I was on stage. I thought it might be too easy for others to find if tucked in my makeup bags in the dressing room. I found a pile of boxes and props behind the stage that looked like no one had touched in years. The building must have been a theater they'd retrofitted into a strip club. When no one was looking, I stuck my passport in there, and then got ready for my performance.

The club was packed, wall to wall, with people. The music—American hits with a Latin flair, like Ricky Martin's "Livin' La Vida Loca" and Carlos

Santana and Rob Thomas's "Smooth"—throbbed and the lights flashed. Jacey and I watched the feature open up the night from behind the stage with her Marilyn Monroe show, watched the patrons dropping bills at her feet, and felt like we were about to become *rich*.

That night, we all took our turns on the stage, making what appeared to be huge amounts of money. When the show was over and the crowd thinned to no one, a car took us from the club back to the compound. Then the three of us sat down together and counted our piles of cash. Jacey and I were giddy and buzzing off the energy from a successful and incredible opening night. But right away Heather, our unofficial house-mom, said, "This looks like a lot of money, girls. But if you convert bolivianos to Canadian or US currency, it's practically nothing."

Jacey and I looked at her.

"It's actually worse than the Mexican peso." She tucked her neat pile of bills into her bag. "There's no way I'm staying here for six weeks. I saw a travel agency not far from here. I'm going to get my return ticket changed ASAP."

Breaking my contract hadn't occurred to me, but as soon as she said that, I started calculating how much I'd make if I did stay for all six weeks. It wasn't anything fantastic, and it wasn't more than I could make back in Canada. I liked adventure too, but not more than making money.

The next morning snuck up on me after that busy first night. I was up before the other girls, and went looking for breakfast. The maid in the main house did not speak English at all. A blank stare is all that I got when I politely asked for something to eat. Only after I motioned food to mouth did she clue in and guide me back out to the courtyard garden. I followed her to a grand table setting of a five-star breakfast complete with croissants and fresh papaya and ham. It was glorious and beautifully set in the sunshine. When the other girls woke up, they found me and settled down at the table. We gathered our wits about us, and our conversation quickly turned to getting out of Santa Cruz. Heather insisted that she was slipping away that day, before we went into work that night. "You two should come with me."

"I don't know." I'd seen the travel agency she was talking about. The shabby storefront, papered with faded travel posters, didn't look like the kind of place I trusted to get me where I needed to go. "Maybe I'll wait and see how it works out for you. It's pretty nice here. I might not make a lot of money, but this is like a paid vacation with maids," I quipped.

"Suit yourself," she said, with her cool, characteristic detachment. "Just don't lose your passport, dummy."

The three of us went to work that afternoon, and the subject of leaving didn't come up again. But the next morning, I woke up early. On my way to my private bathroom, I passed Heather coming out of her room, suitcases in hand.

"What are you doing?" I asked, still tired and unaware.

"I got my return tickets changed yesterday and I'm out of here," she huffed. She took a cab to the airport, and I never saw Heather again. This panicked me but I decided to give it a shot. It was only day three.

§

The language barrier made mingling with the crowds after my show awkward. If the men did speak English, it was broken and difficult to follow. Like any crowd in any club, there was a mix of wealthy and blue-collar patrons. There were men who seemed comfortable, and men who seemed like they'd been dragged out by their friends. Whenever I pulled out a cigarette, someone always had a lighter ready. They were kind and treated me with great respect. Even the local go-go dancer girls seemed to be enthralled and intimidated by us. They danced on side stages in between our feature shows to keep the crowd and club vibe going. But since we couldn't really talk, they just stared, awestruck, like they'd never seen anything like me before. Funny to me, when they danced to English songs, they mouthed the words perfectly. Music is borderless like that. These local girls had all those famous Latina curves and perfectly plump bums. They were stunning and I laughed that their own local men didn't seem to notice. The local Latino businessmen patrons in the club treated them like servants and me like a star.

When I came across a white guy with dirty-blonde hair and hazel-green eyes speaking English to his friend, I was so excited I went straight to their table and pulled up a chair.

"It is so amazing to see someone speaking English," I said. "Do you mind if I just sit with you and have a conversation? I need to talk to someone from my side of the planet, just for a bit."

"Not at all," Tom, the white guy, said, introducing himself.

His accent said southern American, so I asked where they were from. Tom was from Florida, and the other guy was from Louisiana. Santa Cruz wasn't exactly an American vacation hotspot, so I asked what in the world they were doing in Bolivia. And that's when they loosely explained, as secretive as cops can be, that they worked for US Customs in drug enforcement. At first, this didn't mean much to me, but Tom leaned in and whisper-explained that they were in town working to prevent large-scale drug operations from coming into the United States. They even carried badges. Not knowing anything about the drug business, I said, "Shouldn't you be in Columbia, then? Isn't that, like, the cocaine capital of the world?"

They both looked at me like I was an amusing but stupid kid. "Yes," Tom chuckled. "But a lot of people don't know that just as much cocaine is grown in Bolivia. And even when they grow the cocaine in Columbia, they move it to Bolivia for processing because labour is cheap and control measures are easy for drug cartels to manage."

"Wow, that seems very serious," I said wide-eyed. I may not have known much about the drug trade, but I could tell that Tom wasn't the kind of guy who usually hung around strip clubs. "Are you enjoying the show?"

"Of course," Tom said, looking sideways and mildly embarrassed. Most men don't object to looking at beautiful naked women, but he struck me as the kind of guy who'd had a hard day at work and ended up check-ing out the new club at the insistence of his friend. You could always tell with a group of bachelor party guys, college guys, or business guys that there was usually one or two who the rest of the group had to drag out. Tom gave off that vibe. "How about you? Are you enjoying your stay in Santa Cruz?"

"Honestly, I haven't seen much of the city. I'm nervous to leave the place where I'm staying because I don't know Spanish, and everything is so different. I'm bilingual, I speak French and that is kinda helping me get by here in Spanish-land," I joked, feeling so good to speak English to someone.

"You know, there aren't many English-speaking girls for us to talk to around either," Tom said. "If you're up for it, maybe I could take you around the city tomorrow."

"I don't know," I said, hesitating because I was, in general, wary of men and offers like this.

"No pressure," he said. "Just a walk around and something to eat. I'll give you my number and you can think about it."

"Sure, that would be great." He was a cop, after all.

He wrote down the number at his hotel and gave it to me.

The next morning, I got up early and excited to get in touch with Tom and his sexy southern accent. I wanted him to talk to me all day. The housekeeper, who barely understood me, helped me figure out how to make a phone call to the La Quinta Hotel where Tom was staying and what callback number I should leave. I left him a message and he called me right back. "Why don't you meet me in the lobby of my hotel?"

I agreed and caught a cab. I never understood what cab drivers were trying to say. I usually ended up tossing a fistful of dollars their way until they seemed satisfied. From Tom's hotel, we set out on a city promenade. I wore an Edmonton Oilers hockey T-shirt and cutoff jean shorts. And Tom wore khaki cargo shorts and a linen button-up shirt with pilot-like Ray-Ban sunglasses. He had a small bulge from the back of his shirt that I suspected was a handgun.

We had an amazing time together, walking around the city, talking, and getting to know each other. I remember many moments of high contrast: we saw vendors selling beautiful tropical flowers, artfully displayed, but then moments later ran across the most deplorable beggars I'd ever seen. A man with no legs and only one arm, his begging cup arm. It looked like polio had ripped through this country hard. It was remarkable how this mashup of natural unkempt vegetation could instantly contrast with the dirtiest of dirt underfoot. We walked across a bridge where below, instead of a river, a solid concrete ravine held only a few inches of dirty, murky water. This was unlike anything I'd ever seen, coming from the clean countryside and cities of Canada.

Tom, as my tour guide, was very experienced with South America. He hadn't told me so, but he showed it in his comfort with being around so many disabled beggars. His Spanish was fluent enough to converse with local vendors or in stores as we browsed and set out to find me a disposable camera. I asked where he had learned all of his Spanish and he noted simply from many tours in and around South America and self-study to help him improve in his job.

I told him that I was pissed with our housemaid as I felt that she was rude and uncaring and stealing our clothes. My upper-middle-class upbringing made me a bit of a cocky kid more often than I cared to admit. As soon as I blurted out my disdain for the housemaid he gently reminded me that perhaps I was being unkind, even a bit self-entitled. I pointed out that she was probably behind our missing clothing pieces, like my beloved vintage Club Monaco sweater and Victoria's Secret pajamas. Still, I felt instantly embarrassed at my lack of empathy; he challenged me gently and did not care to hang off my every word, as was my previous experience with most men. I liked that about him, very much.

I shared with him that although you couldn't tell a lick from sound, that I spoke French fluently with a Parisian flair. Half my family was extremely French, descendants from France, not Quebec. He asked me to prove it, and I prattled off a paragraph asking where I could find a camera and gave a detailed update of the weather, hoping that would impress him and help him forget my previous insensitivity. I didn't want him to think I was rude at the core (although I certainly could be at times, never for sport, but rather self-defence). I was a scrappy, take-your-eye-out kinda girl if needed.

You can tell a lot about people by how they treat others. Tom was friendly, smiley, and encouraging when vendors shied away from speaking any English words. He explained to me that the ability to speak English revealed class. I never thought that knowing English was anything special, but he reminded me about how much of an asset that was to these people. He explained that all these people here desired to know English.

He then reminded me that perhaps the reason my clothes went missing was because the maid thought I was a bit of a princess who needed a correction. Taking Tom's advice to heart, I then resolved the next time that I saw her to exchange English words for Spanish words. This would be my approach to attempt to get her to like me a bit more and to subsequently stop stealing my clothes.

Burger King had just opened in the city, which was a big deal, according to one of the housekeepers at Elena's. Tom and I decided to check it out because I craved something familiar.

Even in such a foreign city, the Burger King looked like every other Burger King everywhere, with illuminated menus behind the counter, bold logos, and drink fountains. We ordered our burgers and fries and slid into a hard booth by the window.

"This is the weirdest Whopper ever," Tom said after washing his first bite down with his Coke. The Cokes were also too syrupy, and the fries were different too.

"It is, isn't it?" I watched a Bolivian woman pass on the sidewalk outside. Her full skirt had faded from wear, and she carried a sling on her back. A small, thin boy walked alongside her, and reached for her hand when they went to cross the street. "The housekeeper where I'm staying said her daughter wants to come here for her birthday party. But she said it would take a whole month's salary. So, it's Burger King, but it's ridiculously expensive for the people who live here."

"Where are you staying, again?"

I told Tom all about Elena our club owner and hostess and her luxurious compound, with the high walls, gardens, and full staff of housekeepers and our luxury breakfasts.

"She sounds exactly like a cartel princess."

"What do you mean?"

"Like she has a well-connected father or uncle or someone in the cartel," he said. "This is South America. Anybody who's got that kind of wealth here, 99 percent of the time that's coming from some sort of drug income."

I never would have made this connection, but his concern seemed to grow when I told him that she'd tried to take all our passports. "One of the girls actually changed her return flight and left after three days."

"Honestly, I don't think this is a safe situation for you," he said. "Maybe take a cue from the girl who left. Please promise me that you keep alert and stay aware of suspicious behaviour."

We finished our lunch and parted ways, making plans to see each other again the following day. The more I thought about it, the more Tom's concern made me nervous. Early the next morning, I left the compound and walked to the travel agency that Heather used, where they helped me book a return flight in a few days. With the end of my Bolivian adventure in sight, I carried on as if nothing had changed. I thought it'd be best to just leave like Heather and to not alarm Elena beforehand. I asked Tom to come see me again that night, which he did, and we made plans to spend the following day—Sunday, my day off—together. And he was the only one I told about my plans to leave. At least at first.

§

In case Elena was not a cartel princess who deserved the benefit of the doubt, I didn't feel right leaving suddenly. I concocted an excuse about my father being sick and my family needing me back at home. When I told Elena that I was leaving, she asked again for my passport. "I need you to fulfill your promise to me that you will stay here and help me open my club."

"I'm sorry, but I can't. I have to go." I looked at the floor, terrified after Tom mentioned the cartel.

"You don't understand how my reputation is at stake." She looked me directly in the eye when she spoke. "It would look terrible for me if only one of the three girls perform for five more weeks. It would be disastrous."

"I'm sorry," I said. "I just can't really make that my concern. Thank you for your hospitality, but I need to get home. And Jacey's going to stay," I said enthusiastically, trying to upsell boring bits Jacey.

Elena's brow furrowed in anger. "I need someone besides Jacey."

"I guess I can think about it."

"We can talk about it more in the morning," she said. "Just promise me you won't take off like the other girl."

"Okay, yes, of course."

The next morning came with sunrise, but even the sunshine didn't make me feel better or less worried. Aside from what Tom told me about her possibly being attached to the cartel, Elena had not been unkind or inhospitable. She'd been straightforward and even admirable in how she handled herself and her business. I got dressed and ready to leave to meet Tom, assuming that I'd run into Elena. Maybe I could straighten it all out with her. When I went downstairs to call the cab, I couldn't find Elena. Then I left the compound to meet Tom.

Before we left on our walk, Tom invited me up to his room as he had to get a few things prepared before we toured. He seemed well-intentioned and I gut-trusted him. Once in his room, he hid something wrapped tightly in a bundle and pulled out his work gun. I had never seen a handgun in my life, ever. Only hunting rifles. I expressed this and asked why he had to hide the mystery bundle, and he explained his distrust for hotel room privacy.

"What about here?" I motioned to a wall cupboard.

He said most people would easily guess that spot if they were looking for something valuable. Then he pulled the chair over to the wall and stood on it to reach a high air vent near the ceiling. He popped the vent cover and hid the mystery bundle there.

I was blown away at what my naïve self just witnessed. Guns, handsome, strong, tall, and safe. This would be a great Sunday spent getting to know him more.

We spent the day together as planned, exploring Santa Cruz and talking about all his travels for work. He never went into detail about his job, and I sensed that I shouldn't ask, although I was completely curious! I took pictures as we walked with my new disposable camera—the kind you click and then have to wind again to set up the next shot. We talked and laughed about how different life at home was from life in Santa Cruz.

Then, I tried to use my ATM card and noticed that it was not linking to my account in Canada. I had lots of Bolivian money from tips from performances and resolved to use that while here. But I noticed that everything cost thousands of bolivianos, even fast food. At this rate, I would be out of bolivianos shortly.

Because he was twelve years older than me, Tom was different from any man I'd ever dated. He didn't ask my age, but I ordered alcoholic drinks at lunch to perpetuate the illusion of being older than nineteen. The drinking age in Alberta, Canada, was eighteen, but I knew it was twenty-one in the United States where Tom lived. During our time, he didn't even once joke about my profession, and he treated me like a lady through and through. And I found myself completely smitten with him. He had a fabulous vocabulary, an even better body, and his southern syrupy drawl was completely disarming. He was strong and capable, and made me feel incredibly safe. While crossing the street, he stepped ahead, cleared the way, and grabbed my hand like a gentleman.

After our walk we returned back to his room. I knew instantly that I wanted him to touch me and hoped that he wanted to. Without saying a word, knowing and feeling our joint desire, we collapsed into each other's arms and made love over and over again throughout the night, stopping only to catch our breaths and to learn more about each other with our hands and head-to-head whispers. He didn't mind that I smoked cigarettes during our breaks, even though he only smoked cigars occasionally. Cigars, of course. He was a debonair combination of Ralph Lauren and GI Joe.

I never thought I would see him again. We had such a great, fast-colliding time together in an unlikely circumstance in an unlikely place—a first for me in many things. He was unafraid and unbiased about my job. Almost every man is off-the-charts insecure if their girlfriend is a stripper. But Tom was unconcerned and very mature within himself. This shocked me; a total first in terms of how I looked at men. Knowing I was leaving in a few days and that I had no money, except for what would exchange to about twenty-five dollars, Tom offered to give me money to travel home. I was instantly mortified. I refused it. I could not possibly think of taking money, not even with the promise of paying him back. The idea of taking his money abhorred me even though I would snatch it from scads of other men in the clubs before they knew it was missing. This was how I knew that I felt differently about Tom.

He was worried that I might have trouble leaving Elena's if I didn't play it cool enough. He worried that she was smart and cunning. I told him not to worry and to shush as I started to kiss him again. I gave him my phone number in Canada, and he told me that he'd looked but couldn't find a Canadian embassy in the city. So, he gave me the address for the US consulate office in Santa Cruz and said that the United States had an agreement to help Canadian citizens abroad. So even though I wasn't American, if I got into serious trouble I could contact them, explain my situation, and they would have to help me. He said I should call them for an escort instead of taking a cab to the airport and waiting in the terminal—where I could be in trouble if Elena decided not to let me go.

But even though he offered, I didn't see any need for all that. I was tough; I could handle it. I said goodbye, and he reluctantly let me go.

§

I didn't see Elena again until that night at the club. Our dancer dressing room was up a small flight of stairs in a windowless loft. Along one wall, five mirrors surrounded by incandescent lightbulbs hung over a continuous counter. A long, musty and dusty purple velvet sofa lined the opposite wall, covered in the same velvet as the club walls.

With a special I'm-outta-here show in mind, I was determined to take Heather's place as the feature entertainer for the last few days at the club. I would knock their socks off tonight with my water show and I would keep Elena fooled that I would stay. This would shake her off my back, I was certain. I instructed the stage hands to fetch me a sizable pail of water with a string long enough for me to reach it and instructed them to mount the full bucket of water at the top of their centre stage brass pole. Then I set to work getting ready for my show-stopping set. I applied extra-heavy smoky eye makeup and reached for my curling iron to smooth my very long humidity-attacked chestnut brown hair. As I picked up the curling iron, the handle felt hotter than usual, but I proceeded to curl. Three curls in, while the hair section was wrapped, the iron portion completely detached from the handle and grey goo dripped out of the iron, almost getting on the rest of my hair and dressing robe.

Jacey laughed so hard and explained that I would need a voltage converter in South America. Their voltage and wattage were completely different here. She lent me her iron. She laughed again; I suspected at me, not with me.

Then Elena exploded into the dressing room and demanded to me, "Where's your passport?"

"Well," I lied, "I don't have it with me here. It's back at the compound, and don't worry I decided to stay."

"I don't think so," she said, confused. Elena's tone was a bit panicked and ballsy. It was the first sign of tough I noticed from her. "We checked your room and we couldn't find it anywhere."

"Oh." I feigned surprise at her difficulty in finding it. This was when all my suspicions culminated in the understanding: She was definitely trying to keep me in the country! She reminded me of a capitalist who was chill and cool as cucumber until you threaten her money-making ability. Kinda like I regarded myself. I had seen her type before—she reminded me of a few Hells Angels biker bitches that I knew from back home. Even though she was fancy, I felt that she was not to be provoked further. "That's weird. I'll have to think about where I put it, but like I said, Elena, I'm going to stay."

Just then the club manager came in and said something in Spanish that I vaguely understood to be a pressing issue. Frustration flashed across Elena's face and she looked back at me. "We'll talk more later."

Because I went on stage last that night, I thought to give this crowd a taste of true Canadian exotic entertainment where no crazy antics would be spared. Upon my third song of a four-song set, down to only a sparkly bra and matching thong, as the signature tempo ramped up to the explosive chorus of EMF's "Unbelievable" pounded in their ears, I pulled the water pail string and was sexily doused with cascading water. Only taking a split second for the full effect to execute, I proceed to dance with an increased intensity acting as if being cold and wet was the sexiest thing in the world. Flipping my long, wet hair from side to side, dropping down into leg splits, rubbing the water all over my slippery body, popping up into a full backbend wheel, raising my right leg to a victory close out of the iconic early-90s song.

Music choice is incredibly important if you want to be a successful and rich entertainer. You don't select music you like; smart girls select music that the audience likes. I learned that night that EMF was a great music choice to make the water show pop. The crowd went wild because they recognized the song and I made more useless Bolivian currency than any other night.

Having managed to brush off Elena, I didn't see her for the rest of the night. But when we got back to the compound, I found my room completely tossed. They hadn't simply "checked my room" as Elena suggested earlier, they'd gone through every one of my bags and left everything dumped out in disarray like a warrant search had taken place. My hand went automatically to my hip, where my passport had been digging into my skin since I'd retrieved it from the pile of props after my show and stuffed it in my pants. That was when any remaining illusions of my legit job in Bolivia crumbled. I had failed at fooling Elena. She was smarter than I'd accounted for. I had to get out of there, and it had to be now before she came looking for me—and I left without Jacey.

§

A tall metal gate surrounded the US consular agency. After shaking it with my bloody palms and discovering that it was, of course, locked, I found a buzzer. I pressed the button, and through staticky interference, somebody answered.

"Hi, my name is Carmen," I said into the speaker. "I need your help. I'm in danger and I'm bleeding. I'm Canadian, please help me."

For all I knew, I sounded crazy. They probably didn't get that many people banging on their gates in the middle of the night. Or maybe they did? After a minute, four heavily armed guards came out to the gate, opened it, pulled me in by my shirt with both hands, and closed it right away. Two of them stayed at the gate, watching I guess to see if I was followed, and the other two shuttled me right into a stark room with only a table and metal chairs. Over the next few hours, I told their only English-speaking agent about where I'd been staying and how I ended up at their gates. I told them about my passport and my room being searched and showed them my crusty-blood palms. One guard presented a first aid kit and tossed it on the table for me to use. I told them about my return ticket. And after I'd explained everything, they agreed to let me stay there until my flight left in two days. They would help me and escort me to the airport to catch my flight home when it was time. Thank you, USA, and thank you for Tom's hot tip about American embassies, I thought.

I felt immediately relieved. They gave me a cozy little barrack-style room. And they showed me where I could find the bathroom and shower, and where to enjoy the grounds. It was a compound similar to Elena's house, with gardens and a fence all around it. The light of the starting day beamed through the window of my room as I fell asleep. Sleep came heavy and full and uninterrupted until a knock at my door later that afternoon. Disoriented, I got up, crossed the room, and opened the door. A guard, though not one I recognized from before, nodded at me and said, "There's a woman here. Elena. She says she needs to speak to you. She says it's urgent."

"She's here right now?" All my feelings about her flooded over me and panic pricked my cheeks.

"Yes. Do you want to talk to her? We don't feel that it is a good idea to talk to her. She is known to us and we want you to stay here, for your safety. We are also keeping a close watch for your other friend."

"No way. I don't want to talk to her, I'm staying right here with you."

I spent the next few days hanging around the US consular agency, worried that Elena found me. While in the compound, with the soldier guys with automatic weapons always in tow (also something I'd never seen before) I felt beyond safe. I felt like I could chillax here, hide out, and they would honour their protection agreement. I caught a few of them staring at me often as if I was an oddity to them for even being there under those circumstances. They knew exactly what I did for work and seemed intrigued that a Canadian girl had ended up in their care. They acted like they wanted to chat with me, so I used some French to translate their attempts at communicating with me. When it started to get frustrating for them, I made them write down what they were saying so that I could pick out words that were similar in French. That kind of worked, but took a long time, and they gave up and headed out to accomplish other tasks on the compound.

The guards were nice. They brought me home-cooked meals of plantains, rice, chicken, and papaya from their little kitchen. I hated papaya until they showed me to sprinkle it with salt before eating it, and they were delighted to see that I liked it better that way.

When the day of my departure came, they presented me with a lapel pin of the US and Bolivia flags. They pinned it on me, and we all hugged. I insisted that we take a picture, one of the last few left on my disposable camera. They must have liked me, because that was strictly forbidden, and they made an exception. We loaded up in their unassuming transport van, and four armed guards, weapons held comfortably across their chests, drove me to the airport and left me safely at the American Airlines counter.

Unfortunately, they didn't stick around.

§

"Your flight has been bumped for three days," the American Airlines representative said from across the counter.

"What do you mean, my flight has been bumped? How can that happen?"

"I'm sorry, but you missed the early check-in required for international flights. We had to bump your flight to Monday."

"And that's not for three days?"

"I'm sorry. This is Easter weekend. The next available flight leaves on Monday."

Desperate to avoid any further delay, I tried to explain that I didn't know I had to check in so early, and I'd been in the custody of the US government for the past two days. But they didn't care. So I would have to spend the next three days, broke, with nothing but the clothes on my back and a suitcase I'd packed in a rush. I had a hairbrush, some of my costumes, about thirty-two dollars' worth of bolivianos, and my disposable camera. Terror was all I felt. I started breathing so fast that I thought I was having a panic attack. I cupped my hands over my mouth and tried to breathe. I was afraid I'd never get out of this country.

In a corner of the airport, I found two connected chairs where the arm rest dividing them had broken off and I slept there, feeling foolish for not taking Tom up on his offer of travel money. I had money in Canada, but nothing I could access from Bolivia. My ATM card laughed at me every time I tried to see if this next time it would work.

And the whole time I kept thinking about how, if I just took my last little bit of money and made the phone call back to the farm, back to talk to my grandparents, that all of this could be better. They had no idea I was even here. This would surely scare them and mean conceding that I didn't know what I was doing, that I was in serious danger, and that I was a loser. I held off.

The Santa Cruz airport wasn't very large. I contemplated begging a vendor to call the US consulate soldiers to come pick me up, but I thought I'd asked enough of them already. That's the first time I cried. I cried that those soldiers were stand up Bolivian citizens. I cried for never probably getting to meet someone like Tom again. I cried that I was a loser, and that my school friends back home were in university making their families proud and I was here, doing this. And I sobbed uncontrollably at the thought of likely having to call my family. And if they didn't answer because they were busy with something on the farm, then I'd have no money left to keep trying to call them. Then what would I do?

The next morning the airport came alive with Spanish-speaking travellers at 5:00 a.m. They looked clean and confident and ready to go where they were going. I was smelly, greasy, had brushed my teeth with my fingers in the bathroom, and was growing completely disgusted with myself physically and spiritually. I found it ironic that *I* was the upper-middle-class Canadian white girl who was dirty and busted-broke, and these local travellers were poised and confident in their knock-off designer bags and clothes.

On the second day, two men about my age working at a taco shop watched me all day. Then they came up to me and gave me food. I forgot how hungry I was until that moment. I ate all they gave me and teared up as I tried to thank them. They left and came back before their shift ended and motioned me to come with them.

Searching their kind eyes, I followed, and they led me to a tiny back room in the taco place. They pointed to an oversized steel cart and, placing both hands next to their ears and tilting their heads, motioned that it was okay for me to sleep here for the night. I slept on the steel cart with my hard-shell suitcase as a pillow. I slept hard and sound until they opened the taco shop in the morning. It was so nice to lie down straight compared to the airport connected chairs. I was thankful for their simple kindness.

On Monday, I headed to the American Airlines counter as soon as it opened to see what flight I was going to be on and fully transfer my ticket value. That's when I got the bad news that my spot was cancelled and so was all the ticket value. The value was suddenly non-transferrable.

I cried and pleaded with the agent, who was clearly losing patience with me. She said I was crazy for trying to coordinate flights last minute during Easter week because everyone in South America was Catholic. No matter, I was Catholic too! I proceeded to plead for consideration as a fellow Catholic. None of it worked. Nobody cared.

I'd toughed it out for as long as I could. The possibility of being stuck in Santa Cruz was unthinkable, and I was just as scared as I had been when I jumped over Elena's wall. If this was the way the airlines in Bolivia worked, my flights could keep getting bumped. That's when I had to break down and call my family, who had no idea what I did for a living and no idea that I was here in South America. They thought I was working odd jobs in Edmonton. I begged for a phone call from the American Airlines agent, and prayed someone would answer.

"Carmen, is that you?" My grandpa's voice sounded small and distant through the international connection.

I'd never felt so relieved to have a call answered. "It's me, Grandpa. I'm in big trouble."

My father's parents didn't have a lot of money, but compared to my mother's side of the family, they were the most understanding. This was one of the hardest calls I'd ever had to make, but I was straightforward with them that I was far away, needed to get home, and couldn't get home on my own. They had no idea where I was, but they dropped everything and called the local travel agent while I waited on the line. I put the phone down on the American Airlines counter area and waited and waited and waited. Half an hour later my grandparents came back on the line. Without any questions asked, they booked all my flights on Delta Airlines, triple-confirmed my seats from Santa Cruz, to Mexico City, to Vancouver, to Edmonton, where I had an apartment a few hours away from my hometown.

By the time I landed on Canadian soil, everyone in my hometown knew what kind of trouble I'd gotten in.

2

HILL AND VALLEY RANCH, EST. 1950

"Ain't nothin' much out there, just life at its best.
On that little patch of heaven, way out west."
—K.D. Lang

THE PUTRID SMELL OF BURNT hair and flesh from a branding iron applied to a steer's flank permeates my earliest memory. It layered over the other farm smells and hung in the cold air. The steer, nervous and alert, arrived at my paternal grandparents' farm on a truck and were unloaded into a pen. Then one by one, encouraged by the sharp zap of the electric prod, the steer moved through the chute toward the squeeze to be branded, inoculated, and dehorned. The sizzling sound and inevitable outcry of pain from the huge animals was no matter, as we had 115 more to process before lunchtime.

"Allen, we're starting on yours next," Grandpa Lloyd mumbled to my father through frozen winter breath. He took a sip from his special cup. Then he put down his LK branding iron and reached for my dad's KK iron. My dad nodded quietly. In terms of farm succession, when both the old and new generations worked together like this, grandpas usually run the show. There was always slight tension over methodologies—doing it the old way versus innovating with the times.

My dad, while quieter, was not one to cower easily. He had great respect for my grandpa as the farm founder, but maybe not so much for him as a drunkard. Their relationship was complicated by Grandpa's drinking, and probably for as long as my dad could remember. My grandpa was also taller and bigger than my dad. When the steer—a solid, horned beast—they'd intended to push through next evaded Uncle Ray, Grandpa Lloyd's brother who we all called Porky, Grandpa shook his head in annoyance, as if no one was working fast enough. This was Lloyd's ranch and he gave the directions. That was clear.

"Ray, load him up faster," Lloyd shouted impatiently towards his brother, who was tasked with fetching the scared animals to be loaded into the chute from the adjacent pen.

Porky threw his hands in the air and yelled, "Come on, you whoore," and gave the animal an electric prod into action. With his slight Ukrainian accent, whoore meant whore, or "whoora" in the old country.

I peered over the bottom slat of the pen where the steers were released and free to go. It was dangerous and loud near the cattle squeeze, where the beasts would buck, bellow, and kick through the steel sides, their 2000-pound bodies resisting the cage that held them tight and still while the men worked. The distinct smell of this operation didn't bother me. But the blood squirting from the severed horns in thin, high-pressure streams made me queasy and curious. The fresh cut ends were porous inside, filled with blood vessels and spongy bone; some blood dripped, some spewed. The bewildered cattle bled all over each other and the walls of the pen. The snow below where they worked was cherry red with blood running in swirls.

Complaining of hunger, I stepped into the danger zone of the squeeze, where the steer they'd wrangled kicked hard and rattled the bars fiercely. My dad immediately pushed me to the sideline of safety, sending me, stiff in my one-piece belted snowmobile suit, stumbling back, insulted. Lloyd looked my way and motioned me to come closer to him. I was safe with Grandpa. I waddled over, and he picked me up effortlessly and held me with his six-foot-three-tall frame. Tucked in the safety of his embrace, he brought me closer to the animals in the squeeze. Here I got a bird's view of the tops of animals versus the underbelly view that my toddler height provided.

"You see, Dolly Girl," he said, "this guy's horns are sharp, and he could hurt his friends if they get too close to each other, so we've got to get them cut off."

His face was inches from mine. My Grandpa was in his late forties, a young grandpa, although he looked really old to me. The Kissels migrated from the Ukraine to Canada in about 1915. Grandpa Lloyd, a second generation Ukrainian Canadian, was one of eight siblings born in the 1930s. Ranch-raised men like him were survivors. He started working hard well before any child labour laws governed a new way forward, and it all showed on his face. His skin looked weathered like old cowboy boots. The biting, cold winter day made icicles in his eyebrows and nose hairs. Grandpa Lloyd's breath, even at ten in the morning, smelled of whiskey.

Lloyd explained everything to me in a soft voice, what they were doing to the cattle and why. The work was gruesome and bloody, but essential to taking good care of the animals, and this was my earliest introduction to the fleshiness of life. We watched my dad skillfully load up huge needles with milky liquid, as Porky sawed off the horns. Then my grandpa gently brought me back to the ground, instructed me to head over to the house for a snack, and reassured me that they'd be in for *The Flintstones* and lunchtime soon.

Lloyd Kissel acquired the land for his farm, Hill and Valley Ranch, in 1949 from the Hudson's Bay Company through the Canadian Homestead Act. The land was subsidized by the Canadian government as part of westward expansion. Lloyd got two quarters of land, and Hill and Valley Ranch was established in 1950. He and his wife, Elizabeth, my Grandma Betty, started in a tiny 650-square-foot home in the center of this property, wedged between the highway and Kehewin First Nation Reservation. My dad, Kenneth Allen, was born, and Gordon and Brenda followed. By Christmas of 1967, when my dad was twelve years old, they moved into a new, more spacious home on the property. They kept the starter house intact, an homage to their humble beginnings.

My mom, Françoise Dargis, met my dad when she was seventeen. She was from the wealthiest farm family in the area—my maternal grandfather ran a large, vertically integrated farming enterprise, with an auction house, four thousand head of cattle, and a meat processing operation. My dad was a hotshot high school hockey player and men's league baseball slugger who'd tried college for year, but came back to help on the farm. Hill and Valley Ranch at that time was at its peak. They'd recently won the prestigious Alberta Farm Family Award, and my dad was in line to run it. Most people from that time and from rural areas started drinking at bush parties in high school or after pick-up games of various seasonal sports. It was chalked up to kids having fun. The problem festered and grew from there. Not long after they first met, my mom, still only seventeen, got pregnant with me. Although they were both very young and barely knew each other, the marriage seemed to be well enough matched, at least at the time. They got married in April, and I was born in August. Both my grandfathers collaborated together on building my mom and dad a house on Hill and Valley Ranch. And especially in those early days, Lloyd and Betty helped raise me. They were the ones exposing me to the world, tucking me in at night, and reading me stories like *The Blueberry Pie Elf*.

I was never afraid of Grandpa Lloyd. His attention and company made me feel important and safe. His number one pal was his younger brother, Uncle Ray. Uncle Ray—Porky—also had a small farm nearby, also purchased through the Homestead Act. But he only kept a few pigs and helped with the larger Hill and Valley Ranch operations. Porky had a childish intellect. He was a bachelor and hoarder who showered so rarely that you could smell him coming and see the caked dirt on his skin when he took his shirt off on a hot day. We were never allowed inside Porky's house. Ray and Grandpa were thick as thieves, so it was like having two grandpas all the time. Except one was normal-looking and the other was very smelly. Lloyd never had a problem with me hanging around the farm work. Even before I was old enough to start preschool, I couldn't wait to run over the short, grassy path over to the farmyard to see what was going on for the day. I liked being out with the animals, where the action was, where the big trucks were, where they were branding, or inoculating, or processing the cattle, or delivering calves, or feeding them. There were always baby calves, kittens, or piglets being born. Barnyard King, the rooster, crowed every morning to start the work day, and no matter how many times I tried to catch him, he always sped away and evaded me. Life was happening on the farm, and it fascinated me.

Grandpa had a strict rule that we couldn't eat until all the animals were fed, watered, bedded, and doctored, as needed. Life, in all forms, was valued and protected in large part because reproduction on the farm was money in your pocket. Preserving that *bond* between the mothers and babies was important. Mothers needed to have empathy for their babies so they could bond, and not only survive, but thrive. When a mother cow rejected her baby, maybe because she was too young or wasn't producing enough milk, they'd try to pair the calf with a more empathetic mother cow. If this didn't work, we'd try to bottle feed the baby. Sometimes after all attempts failed, the calf would die, and they'd put it in the pile of other dead animals until the gut wagon came to haul them away. I watched the new calves and piglets and puppies and kittens bond with their mothers, and I witnessed, across so many species, this core element of survival. Nobody knew it better than my Grandpa Lloyd, who depended on these mother animals to produce, grow, and maintain his healthy herd.

My grandpa was a more-the-merrier type of soul. He had a giant Norwegian elkhound named Wolf that followed him all around the farm like a shadow. He delighted in telling us Wolf was a real wolf; stories were his way of making the ordinary extraordinary. The Kissels embodied community spirit. They were always reaching out and bringing people in. Not many white men in those days associated with the local Indigenous people, whose government land reservations existed all over the area. But my grandpa, probably over whiskey, befriended them and brought them to Hill and Valley Ranch and gave them jobs. Betty was always bringing people home from school for dinner. The Kissels helped their neighbours. Lloyd believed in being nice to everybody, from feeding the motherless calf to occasionally employing the Indigenous workers on our farm.

The Kissels, like many of the Depression Era, also prized resourcefulness. Once a week we loaded up into Grandpa's red Ford pickup and drove to George Jelshen's IGA grocery store in town. Every farm we passed, Grandpa would tell me about who lived there and how he knew them. Some families were German, some were French. I'd listen, wide-eyed and curious. He considered himself a great cattleman and farmer, so he loved answering my questions. When we got to IGA, where Grandpa had a standing arrangement with his friend, George, there would be giant boxes of slightly overripe and unsellable produce waiting for us. I would jump out of the cab and help load the overflowing boxes, some so malodorous that I'd have to tuck my nose into the collar of my coat to get them on the truck. Anything decent enough to eat, like ripe peaches or strawberries, went into the cab with us. Sometimes we snacked on our ride home, but usually we saved it for Grandma Betty, who turned it into something delicious for dessert.

Overripe produce has a distinct, sweet scent that the pigs could smell as soon as we turned off the road. Nothing delighted my grandpa's pigs more than this weekly feast. They would grunt and squeal, becoming frenzied with anticipation. We'd empty the boxes straight on top of the pigs' backs, and they'd scramble to eat until every last scrap of lettuce had been devoured. Pigs will eat absolutely anything, even the wooden walls of their own pig-pens. I can remember hearing other farmers make fun of my grandpa for feeding his pigs slightly rotted produce, but he was always proud. "It's good for them," he'd say. "It makes their meat taste better."

I spent a lot of time with Grandpa. Lloyd ran a tight, successful family farm, even if, with every sip from his special cup, the operation strained under the wholesome veneer.

§

My brother was born when I was two, and before he was one, Mom was working full-time in the butcher shop and meat processing facility her father set up for her. She was twenty, had two little kids, and she worked all the time. My brother and I had a babysitter in town named Diane, which was where my mom often packed us off to.

But I learned that if I could get up and put my clothes on superfast and rush over to the farmyard, then chances were my grandpa and my dad were already working out on the farm. My grandmother, who taught sixth-grade English at the local school, would be gone for the day, but all I had to do was find them before my mom got up for the day.

I ran from our house, across the yard, and picked up the path that led through the trees that spilled onto my grandparents' yard. The distance felt so large when I was so small, and the plywood-sheeted walls of the workshop towered over me. Inside the vast building, which functioned as the heart of farm operations, the smells of motor oil and sweet grain mingled and lingered. The walls were papered with land maps, showing quadrant after quadrant of Kissel fields; government-issued farm safety warnings, depicting illustrations of long hair and loose clothing getting caught in PTO drive equipment; and a few giant sized late-70s nudie-girl posters (my dad's). During the winter, the tractors were parked inside over a pit in the floor where they could get down under and work on the machines. There was a medical shed attached to the back, where long stainless-steel needles, strong enough to pierce a steer's hide, and other pieces of veterinary equipment were kept. The radio was always on, tuned to the Edmonton country station, 790 CFCW, and played old country songs about drinking and lovin' from artists like Merle Haggard, Hank Williams, George Jones, and Tammy Wynette. A classic and rugged rotary dial phone—the only one in the yard—sat on the top of an old wooden bureaucrat's desk. The telephone horn mounted at the roof-pitch outside the workshop had a World War II-era bomb siren sound to it and rang loud enough that you could hear it no matter where you were on the farm—drop everything, and get to the party line phone. Two short blasts from the horn meant a call for our family, and other horn blast patterns meant calls for other farm families down the road. Here my imagination and curiosity were piqued by farm talk, swear words, and gambling lessons. Grandpa taught me about the lucky "Dutch Poke" prior to dealing out everyone's card hands.

One day, while Grandpa chatted up the clerk at Matichuk Equipment in Bonnyville about whatever tractor part he needed, I wandered the aisles. The shelves were filled with box after box of shiny machine parts, so clean they looked like jewels. I slipped thin black rubber O-rings on my fingers and silver adjustable hose clamps on my wrists, stretched my thin arm out to see my new rings and bracelets. Thrilled, I ran to show Grandpa. I hoped that he would buy them for me.

"Dolly Girl," he exclaimed, delighted by what he saw as my endless imagination. "Look at that!"

He thought I was so inventive, he bought me the O-rings and bracelet hose clamps, and we left the store smiling.

When we got back in his truck, Grandpa turned the ignition and let it idle while he reached for his travel mug. The sun had started falling, casting long afternoon shadows across the front of Matichuk's. We'd been out for a while, and by this time Grandpa's cup was empty. He tipped it all the way back, letting the last drops fall into his mouth, then placed it back in the cup holder between us. He checked the rear-view mirror, and pulled away from the parts store.

Another popular errand with Grandpa was stopping by the Bonnyville Hotel, and that's where he headed after Matichuk's. He parked the truck behind the hotel, turned to me, and said, "Now you stay put, Dolly Girl. I'm going in to take a look at the *shiny bottles*. I won't be long."

I didn't mind waiting in the truck. I fiddled with my O-ring jewelry and pressed the thick buttons on the radio to change the a.m. stations. Grandpa never seemed to worry that I'd break them or wear them out. The Bonnyville Hotel was a narrow, three-story building on 50 Avenue, with a bar on the first floor. I liked watching other people come and go from the hotel because once a fight had broken out between two men, who came stumbling out, pushing, swinging at each other, and yelling in their native tongue. Today was quiet, and after a while Grandpa emerged from the swinging thick wood door. He always came back from the old hotel a lot happier than when he entered.

"How are you doing, Dolly Girl?" His watery cornflower blue eyes gleamed, and his face flushed.

"Hi, Grandpa."

He started the truck, and we drove back out of town to the farm. This particular trip stuck in my mind because of the O-ring jewelry, and because Grandma was so angry when we came in. I was too young to understand why.

"Look at my new bracelets, Grandma," I said as soon as I saw her. She had her apron tied on, a kerchief over her hair, and two pots steaming on the avocado green stovetop.

"Aren't those nice." She looked hard at Grandpa, but lovingly my way. She wiped her hands on a towel and placed it on the counter. Then she said to me, "Why don't you go show your Aunt Brenda."

My Aunt Brenda Laurianne came home from college at the University of Alberta in Edmonton about once a month, which thrilled me. Only fourteen years older than me, she was my sister-auntie, and she treated me like her doll. She was a farm 4-H queen who'd won dairy princess pageants and had been a top three contender for Miss Edmonton Eskimo for Edmonton's CFL team. To me, she was the coolest person in the world and the perfect person to admire my new jewelry. But as I left the kitchen to find her, I overheard Grandma boom, "Lloyd, what the hell are you doing?"

I stopped to listen to them. Grandma was the kind of woman who quietly held it together, and I'd never heard her utter the word hell.

"What, Ma?"

"You know exactly what I mean. Buying tractor parts for a child to wear as jewelry. You're drunk!"

"They cost a few cents, Betty. And we had a great time in town."

"You usually do," she said. I could hear her anger through the wall. "Did you leave Carmen in the truck this time when you went drinking at the hotel?"

To me, our errands had been a fun outing, not unlike any other outing with Grandpa. I didn't feel unsafe or worried ever. But I did know Grandpa was always drinking from his travel mug, from first thing in the morning, and all day long. Silk Tassel Vodka and Royal Reserve Whiskey were his favourites. He kept mickey bottles on his person or in his vehicle, tucked under seat, and his stash of full-sized glass bottles was stored under the kitchen sink. When he needed a refill, he gave his signature whistle. That was the cue for my brother and me. We would race each other to grab the bottle to be the first to bring it to him. Whoever brought the bottle got his unending praise. This was the early 1980s, before kids wore bike helmets and rode in car seats. The societal push to end drunk driving was just beginning. And not long after this day, my grandpa got three impaired driving violations in just as many years, not for driving fast and reckless, but flagged for driving so sloppy and slow. Lloyd's drinking and driving with me or my brother in the truck was the only time I ever saw my sweet, quiet grandma get mad.

Elizabeth Kissel, Grandma Betty, was a teacher, farmer's wife, and accomplished seamstress and homemaker. She was known in our area as the queen bee of homesteading women, a master of all the dying crafts, like gardening and canning as a means of producing and preserving your own food. Her quilts took home all the blue ribbons at fairs, and her sewing room produced a high volume of goods, all professional tailored quality. She wrote and published a book about the history of our Eastbourne and Rife community, with details about the founding families. She made cinnamon toast on white Wonder Bread slices with gobs of butter and brown sugar anytime we wanted and indulged us with two or three rounds of it, if we fancied. She played the piano at her church, even though she was the only one in her family that attended. But she was humble and brushed off the attention, never resting on her laurels. Her husband's drinking was a mark of shame that she wore silently. She was able to do it because she stayed involved in the community and was so universally adored and well liked. Her never-ending lonely nights were spent in her sewing room or chasing Maurice and I down for a much-needed bath.

§

My grandfather loved nothing more than to instigate fights between my brother and me. We were always bickering about who was tougher, and Grandpa turned it into entertainment. My brother and I would go at it, and he'd say, "Wow, what a tough kid. That was a good hit."

"Whoa, that was a good shot, Dolly Girl," Porky would chime in.

They were weird that way, but wonderful and loving and drunk. They taught us about good *fisticuffs* and the proper way to deliver an effective upper-cut. If I hit my brother too hard with my little fist, and he bellowed in pain, my grandfather would say, "Okay, we've had enough here." I remember he used to make us have contests where we'd stand on our heads against the pantry door in the kitchen, and I'd stay like that, my head on the thin orange and brown carpeting, until I fell over. I was better at it than Maurice, and I would get the praise and get to select a treat from the pantry.

And Betty thought it was all cute to a certain extent. But she didn't let it go too far because my grandfather was usually just drunk and looking to entertain himself. She'd sometimes run up the stairs from her sewing room and bellow, "Cut it out, Lloyd. That's enough." She didn't pipe up often, because her world was very pink and blue. So when she did, everyone knew that Ma was serious.

Because Maurice and I were so competitive and only two years apart, they tried to appease us. When it was my birthday and my brother's nose was out of joint, sulking and sad that it wasn't his birthday, Grandma made sure she had a little present for him too. She did the same for me. They made us feel like we were so noticed, so loved, and always so cared for.

§

I started school when we still lived on Hill and Valley Ranch. First came preschool—three half days a week—at the French Cultural Center. My mom was French and so was her family; it seemed important for me to be bilingual. My name sounded weird in French. It was pronounced "Carr-eu-mène." But kindergarten brought me closer to Grandma Betty, who worked in the same school I attended, though she taught in the English wing. Then when I started full-day kindergarten, I rode the bus. My mom, who I have so few memories of during this time, was working long hours managing the new meatpacking plant and butcher operations. Dad was working on the farm and driving a commercial truck during the off-season for B & R Transport for extra income. Dad would often take my brother and me on half-day trips and indulge us with arm-pumps of the highway tractor's air horn anytime we liked. We played tag on the loading docks at the transport terminal while he unloaded freight. Although I didn't recognize it yet, my parents' marriage had already started to deteriorate.

By this time, as my grandpa's drinking and carousing habits intensified, Grandma Betty's teaching salary largely supported the farm as reliable income. When the farm work finished, Lloyd would go off with his brothers in Glendon, where they were all raised and still lived. In the summer, when there was more farm work to do and the daylight hours stretched until eleven at night, he wouldn't get home until late. In winter, when the work day and daylight hours ended early, the party and visiting moved into the workshops or kitchens. Horse-trading business negotiations between farmers took place over drinks and card games. Lots of times my great-uncles, Bill or Johnny Kissel, would stop by our kitchen to have a visit and a few drinks. The women were expected to entertain, make snack food, and smile and be pleasant. If they didn't feel like doing that, the women kept busy with the kids or house chores.

Betty's kitchen was the domestic hub of the farming operation. Her food was filling and creative, and her repertoire included borscht soup, pan fried meats, cold pasta salads, and canned relishes. There was always a dessert, something simple like instant pudding or a homemade fruit pie. And all condiments were available on a lazy Susan in the center of the table, replete with instant coffee for Porky and honey for tea. We all came in for lunch at noon, and Dad turned *The Flintstones* on the ten-inch television set on top of the fridge for all of us to watch while we ate.

In a group of ladies in a round circle, Betty would be quieter, but when she spoke she had value to offer, insight or a new trick or solution. She was the respected wise owl. She was different from her sisters-in-law because she was educated, beyond a farm wife and accomplished on the piano, recorder, and accordion. When Aunty Brenda was very little, Betty earned her bachelor of education degree from the University of Alberta and lived with her parents in the city of Edmonton to earn that degree. She valued her education degree and it was hard to earn as an adult farm family woman, so she was serious about her children getting formal post-secondary educations. Learning new things was highly prized by Betty; she lived it and walked that ideology in her own life. When she was with her fellow teaching colleagues from her school and other schools, she was truly at peace and with her kind. Lloyd, his drinking, and his humble family members were none of those things. Betty stood out and blended in all at the same time.

But her religious devotion, love for her family, and level of commitment were why she stayed instead of bolted. Hers was a moral compass like no other. As long as she could create and have freedom to be who she was, she loved her farm woman life. She was reliable and always there if anyone needed her, even Lloyd.

Farm income could be feast or famine. The power, heating, fuel bills, and feed bills are steep on a farm. Lloyd had a larger farming operation and when a tractor or a harvester or a grain mixer would break down, the parts and repair bills could be costly too. Especially if you had to hire a fancy mechanic instead of the neighbour mechanics down the road. And Lloyd's alcohol expense wasn't insignificant. But because Lloyd was rarely sober, he wasn't overly concerned with finances and paying the bills—that worry-burden fell mostly on Betty.

And in the hours between supper and Grandpa passing out, the drinking caused tension and arguments. But the next morning always seemed to start fresh, without discussion or notice of any rifts from the prior evening. Everyone moved on with the day, for better or for worse.

Hidden from my child's view, the underpinnings of my life on Hill and Valley Ranch were crumbling away. But the bus stopped at our house every morning. And the school day unfolded in French immersion. Every afternoon, without fail, Grandpa Lloyd and Porky waited for me at the end of the driveway so I wouldn't have to cross the busy Highway 28 that bordered our farm. I'd see them through the window as we pulled up, chatting and kicking their boots at the gravel, shielding their eyes from the gleam when the bus eased to a stop. I'd spring from my seat and clamor under the weight of my backpack off the grumbling diesel bus. Grandpa and Porky would each take one of my hands, and they'd walk me across the major highway to home, just in time for cinnamon toast and a shot of whiskey on the shaded veranda.

3

DIVORCE, CONGLOMERATES, AND DARGIS LAND & CATTLE

"It is not from the benevolence of the butcher, the brewer, or the baker that we expect our dinner, but from their regard to their own interest."
—ADAM SMITH

I'D NEVER NOTICED THE HOUSE that sat right next to my other grandpa's auction mart, not until Diane, our occasional babysitter, brought my brother and me to it one day. White paint flaked off the exterior. The main floor had brown '70s-era carpet everywhere, even in the kitchen. A creaky wooden staircase led up to two bedrooms. The basement was a giant dirt hole, and the house looked like it had been placed overtop to cover a hole in the ground. And it was right down the road from my mom's meatpacking plant, just a few kilometers outside of Bonnyville. When she was watching us, after school or on the weekend, Diane was always taking us along on different errands with her daughter, Christine, who was my age and my first best friend. I was so excited to play with Christine that I never thought to ask whose house it was.

Diane had two other children and was married to a mean old meat cutter named Marcel. He was a bit of a drunk, too, who was never very affectionate towards his three children. When he came home for lunch from Hamel's Deli Shop, we'd all have to sit and eat in another room at a kid-sized table because he liked it quiet. They were a French Catholic family, but when Marcel died suddenly of a heart attack, Diane instantly converted to the Jehovah's Witness faith.

That day, Diane filled a paint tray and dipped the roller in, then rolled on the bright white, covering the stained old surface with a clean start.

"Can we paint too?" I asked, watching the roller spin across the wall.

"No, no. You guys go play." Diane's cigarette hung from her mouth as she talked. "I brought you snacks. Go play."

Christine, my brother, and I played around the house and in the yard, making our own fun. I watched for signs of my other grandpa next door at the auction mart while Diane painted the inside, room after room. We returned to the painting project several times that week, until the job was done.

By this time, my dad had started hauling freight as a truck driver for the same local company called B & R Transport during the winter. He already had his Class 1 license, because he needed it to operate some of the equipment on the farm. He'd leave Bonnyville with his big blue and white highway tractor, drive to Edmonton three hours away, and pick up a load of liquor, produce, or whatever was coming back. These were long trips that kept him away sometimes for the whole day.

But business at the meatpacking plant was booming. This inflated my mother's ego and further strained my parents' marriage. Meanwhile, Grandpa Lloyd's drinking continued to degrade the situation on Hill and Valley Ranch. Even with my dad helping, it wasn't doing as well as it should, hence the need for Dad's trucking income. And when all the other truck drivers met up at the bar after a long day on the road, my dad was always there with them, perpetuating the previous generation's drinking habit.

§

A few days after Diane finished painting the house, my brother and I just *woke up in it.* I'd gone to sleep in my bed on Hill and Valley Ranch, but during the night, my mom had brought us into town to the house she'd had Diane working on. There was furniture in it now. We had beds, though not the same beds from home. I found some of my toys and some of my brother's toys, and felt like everything was wrong and strange. My dad wasn't there. There was no sign of him anywhere.

"What about Dad? Does he live in the new house with us?" I asked my mom.

"No, this is our house now. He doesn't live here, he lives at the farm."

"What about Grandma and Grandpa and Porky? Can we go see them?"

"No. This is our house now. We don't go there anymore." My brother, who was four at the time, and I had so many questions. But that was all the explanation I ever got. We didn't live on the farm anymore. That was it. I don't recall a hug. Just a blank and bare statement. My fingers flew to my mouth and I started to get nervous and sweaty.

My mom ended her seven-year marriage by sneaking out in the middle of the night. She set up the house in secret, and then took my brother and me, in the middle of the night, and put us in these beds. Waking up, suddenly full time in my mom's care when we didn't know her and she didn't know us, with no explanation except that this was our new life, felt like half our world disappeared. We knew our mom, but we didn't have a strong bond with her because she was always working. She didn't read us bedtime stories or tuck us in. Did she know how to make cinnamon toast? We were so young at the time, but I can remember a feeling of alarm settling over me as I desperately asked for answers.

When I saw Diane, I'd ask, "Do you know my grandma and grandpa? Do you know my Grandpa Lloyd?"

"Yes," she'd say, distracted by whatever she was doing.

"Well, can you take me to them to see them? I haven't seen them for a long time." It's hard to say what I considered a long time—it could have been a few days or a few weeks. But they'd been my daily life for my whole life, and any span of time without them felt like complete heartbreak.

Diane, who was good friends with my mom, dismissed these requests without elaboration. "No, not today."

I even asked Christine, who was also six years old, "Can you ask your mom about my mom so I can figure out what's going on?"

When my mom wasn't looking, I used the phone at our house to call the farm. I knew the number by heart, 826-5317, and sometimes someone on the other end would answer and talk to me just like normal. I can remember Grandma would say, "Oh, hi, sweetie. How are you?" She was so soft-spoken and gentle and kind, but that only confused me more.

When I'd say, "Grandma, I miss you. Why do I live here? What's going on?" she would patiently tell me that she was making plans to come see me or that on her teaching breaks from school she'd come for a quick visit. She never answered my questions. And as busy as teachers are, she dropped by my classroom to see me. She always brought me fresh strawberries or a fruit roll-up or some other little treat. She never had much time, but she'd sit with me for a minute and give me a hug to let me know that I was still loved and cared for. Seeing Grandma at lunch was the brightest spot in my day and otherwise very confusing new life.

But aside from these small, stolen interactions, we were cut off from the Kissels for a long time. And life changed. Divorce was uncommon in our small Catholic town. Now we were from a broken home, and everyone in town knew what had happened. The pity and stigma of the broken home attached to me. Everything that I'd ever known and shaped me as a person was turned on top of its head. And for the first time in my life, I felt isolated. That's when I realized that no matter what, no matter how, nobody was coming to save us.

§

Perhaps my parents' marriage, being so rushed and happening so young, was doomed from the start. Perhaps my other grandpa, Pierre Dargis, saw it coming and gave his daughter a business so she could stand on her own two feet regardless of her husband. Mom didn't need Dad's money because she had her own. And I think she was angry because he ended up being a poor performer instead of a life-conquering partner. She was a tough worker, and he was drinking and not taking anything seriously enough for her. She may have been young, and not an angel herself, but she was driven. She would have done anything to please her father and succeed at her business, possibly to repent for the shame she'd brought her parents with her teen pregnancy.

At twenty-three, my mom, was a single mom of two kids, working as the general manager of a large business that serviced five counties. Her dad, Pierre, bought her the house next to the auction mart and the butcher shop. It had to be close to her work because, at the time, she didn't have a driver's license. Always in a hurry, Françoise had enough speeding tickets to get her license suspended for thirty days. Then she got caught driving during that suspension and lost it for another year. But now she could bike to work or hop in with a coworker.

Even though she was okay without the money, my mom used child support against my dad and his family. I think my dad tried to make a child support arrangement, but that would have ended with him having access to my brother and me. My mom wouldn't allow that; she wanted to stick it to him, it seemed, in a big way. She appeared angry and vengeful, and she didn't want him to see us. She said he was a drunk, just like his father, to justify cutting him off. The child support was just an excuse for keeping him away from us. Our welfare had little to do with it, based on the way she treated us. I became very scared of my mother.

§

In second grade, I was hanging upside down on the playground at school. For a few moments, I felt light as the world tilted and tipped around me. Then a kid knocked my legs loose, and I fell down to the ground. I landed square on the top of my head and was knocked out for several minutes. The school shuttled me to the infirmary and suggested that they call an ambulance, as I was talking gibberish. But when my mom arrived, she insisted there was no need for that. I was awake by this time, foggy and in pain from the fall.

"I'll drive her myself," Mom said. In the car, her frustration was palpable even through my haze. She fussed about how inconvenient this was, how busy she was.

"I don't have time to take the day off, Carmen," she said. "There's no one to answer the phones at work but me today."

When he saw me and checked me, Dr. Ruiter determined I had a concussion. I could go home, he said, but someone would have to watch me very closely. He explained the aftercare to my mom. She needed to wake me up periodically for a cognitive lucidity test to make sure I hadn't lost consciousness again. My mom nodded her head in compliance and said okay. Then she took me home, propped me up on the couch with a blanket and went back to work. Feeling more tired than I ever had, I slept for the next fifteen hours without being woken up or checked on once.

By the time my brother and I were both in school, Mom would be gone to work by six in the morning, and I'd be getting us up and ready to catch the bus to school. And then after school, the bus dropped us off at the meatpacking plant, which was along the same route as our house.

A meatpacking facility isn't exactly the safest place for young children to be running around in, and my mom wasn't the kind of mom who'd think to prepare a fun activity to keep us busy. She never asked if we had any homework or a book to read. As soon as we got dropped off, she put us to work. And my brother and I got to know our mom by seeing her work every day.

She ran a large operation from day one—and to her credit, she did it without any formal training or experience, which couldn't have been easy for such a young single mother. But people would come from far and wide to my mom's meat processing plant because she had the only operation in the area. She was also known for having the best cured meats. We made rings of garlic sausage, beef jerky, and all the delicious smoked and cured meats that people get from the deli.

The live animals were kept in the far back of the building, and they were kept comfortable before their impending slaughter. We understood our role in these animals' lives. We raised farm animals so that we could consume them. And that ensured our own survival. As farm kids, we didn't care for them any less. Grandpa Lloyd taught me to respect our food source, taking good care of the animals up to the moment they were culled and doing so humanely. Even Mom, who viewed animals as nothing more than a dollar sign, knew the importance of keeping them well. Once the local animal rights activist group targeted our meatpacking plant, demanding to inspect where we kept the animals. My mom welcomed them and assured them that the animals were bedded and watered and well cared for. "If you'd like to take a look," she said when they came to the store, "you're more than welcome to." They still looked at the whole operation with disdain and bias, but my mom showed great moderation with them.

People had until Wednesday to bring their cows and pigs, and whatever other animals they had, for slaughter on Thursdays. Meat inspectors, who worked throughout the region, had to be present on slaughter days, so it happened on the same schedule every week. On Thursday, all other cutting and processing activities stopped, and everyone helped slaughter the animals. And Vivianne and her apprentice came in to inspect the meat. I loved when Vivianne came because she was a middle-aged jovial farm girl. She'd taken special education and training to recognize different diseases in the meat, or abnormalities that would not make it safe for food consumption. And Mom was vigilant about food safety to the highest extreme because her business's whole reputation depended on it.

On slaughter days, we started with pigs first thing in the morning. Pigs were the easiest to process, and there were usually far more of them to process compared to the cattle. We usually had ten to fifteen pigs and two to six cattle. I would stand and watch at the door in the slaughter studio room, which was a concrete room with painted walls that could be easily cleaned and sanitized. Slaughtering is very messy, messy business with blood, bacteria, filth, and fur. The butcher would bring three or four pigs, squealing and frantic, into a cramped area in the slaughter room, and shoot them in the brain with a .22-caliber rifle. I'd hear their frantic screams, pop, pop, pop, pop, and then silence. Dead silence. Loud, then eerily silent.

A hatch would open low to the ground and the pigs would spill onto the kill floor. Here, a giant hoist attached to their hooves and lifted their floppy, lifeless bodies from the floor into a giant tank of boiling water to clean off all the bacteria and filth. Then the same hoist lifted them out again and brought them to the other side of a huge steel processing machine, where it laid them flat on a bed of cylinders that spun. This was the dehairing machine. The butcher, with a foot-operated control, would turn the machine on, spinning the pig bodies around, while he used a propane-fueled fire wand to burn off the animals' hair. The rotisserie machine made a heavy clunking noise as it turned under the heavy pigs, and the smell of burned hair and death hung in the very humid air.

Next the steel hoists grabbed the pigs by their back hooves and moved them upside down to an area known as the kill floor. Here, the butcher sliced their necks, and, with a whooshing sound, the blood would spill into a pail. They saved some for blood sausage, and let the rest run out onto the floor and down the drain. After the blood stopped running, the butchers started with the head, cutting it off completely. Then they sliced open from the anus to the throat, cracked open the ribs with their hands, and let all the organs fall onto the floor. Once all the innards were removed, they'd cut the pig in half lengthwise with a ceiling-suspended steel chainsaw and mount each half pig onto new shanked rolling hooks by their rear ankle tendons and lift them onto a steel rail track mounted to the kill floor ceiling. This ceiling track allowed the butchers to push the sides of pork into the next room, which was an industrial cooler, like a giant fridge room.

We'd wash the sides of pork with hoses tipped with sprayers, and the meat inspectors would look at it. If the meat passed inspection, Vivianne stamped each one with her heavy, gavel-shaped, spiky steel stamp. Then the butcher pushed them into a cooler where the meat cured until it was ready to cut into salable pieces.

They processed all the pigs this way, in groups of three or four at a time. Then, usually after lunch, they'd start the cattle, which was a little different. They took the cattle one by one, through the same network of pens outside and into the kill chute with a larger swinging hatched door. The butcher used the same or a higher caliber rifle to shoot the steer in the brain. Butchers always go for the brain because it doesn't damage the meat. But a steer has a thick skull and it must be shot at near point-blank range. Once the steer was killed, the hatch opened and the animal spilled onto the killing floor, where the three-ton hoist grabbed it by its rear tendons and lifted it into the air, hanging upside down. Instead of boiling and burning off the hair, the steers were bled, the heads removed, and the leather skinned off. The hoist dropped the animal down on its back into a cradle with the legs in the air, and the butcher removed the hooves and cut the skin from the ankles, up the inside of the legs, across the under-belly. And then they peeled back the furry hide, slicing the connective tissue with knives to separate it from the fatty carcass. Even after their hide was completely removed, the thick layer of fat underneath it often twitched and jerked as the nerves died. Sometimes the fat would twitch for up to two hours after! This fascinated me. How did this happen when there was no head and brain even attached to the animal anymore? What was sending the nervous system signals?

Then they hoisted the animal up again to remove the innards, slicing it from anus to throat and reached in to scoop the web of organs out on the concrete floor—all the many stomachs of a steer on display. Some stomachs held freshly eaten hay that you could see through the transparent stomach tissue. Customers usually wanted the offal—the heart, tongue, liver, and kidneys—which we kept aside and prepared for them with the rest of their meat. But all the rest of the mess went to the gut room—the most putrid smelling place in the whole meatpacking plant. There were piles and piles of animal innards in there, plus hides salted and stacked on top of each other. Then every couple of weeks, the same gut wagon trucks that visited all the farms to pick up dead animals came to pick up all of the innards. That was the only room in the whole place where the smell made me feel like I couldn't breathe. Pete, my favourite butcher, told me the only way to survive it for any amount of time was by breathing through your mouth. Yeah, indeed, it makes a difference that way.

§

I noticed irony at a very young age. The essence of the meatpacking plant was taking life away; but it provided for our lives and allowed us to survive. I learned so much during those days, like where food from the grocery stores actually comes from, the different grades of meat, and how fat marbling and marrow make the meat taste better. And how freshly slaughtered meat was too squishy to cut. They'd cure it in the big fridge cooler for at least twenty days before sliding the sides of beef on the rail system into the meat cutting studio. There, they used a primary industrial bandsaw to further cut the four-hundred-pound half-sides of beef into manageable chunks. The meat cutters—always large, muscular men—used the sharpest knives to cut the meat to the customers' exact specifications.

One of my jobs was grinding the beef scraps. Any pieces that weren't usable for a steak or roast or stew meat would be thrown into the hamburger-making bin, because clients always wanted loads of ground beef.

I fed those meaty chunks through an industrial hamburger grinder, then pressed the meat into a rectangular tub mold, and cut it down into one- or two-pound pieces. We'd wrap them in paper, label them, and pack them into boxes with the rest of the order. After the meat had been in the freezer for at least twenty-four hours, Mom would call the customer and tell them their order was ready for pickup.

Even as a little kid, the whole process captivated me. When the local farmers started experimenting with bison and ostrich, we butchered those animals as well. It wasn't exactly a normal environment for children, but there were always little jobs for me to do. I was never afraid of the blood and guts. At nine years old, I suited up in rubber boots, rubber apron, and safety goggles, and used the hose to wash the sides of beef on the kill floor. And everyone kept an eye on me because I was Françoise's daughter. Vivianne and Pete and I used to talk on her smoke breaks, and everyone seemed happy to have me around. They would make me speak French and glee at how cute my progress was coming along. I felt helpful and useful and wanted. And I felt like hard work was something that I enjoyed doing because it passed the time, and I could feel proud of myself. Just like I was as a young girl on the farm with the Kissels, I didn't want to be in the house with my grandma making cookies. I wanted to be where the work was happening. I always found the machinery, the sounds, the hustle and the bustle of the man's work more exciting. And I think my mom did, too.

Mom never worked on the kill floor with us; she was the manager of everything from the butchering and meat processing to the deli retail operation at the front of the building. She supplied large work camps for the oil companies in our area, keeping their kitchens stocked. And hospital and university cafeterias would also order large amounts of meat from my mom. My grandfather, Pierre, planned and set all this up for her; all Mom had to do was step in and run it.

§

The meatpacking plant was only one piece of Dargis Land & Cattle, which was my grandfather's giant conglomerate operation. My other grandpa, whom we called Pépère, valued discipline, decorum, and capitalism, and in turn, he was a very good businessman. He started off broke, just like every other grandpa whose lineage came via the European exodus to North America. He acquired his first piece of land privately and by saving up to purchase it out of pocket. He spent time as a teen working in hard labour lumber camps in British Columbia, and he was very disciplined and savvy with his money. Like the Kissels, Pierre and Anita Dargis were survivors from the depression era and kept a garden and believed in being resourceful. He was a pay-cash-for-everything kind of person and saved all his money. He never bought anything unless he could pay for three quarters of it, which was different from everyone else, even then. And habitual reinvestment led to his good fortune.

Because he was so disciplined, when a recession hit in the late '60s and early '70s, he had a little bit of money. During that time, he took advantage of everyone else's bankruptcy and bought land all around the area for pennies on the dollar, amassing a land wealth that increased in value over the next twenty-five years by about 500 percent. Pierre used that capital upgrade to diversify his business and grow the farming operations vertically. Where Lloyd Kissel had about two hundred head of cattle, Pierre Dargis had two thousand and about four times the amount of land and three strapping sons to help succeed Dargis Land & Cattle. He had the auction mart in town, where everyone came to buy and sell livestock. And he had the meatpacking plant that my mom was running like a good soldier. But he may have built it all by taking advantage of desperate times and situations—as a good capitalist does.

In the Bonnyville and St. Paul communities, Pierre was important—the wealthiest and most powerful man in area agriculture. He was the man who would buy your farm if you needed to sell it. But he would buy it only if it was a good cost-saving deal or if it was close to his existing infrastructure. Pierre was an innovator who kept his eye on emerging trends in agriculture and was the first in our corner of the province to bring in zero-till crop seeding technology, a process that used cutting edge machinery to preserve the surface soil integrity for advanced seeding methodology. He was an unassuming humble man. He dressed in clean, everyday plaid GWG shirts, always with a cloth hankie in the pocket and jeans that my mémère pressed for him.

Anita Dargis, my mémère, was a classic no-frills French woman. She never wore makeup and kept her hair short and plain, but she could bake and cook and garden expertly. The story goes that Pierre fell in love with her because of her meat and fruit pies. She was a domestic expert, very talented in the way of running seven children in a large household over the years, a true *chatelaine*. Mémère was similar to Grandma Betty in so many ways, with her quiet, kind nature and homemaking skills, but she was also a product of living with a driven and disciplined and often unrelenting husband. If she disagreed with anything that happened, she knew better than to say it. She was a subservient wife and mother, which was expected in French Catholic families.

The Dargises lived in a big, beautiful house. Their wealth was blatant. His fortune made allowed my grandpa to pursue hobbies, like flying his new Hughes helicopter. He went to flight school and had a hangar and platform built for it in the yard. He used the red and white helicopter to fly around and check on the cattle on his faraway ranchlands, just like on his favourite show, *Dallas*. As kids, we'd hear the familiar electric sound of the platform rolling out of the big hangar doors, bringing out the chopper to an area where he could warm up the rotors and get it ready. And Maurice and I would run to see if we could ride with him. It had four seats and a weight limit, but we argued that we were small enough to come along. Sometimes he allowed it, but most of the time he said no, perhaps not wanting to put us in danger. As we got older, and my brother spent more time with him, he got to accompany Pépère on his rides more frequently. Owning and maintaining the helicopter was expensive, and learning to fly it took discipline. On quieter summer days when all the crops were growing, Pierre taught Maurice how to golf. So, my brother just thought my grandfather, Pierre, hung the moon.

My brother and I spent a lot of time with this set of grandparents after the divorce. In the French tradition, Mémère made a fresh dessert every day, always saving the first piece for my pépère. Days with Anita started early and busy. The house needed to be spotless; we needed to do the shopping. We prepared the dessert every morning from scratch and then created some sort of delicious lunchtime meal and suppertime meal every day. Pierre detested leftovers for dinner. When the work was done, Anita and I picked berries in the summer and went ice fishing in the winter. My brother, when he would wake up in the morning, spent all day with my grandfather, overseeing the business operations, stopping for coffee in town. Their adventures always sounded more fun than mine. It was just a lot more fun than the work that Anita and I had to do every single day. I was used to being with actionable men and, at first, full-time domestic duty was excruciating. But my mémère and I became quite close. Both my grandmothers were very much the same. Betty taught and prized academics, and Anita always admired that about Betty. And Anita never spoke poorly of Lloyd, even when everyone else did. I loved her even more for that.

§

My mom's siblings, my three aunts and three uncles, had a different life than Françoise. They didn't have a teenage pregnancy or the wrath of their embarrassed and disappointed French Catholic father, so they went off to university or started their own farms and lives. Unlike her very pretty and glamorous sisters, my mom was a heavy, masculine woman who never wore makeup or did anything with her fine, thin blonde hair. She always seemed to believe that she had to make up for her sins and do right by her parents, and she believed the only way to do that was to make a lot of money. In our town, whoever had the most money had the most power and respect.

My Aunt Martine, who was the baby of the family and about fourteen years older than me, was an opera singer. Another sister-auntie. She was pursuing her master's in fine arts at the University of Salzburg in Austria and singing her way across Europe. She was beautiful and sophisticated, and her career was gaining momentum, and my grandfather always encouraged the pursuit of fine arts and higher education. He bought her a baby grand piano to play in the mansion for when she was home. She made everybody feel like they were the most beautiful person in the world. She was truly a lovely and elegant person. Her favour as the baby of the family was obvious whenever she came home from Europe, because Mémère and I always polished and cleaned her room, with its parquet flooring and a brass four-poster bed. When Martine was there, she spent much of her time with me, painting my nails and curling my hair. She made me feel beautiful. When I struggled with my times tables, she spent a summer building custom flash cards for me and played Chopin on the piano. She elevated all of our acuity with the study of fine art. One summer before my breasts had sprouted, Martine taught me how to soften the stiff lace of a French balconette bra and exposed me to movies like *Fiddler on the Roof*, *My Fair Lady*, and *Oliver Twist*. She was born elegant, I was sure of it.

When I got lonely for Aunt Martine, Mémère and I wrote her letters. My handwriting was boyish and sloppy, and I'd often write, scrap, and rewrite those letters to produce only the best cursive text for my Auntie Martine to read abroad. Then we used special Airmail envelopes with the blue and red stripes down the sides to send them off to her in Salzburg. She always wrote back and my mémère saved them for the next time I came over.

Divorce was uncommon in those days and judged poorly by our Catholic church. Pierre was a leader in the Knights of Columbus and an all-encompassing man in the community who was successful and a very strong leader, and he had this poor daughter who was always causing him trouble, getting pregnant so young and now recently divorced. But Pierre and Anita never made my brother and me feel that way. I felt the stigma at my Catholic school, but I still loved going to church, especially on special occasions when all my glamorous and beautiful aunts were visiting or home from university. We were quite the tribe to roll into Sunday Mass in our polished attire, occupying two full rows of pews. I liked it. I felt strong and safe amongst them.

Christmas was always special because everyone came home to the Dargis mansion just like on the show *Dallas*, and Mémère and Martine would decorate. Martine added ultra-chic touches of decor pieces discovered in Europe. The Dargis sons came from their farms, and the daughters came with their new husbands or boyfriends at the time. When I was nine, my first cousin was born. Her name was Leona, and her dad, my Uncle Jean, was closest to my mom of all the siblings, so we spent lots of time together with Aunty Joanne and Uncle Jean. I absolutely adored my baby cousin. But the next year when her father stood at the Christmas dinner table to announce they were pregnant again, I saw the tense undercurrent that affected this otherwise perfect-looking family.

We were all gathered around the extra-large table in my grandparents' dining room, dressed to the nines and ready for midnight mass later, when Uncle Jean stood from his seat and said, cheerfully, "I have some special news to share."

When he explained, joy overcame us all and everyone cheered, except the second-eldest brother, Uncle Joe, who was co-successor to the family business. He and his beautiful wife, Cheryl, had been struggling with infertility, and when he saw Grandpa Pierre's face light up, Uncle Joe took their pregnancy as a personal slight. They were always competing for my pépère's favour.

"You think you're so great, with your perfect family and new baby on the way." Joe stood up, face-to-face with his brother. "The only reason you're bringing this up now is to show off because we're still without children."

"That's ridiculous," Jean said, never one to back down. "Not everything is about you."

But Uncle Joe didn't let up. The argument escalated and Joe threw a punch across the gloriously decorated Christmas table and the dinner my mémère had prepared and served on her best china. When Joe's fist skimmed the side of Jean's face, he threw one back at Joe, which he ducked. The table rattled between them, and a water glass fell and spilled, shattering next to me.

Then Grandpa Pierre stood up and slammed his fist into the table. "This is not what Christmas is about. We need to put our struggles aside and observe the holiday in our Lord's name." He had a slight French accent when he spoke and a very deep commanding voice.

Everything settled down after that, and we went back to our prime rib and lobster meal; but the turbulent undercurrent of strife that existed among my mother's family never ceased under Pierre's constant scrutiny. My mom was born and raised in this take-no-prisoners, opportunistic capitalism value system. Her father put pressure on her to succeed and make money to grow the empire. And that pressure wore on her and my uncles.

§

Françoise was very charismatic with people who came in the shop, and people loved getting their meat from her. She always smiled and chatted up the customers; for them, she made a show of being amazing. But as soon as that customer walked out the door, she often became a different person.

Mom didn't handle stress very well, and she shouldered quite a bit with the day-to-day operations and constant need to satisfy herself and her father. Being an entrepreneur and building a business is not easy. It was a classic corporation that needed balance sheets, budgets, growth, space, and employees. Something had to fall by the wayside in my mother's life, and that was being a mom and raising her kids. Even if she wanted to do that, she didn't have time. Her annoyance and anger always ran high. Everybody who worked for Françoise was quite a bit older than she was, but they had to take orders from her, and she wasn't the best manager. Nobody was ever working fast enough for her. But really, she didn't understand how to manage people, workflows, projects, all the things that you might learn if you grew up in a family business or you went to school for formal training. She demanded more than they could give, even with my brother and me.

She either treated my brother and me like we were in the way or made us work harder. Every day, when we arrived after school, there would be hours of work to do. On most days, our job was processing cured meats and packaging them for retail sale in the butcher shop. We would have anywhere from one hundred to a thousand pounds of sausages to place in thick plastic bags and vacuum seal, before 9 p.m. Vacuum sealing was a new technology at the time, and in 1988 we had a state-of-the-art machine that processed only three packages at a time. We'd work until eight or nine at night, long after the regular employees left for the day, to get all the deli-counter meat ready.

Mom would do paperwork in the office and when she was almost ready to go, she'd come back and check on us. She would click the face of her watch with her finger and say, "Where are you with this, guys? We've got to go." We were ten and eight years old.

When we weren't vacuum sealing meat, we were folding endless boxes that the meat would eventually be packed in, each one printed with the DLC Meat Packers logo. And if my brother was goofing off or not getting the work done, I'd have to tell him to keep going. During those days, Françoise worked us like we were undocumented immigrants.

And her father was fine with that, even encouraged it. He loved nothing more than to show up at the facility to check on operations and see my brother and me working hard. He would dole out little bits of love and acceptance to Françoise, which was what she craved the most. My mom worked tirelessly for him. And while he expected a lot from all his children, he relied on Mom to help build this leg of his empire. He needed her because he had his hands full already with the feedlot and auction mart, and he may have taken advantage of her debt to him. The only time my mom was happy was when business was going well and her father was pleased. But on most days, she was difficult to be around and verbally abusive.

My mom felt self-conscious about her weight and was always trying Nutrisystem or Weight Watchers, any new fad diet. She was an emotional eater. Any attempts my mom made toward improving her looks, like her tight perms, were largely ignored and akin to me shaving my unibrow. She started taking me for the same super tight perm. It was so tight I looked like a sheep. But I learned from listening to the ladies in the salon that I could wash it in the next six hours to relax the curl a little. When I tried this, my mom was furious that she'd spent her money at the salon only to have me ruin it by washing it out. She had moments of abusive rage, like the time she shoved me, sending me falling face-first into a door. I hit my face on the knob and got a black eye.

§

On rare weekends, Mom let us spend time with my dad and my grandparents at the Kissel farm. When Aunt Brenda came home from studying to become a dental hygienist at the University of Alberta and running for Miss Edmonton Eskimo, Grandma Betty made such a big fuss out of it, just like Anita did when Martine came home. That's when my grandmother really worked on my mom to let us come to the farm. Brenda loved to bake cookies, read stories, and take us for rides around the farmyard on the smaller garden tractors. She was one of those light-up-your-life kinds of people, and my grandmother knew that. And she knew there was no reason that my mom's biases against my dad and grandfather should apply to Brenda. And once in a while, it would work.

One Friday in October when I was going to Dr. Brosseau Middle School, Mom told Maurice and me that Brenda was going to pick us up from school and take us for the night. It was close to my brother's birthday, and Brenda had these amazing things planned for us to celebrate. The Kissels always tried to see us. It just never really worked out well. So we were so excited. All day long, I looked forward to my aunt picking me up and spending the night with her at the farm.

At the end of the day, I waited outside for Brenda. And when she pulled up and got out of the car, I ran to her and embraced her in a huge hug.

"How are you?" She hugged me hard. "I've missed you so much."

Then just as we were getting in Brenda's car, Mom pulled up and said, "Carmen is not going anywhere with you. Carmen get inside my vehicle."

"What are you talking about?" I said, baffled. "I want to go with Brenda. We're going to pick up Maurice." Then I noticed she already had Maurice. He peered at me, in tears, through the backseat window.

"What do you mean?" Brenda said. "Why?"

As my schoolmates caught their rides and loaded into buses, I watched in tears as my mom launched a verbal tirade against Brenda, who was the nicest and sweetest person. I don't know what happened to change my mom's mind, but Brenda left the school in tears, and Mom whisked Maurice and me off to the meatpacking plant and put us to work. And after that Betty never used Brenda ever again to try to lure us for a visit, and Brenda never tried either. Françoise had won.

§

Some days, as soon as the bus dropped us off at the meat processing facility, my brother and I could see the stress on her face. She would be impatient and short with us, and we learned to put our heads down, work, and stay out of her way. But we were also old enough to recognize that she was in a stressful situation—a single mom, with a father she wanted to please more than anything, and a large operation to oversee. I'd see my classmates' moms come into the classroom and bring cookies or help for the afternoon. My mom was never that mom. But I was old enough to understand my grandpa's stature in the community and my mom's role in it. And working all those nights to help, I became proud of what we did. I could look back at five hundred pounds of processed garlic sausage and feel good about what my brother and I had accomplished. We got to take our product and move it to the display coolers, and I learned how to talk about it with the customers. I could make recommendations. Selling came naturally to me. And I was proud.

Mom had business cards with this cool hologram DLC logo on it, and I'd taken them to school to show my classmates. They ooed and awed at the business cards and my stories about owning your own business. And when the school highlighted the local business community with field trips to see the operations, they asked to tour my mom's business. My mom was so excited that her daughter's class was coming to see the facility, and I was excited too.

When the day of the field trip arrived, I couldn't wait to show everyone where I worked and what I did. But as soon as we walked inside the building, everyone cringed and held their noses at the smell. The meat cutters, who had become like family to me by that time, were working that day, slicing a side of beef. All the kids winced at the high-pitched sound of the saw cutting through bone and turned away from the sight of something that had become such a huge part of who I was. Their abhorrence to see animal flesh crushed me. I showed them what I did after school, and what was a big part of my life, only to be met with jeers and sneers. And once I showed them, they never let it go. I was known from then on as *the dirty butcher shop girl*.

I learned to never talk about those parts of my life at school ever again and I became a social pariah. But I never told my mom about it. She probably would have laughed and told me that they were being ridiculous, and I should be proud no matter what. But I didn't want to hurt her feelings because I thought what the kids were saying was cruel. And my brother and I were always in Mom's way anyway. I assumed that she wouldn't care in the slightest.

"I'm hungry. Is it time to go home yet?" I whined one night, hanging in the doorway of her office. Maurice and I had finished our work.

"Don't you have anything to do?" Mom growled over a stack of paperwork on her desk. "Children should be seen and not heard." This was one of her favourite quotes.

I knew this meant we weren't going home anytime soon. And I'd already skipped through whatever homework I had. I was never much of a student because that wasn't a priority in Françoise's house. Any homework help or questions bothered her. If I did miss an assignment, I figured out how to leave class for an extended bathroom break when it came time to turn it in. I said to Maurice, "Let's go check on the cows and pigs."

Even if I knew where they were headed, I always wanted to be with the animals out back. The cows, with their herd mentality, could be in a pen anywhere and still be chewing hay and swishing their tails. But the pigs knew what was coming. They were dirty and grimy, but they were vocal and frenzied and *smart*. I had grown up around pigs, but these pigs were unlike any I'd seen before. They were so scared. It seemed like they knew that they were about to die. And we'd been told never to approach farm animals that we didn't know, but Maurice and I didn't care. We were livestock whisperers. It was here that I learned that steers about to be slaughtered were oblivious, but pigs always sensed when something wasn't right.

It was early in the week, so the pens were mostly empty, except for two very frightened pigs. They cowered in their small pen, rooting for comfort and were oddly quiet. I had an apple left over from my lunch at school, which I cut in half for them using the sterilized butcher chopping knives, while Maurice refreshed their bedding. By the time Maurice and I were ten years old, we were both experts with large knives. We understood that these animals were coming to the end of life, but that didn't mean we couldn't make their last moments as good as possible.

"It's okay," I said when I offered the snack. "You had a pretty good life." The pig shook and pawed at the floor. Maurice and I sat with them until we heard Mom call for us.

"Let's go," she yelled from the other room.

"Finally," I groaned at Maurice.

"I hope you weren't back there messing around with those pigs. You know better than to approach animals you don't know," Mom said when we joined her.

"We were just checking on them," Maurice said.

"Ridiculous," she said, turning off the lights. "Get your things."

My mother often scolded us for spending extra time with the animals. To her, they were just one more burden, and we could have been sweeping the floor instead. Although our life at the meat processing facility had a few bright spots, the work and stress took its toll on all of us.

4

LIFE AT HOME

"Because of you I find it hard to trust not only me, but everyone around me. Because of you, I am afraid."
—Kelly Clarkson

FRANÇOISE'S BITTERNESS OVER THE DIVORCE and against my father never subsided. It proliferated and continued to grow. Because she came from money and power, she let that justify and fuel her abusive outpour. She was constantly annoyed and never had a good thing to say about my father or Grandpa Lloyd. He was just a drunk and he was going nowhere, and the only good person worth half a shit on my dad's side was my grandmother, Betty. Françoise often quoted with a sneer, "If it wasn't for Betty's teaching salary, that Kissel farm would go under."

Françoise was a death by a thousand cuts type of person, always taking verbal shots at us—destroying opportunities to create a kind inner voice. And she used the guise of good character development and the ten commandments to instill the fear of God into us, that we'd better be good people. Lying was the worst. If you lied and you got caught lying, you'd face the full brunt of her rage. Even at a young age, I suspected that she liked being mean, *for sport*.

She made threats about throwing away our most treasured possessions, like my brother's hockey cards. He'd been collecting them with Dad, an ex-hockey player with a huge card collection, since he was old enough to talk. Before the divorce my brother used to love to sit down with my dad and look through his collection and reminisce about the Edmonton Oilers' glory years winning multiple Stanley Cup championships. The cards came with a hard, powdery stick of pink gum that my dad always saved for Maurice. And Dad kept the connection alive after the divorce by talking to him about cards on the phone or in letters. He sent Maurice a full set of Upper Deck cards, which my brother treasured. Full sets were like winning the lottery and very costly to buy. With a full set you didn't need to buy individual packs hoping for the cards you needed to create a full set. But my brother and I were unsettled, rebellious kids who frequently acted out, or in my instance, talked back.

One day, after some minor behavioural infraction, Mom threw away all of Maurice's hockey cards. I came upon her screaming in the kitchen at him and saw her exit the back door of the house to access the outside garbage bin. There, she gleefully lifted the lid and rammed his binder and shoe box of cards in the bin and slammed the lid down. My brother cried and cried for days, as if his heart was ripped out.

Maurice was never the same after that. He became hard to engage with and hard to play with. He became depressed. That was when I knew I had to take care of Maurice. Seeing him so little and so upset about his cards, I was equally as crushed, and I vowed to be that big sister who would protect him. Even though they were just cards, my mother crushed his tiny soul when she tossed them in the trash. She didn't just throw away his hockey cards that day, she also threw away the relationship he had with our dad, straight into the garbage.

My dad still tried to break into our lives through holiday events like Christmas. He knew that we would most likely not be coming to visit, so through letters exchanged with Grandma Betty at school he asked us to provide a Christmas "wish list" of present ideas. I populated my list with at least twenty hot-ticket items like Jem and the Holograms, a rocker

Barbie-like group that had earrings that lit up and flashed by activating a small switch on their backs. I liked Popples too, and board games.

After the divorce, Maurice and I missed a few Christmases with the Kissels, and became delighted to learn that this one Christmas, we'd be able to go. But my mom would have to attend as well and so Françoise was invited too. Mom burned with rage as Maurice and I unwrapped every single one of our wish-list Christmas gifts with sheer delight. I'm sure she felt that our dad was trying to position himself as some sort of "Disneyland Dad" and it worked for us. We were gobsmacked to receive every requested item.

§

By the time I'd reached preteen age, I began to view my mother with complete disrespect. She disgusted me. As she became mean for sport, I manipulated her, knowing what to say to keep her in the right mood. I learned how to insert myself to protect my brother from her. He was a little kid, he couldn't always control himself or his outbursts, but I knew that if I could be there in time, I could interfere so that my mom went after me instead. I wanted him to have someone to count on, when it seemed all the people we'd counted on before—the Kissel side of the family, including my dad and grandparents and Porky and Brenda—were no longer available to us. We never saw them. Phone calls were irregular and infrequent. And for some reason, it seemed like they couldn't ever come get us. I had to be the person in my brother's life who loved him and gave him affection and attention. I helped him with his homework and loved him so much. And in the morning, I got us both ready and off to school.

My mother's lack of involvement in our care became obvious when we'd show up to school in the same shirt we'd wore the previous day, hair unkempt, teeth not brushed, with nothing to eat but a box of Sunripe Apple Juice or, oddly enough, a pack of just twenty powdered mini-donuts. And it wasn't because we didn't have money to buy groceries; Françoise just didn't prioritize having groceries in the house at regular intervals. When I talked to my dad during this time, I begged to see him. "Mom says that if you just give her money every month, she'll let you see us. Can you do that?"

"Carmen, it's not that simple," he said. "No matter how much I give her, she won't let me see you anyway. Are you still getting my letters? I'm still keeping all of yours." He knew how cruel and neglectful my mom could be, so he asked if we were hungry and if we were okay. Our teachers probably saw it. My grandma, who was at the school, probably saw it. Then one day, summoning up all his gumption (I'm sure), my dad called Child Protective Services for a welfare check. This scrutiny and embarrassment only infuriated my mom. Behind closed doors, as secretive and dirty as could be, is when she became physically abusive.

Little slaps across the face when we talked back or weren't working hard enough became heavy blows that sent our small bodies stumbling. Stress triggered her. If she felt overwhelmed, she'd lash out. Her verbal abuse worsened. She stopped using our names altogether, further severing any connection or acknowledgement of us as individuals. "Shut up, *girl*. You don't know what you're talking about, *boy*," and, "You better listen when I tell you this, *girl*."

Once, after a long night at the butcher shop, we all came home exhausted. I had been in a hurry that morning and left the peanut butter on the kitchen counter. I had forgotten all about it in my rush to get my brother and myself out the door. But Mom saw it and exploded. "I am so sick of you not doing your part," she yelled with her finger in my face. This launched her verbal tirade against me.

"That's not true. I do my part," I yelled back at her. "You're just too busy to notice."

She raised her arm high and slapped me across the head, knocking me to the ground. She was a heavy, powerful woman, and I was a scrawny, slight child. Crouching there on the ground, waiting for her to either hit me again or storm off, I would *never cry*. But I wished I was a bigger person so I could fight back. I wished I could be the one to save us.

When I started noticing that all the other little girls in my class had braids in their hair and looked pretty, the pain of my own physical awkwardness increased. Those girls had moms who did their hair every morning and kept them groomed and packed a healthy lunch. I had a unibrow and my mom cut my hair herself in a mushroom-shaped bowl cut. I was never allowed to get my ears pierced or try lip gloss like the other girls. I looked like a boy, and I yearned to look the way the other girls looked. Even the kids at school picked on me for my eyebrows and androgynous looks, so much so that I decided to do something about it.

One morning, when I was getting ready for school, I found my mom's razor in the bathroom and thought that if I could just shave a little away in the middle to separate my eyebrows, I would look much better. As careful as possible, I took too big of a swipe and shaved off halfway over my eye. I went to school, and all day was horribly made fun of. When my mom noticed later, we were standing in her bedroom.

"What the hell happened to your eyebrows?"

"I don't know, Mom." Embarrassment flooded me. "There was an accident at school, and someone got too close to me with scissors, and it messed up my eyebrows a little."

She knew I was lying, and kept berating me, demanding to know what happened, threatening to call the school in the morning, not letting up until I gave her a name. "Who did this to you?" she yelled.

"I don't remember."

A hot rage came over her and she grabbed me by my neck and shoulders with both hands and lifted me up off the ground. She brought my face to hers. Sweat glistened on her brow, and her eyes were inflamed with anger, like they might bulge out of her head.

"You're a little witch and a liar," she said, and she threw me across the room, where I crashed into the wall and slid to the floor, crumpled in a pile.

§

By the time I was in fifth grade, the butcher shop was doing so well that Mom had enough money to buy a brand-new house outside of town. She had gotten her driver's license back by then, so she didn't have to be as close to work anymore. And she had a new car. She didn't have the house built, but the house wasn't finished either. Outside, white wide plank vinyl siding covered the house. The front had a big living room window and two smaller bedroom windows on the main floor. We always used the back door, which opened into the utility room, next to the kitchen. The kitchen sold the place, with a rectangular ceiling light with fluorescent rods behind a frosted piece of plexiglass that gave the room a backlight feeling meant to mimic sunshine. It had solid oak cabinets, and the basement was concrete—a big step up from our dirt hole in the ground. Maurice could shoot plastic hockey pucks without denting the walls. We thought we were lucky with this new home.

We lived off Township Road 631 also known as Lessard Road. Lessard was an intersection on the top of a hill with a tiny graveyard on one corner and a county baseball diamond on the other. Down the other way, at the bottom of the hill, the Beaver River flowed under a little bridge where my brother and I would ride our bikes and search for river clams. It was a beautiful mixed boreal forested landscape, like a John Denver song.

People assumed that Mom got the house because her dad paid for it with the Dargis family fortune. He likely supplied a deposit or down payment though. But he didn't buy her the house; he may have helped each of his children get started, but he didn't spoil them. Mom earned her money and paid for it herself. But at the time, Bonnyville was experiencing a bust, as oilfield towns tend to do, and mortgage interest rates steeped near 20 percent. And it turned out that the people who'd started building the house went bankrupt and couldn't pay for it. Mom, like her father liked to do, swooped in with a rock-bottom offer they were desperate enough to take.

Mom owned that home proudly. She was a single mom, but she didn't have to depend on a man. And she took that very seriously. Moving into the new house and finishing it, room by room, was going to be awesome. The bare yard was a blank slate where we could plant trees and grass. Because clay hardened the ground, trucks brought in loads of topsoil for a fresh start. We were finally going to have a decent life. Mom was so happy, and she was financially secure. But that's really when things started getting worse. Nothing grows in clay, it turns out. Mom only had about two inches of topsoil put down, and subsequently everything struggled to grow.

The first morning after we moved in, as I waited for the school bus at the end of the driveway at the new house, there was a girl waiting across the street. I could see her, kicking at the gravel and watching me. But I was too far away to talk to her. We stood there looking at each other for a minute, chilly in the morning air. Then she waved, and I waved back. When the bus came groaning to a stop and I climbed aboard, I sat near Crissy. I wanted nothing more than to be friends with this girl, who looked nice and was curious about me, the new girl. But the first thing she said to me on our ride to school was, "You live in my cousin Amy's house, where she was supposed to live with my aunt and uncle. They couldn't keep their house anymore, so the bank took it, and now you guys have it." The way she said it, I knew she wanted her cousin Amy to be her neighbour, not me. And I knew her family had suffered an unfortunate loss that gave us the opportunity to live there. Crissy had a sister who was fifteen and pregnant. When my mom found out about this, she said there was no way I could be friends with them. But Crissy and I became friends eventually anyways. One school bus ride home at a time.

Now that my brother and I were older, we could take the bus to the new house and stay by ourselves instead of going to the meatpacking plant every day. This is where I fell into books. I would read anything and everything from Nancy Drew to the Hardy Boys and anything by Lucy M. Montgomery. Mom still worked late, but she had more flexibility and time to spend with us. She even started giving us rides to school in the morning, which she seemed excited about. Instead of spending that time enjoying our company, from our driveway to the school, she preached to us about her feelings on anything and everything. And she grilled us on any small chores left undone or for slipping grades. If we raised any sort of questions or counterpoints, she'd try to smack the insolence out of us. But if we didn't talk enough, she berated us further.

"What's wrong with you?" she'd hiss. "Why won't you talk to me?" But we were simply terrified. We couldn't seem to say anything right. And everything ended with the back of her hand across the face. Because of this, Maurice and I would often fight for the back seat, as someone was always expected to ride upfront, with her.

One winter morning, I went outside early to warm up the car. I turned the key in the ignition and the engine came to life, then I moved to the back seat. A minute later, Maurice came out and got in the back seat with me. The defrost had made two oddly shaped circles of ice melting to water on the front windshield. When Mom came out a few minutes later and saw us in the back seat together, she took offense.

"What are you two doing?"

"We just want to sit in the back this morning."

"How's it going to look when I pull up to the school and nobody's sitting up front with me?" she huffed. "One of you has to move up here."

"I'm going to help Maurice with an assignment," I lied.

She didn't care about our feelings, but it did seem like she cared very much about what the community thought of her. She could be smacking my brother and me one minute, then putting on a show as soon as a customer walked into the shop. It was like flipping a switch. She was a fraud, and I could see at a young age that she had everyone in town fooled. She didn't care about what she was doing to us in the front seat on the way to school every day. She just cared about what it looked like when she rolled up to the school and nobody was in the front seat with her.

§

One day after church in the hamlet of St. Vincent, we ran into someone Mom knew from high school. Maurice and I were sitting in the back seat, and the woman, who was walking through the parking lot when she stopped to chat, peered back at us through the window. "Oh, Françoise," she said, "are these your two boys?"

I was wearing an unremarkable pink dress; I was expected to wear a dress for church, but I loved any reason to dress up. This woman's mistake mortified me. The kids at school had been saying it for years. But if even adults thought I looked like a boy, then it had to be true.

"Oh, no," Mom said, not skipping a beat. "Carmen is my daughter and Maurice is my son."

The woman looked again through the window and saw her mistake. "Oh, I see," she said and then changed the subject to someone else she'd recently run into.

I didn't know what to think. I looked at my hands in my lap, at the fingernails I'd bitten down to the quick for as long as I could remember.

I became desperate to look better and dove into teen magazines and beauty tips. I hid them from my mom under my mattress. I was of French Mediterranean decent, dark and hairy, and I learned about tweezing eyebrows and bleaching my shadow mustache. I started to save up all my money from babysitting my cousins and the neighbour kids, and the odd time when my mom would throw my brother and me twenty bucks for working like dogs at the meatpacking plant. We never asked for money. We never got allowances or anything like that. It was just all-hands-on-deck, everybody helped. And if she felt benevolent that week, we might get some money. And I used my money to secretly buy makeup and clothes.

Crissy, the girl across the road, and I became good friends. She had cousins in the area and we all hung out together. And they were always curious to see the inside of our house and what we'd done to it—remember, it was supposed to be their cousin Amy's house.

One night we came home late, tired and hungry from working all day in the meatpacking plant. There was always meat in our freezer, but there was never food ready to eat. No boxes of mac and cheese or TV dinners. So we were all groaning about not having anything when my mom remembered she bought a box of pizza pops and put them in the freezer. She went to look for them and they were all gone—nothing but an empty box.

"Who did this?" she screamed. She looked at me, and she looked at my brother. Then she zeroed in on him. "You ate them all, didn't you?"

"No. I didn't eat them," he said, looking at me frantically.

"I didn't eat them," I said, and I really didn't. My brother didn't either, but we had no explanation for my mother, who flew into a rage.

She believed my brother had eaten them, and when he denied it, she believed he was lying to her. She took him into his room, closed the door, and made him beg on his knees for forgiveness from God for lying. I paced outside his door, listening to her yell and hit him, demanding he admit to his lies. When I tried coming in, she told me to mind my own business. "I'm teaching him a lesson," she yelled.

Years later, I learned that Crissy and her cousin, Ryan, had stopped in a couple of nights before the pizza pop incident. We never locked the door, and they let themselves in. They walked through our entire house, and the only thing they took or disturbed was those pizza pops. They were hungry, so they ate them all. But at the time, we had no idea what happened to them. I was too embarrassed to admit I lived with an abusive mother to tell Crissy what my mom had done to us when she found them missing.

§

When I was in sixth grade, everyone in my class assembled in the music room at Dr. Brosseau Middle School for a special presentation. They talked about all these different scenarios, where the adults were hurting the kids in the family, explaining verbal and physical abuse in ways that rang familiar. And as the presenters were going through all of these situations, I remember sitting on the floor amongst my classmates with my knees drawn tight into my chest, just listening and taking it all in. Everything they said confirmed my belief that I lived a pretty horrible life in my own home. Based on what they were telling me, my home life was abusive, and I should tell someone I trusted—like a teacher or relative. They said that's the only way it would stop.

I thought about that every day as a kid, wondering if I should tell someone our secret. But I also knew that even if I did speak up, probably nothing would change. My father was a drunk. His father was a drunk. And no one would believe their word against my mom's; she was an upstanding businessperson and member of the community. Whenever I told my aunts and uncles that she was mean or cruel, they told me they were sorry. But my aunts and uncles were always mad at each other, often trying to best one another. I can remember my Aunt Lois saying to me, "Your mom is just a difficult person, Carmen, even for us."

My aunts and uncles did, however, take me in. I lived with Uncle Jean and his family for the whole summer, watching my toddler cousins: Leona, Lynn, and Sarah. Maurice and I helped out around their farm however we could. Uncle Jean taught me how to drive automatic transmissions when I was twelve so I could load up all the girls and take them for a picnic. We'd pack juice in mason jars and make sandwiches and wrap them in wax paper, and then deliver lunch to the people haying in the far-flung fields. And at the end of the summer, when it was time for me to go back to school, Jean and Joanne gave me five crisp $100 bills for all the work I'd done. That was the most money I'd ever seen! This set of auntie and uncle was such fun and so young themselves. Forging their own farm and raising their babies. They were cool. Prior to marriage, Aunt Joanne, who had farm girl legs for days, was a model for a short while with John Casablancas Modelling Agency. She would let me study her old promo and photoshoot contact sheets and helped me with hair and makeup tips.

I matured during that time, and I started demanding that my mom pay me for the work I did at the meatpacking plant too. I already cleaned our home, cooked, and processed all of our laundry too. She did start paying me, I think to keep the peace. I was getting bigger and definitely sassier. If she hit me, I knew I could hit her back, even though I never did. But she stopped picking on me as much, and doubled down on my brother instead.

He got caught stealing something small from 7-Eleven. She closed him in his room, demanding he repent for his sin of stealing, and started berating him. A protective rage flooded me, and I slammed myself into his door, and yelled, "If you hurt him, I'll hurt you."

But she stood on the other side, holding it closed, laughing at me. "I'd like to see you try," she hissed.

I slammed myself into the door again, but it was no use. I couldn't do anything. I didn't know what to do. She only laughed louder, like the idea of me hurting her was the most ridiculous thought in the world. All I could do was beg her to stop, and she eventually did. When she opened the door, my brother was bruised up and crying.

I started escaping into books more. I read *The Baby-Sitters Club* and *Sweet Valley High* books. When I read *Are You There God? It's Me, Margaret* by Judy Blume, I felt like I'd been seen for the first time in my life. I brought home stacks from the school library and piled them on my night stand. I learned about my period and what to do about it from books and magazines.

I took ballet lessons and spent the weekends studying with an accomplished Russian instructor named Staszuik, learning to dance first on demi-pointe then on to full pointe as well as jazz and hip hop. I always love the discipline and the choreography and the elegance of our theatre classroom: 5,6,7,8 . . . ! And ballet was something my auntie, Martine, just absolutely loved too because it was a classical art. She even made it to some of my recitals. Ballet was very expensive, and I learned that my grandfather, Pierre, was footing that bill. I wanted to make him proud. And I excelled at sports, and went out for any team that would keep me out of the butcher shop in the evenings. I played volleyball, basketball, badminton, track and field, baseball, and I was in synchronized swimming. My mom loved that I was in all of these activities because it kept me busy and it was like a babysitter program.

But she was always late to pick me up after practices and games. I'd be waiting after all the other kids and coaches had gone home. The janitors would be ready to lock up the building, and I'd still be sitting there. The first time this happened, they didn't want to leave me alone.

"Are you sure your mom's coming?" they asked.

"Yes," I said, embarrassed.

"Are you sure you're okay if we leave?"

"Yes. I'll be okay."

After it happened several more times, they knew just to wave and leave me there to wait. But once I was in sports—and as good as I was—the kids at school started seeing me as something other than the dirty butcher shop girl. I liked being part of the team, and I took advantage of every opportunity to be away from home and to smash a volleyball or sink a basket.

§

When we were old enough, Maurice and I joined the Bonnyville 4-H Beef Club. My mom really wanted us to participate in this program because, as a business owner in the ag community, our participation reflected well on her. And she had become more tolerant of the Kissels lately, as their farm was close by and the perfect place to raise our steers. So my dad donated us each a calf from his farm, and we kept them there, which was a big deal because it meant spending more time on Hill and Valley Ranch. And my mom didn't have to take care of a farm animal, so she didn't mind us going over there. My dad would feed them every morning for us during the school week days.

On weekends, Mom took us by the Kissel farmyard—never the house or my grandparents' house—and let us spend the afternoon taking care of the animals. That first year, I named my steer, a black angus, Blackie, and I'd never loved an animal the way I loved that calf. Getting to spend time feeding him and petting him and talking to him was the best part of my week. I loved being back on this farm. I loved being around the animals. I loved that for once my mom was starting to lighten up about my dad. She didn't say as many mean things about him to me anymore. My dad and Grandpa Lloyd would come into the barn while we cleaned and bedded the animals, teaching us about how to be successful in 4-H. The Kissel family members had won many 4-H trophies over the years, including my dad, Uncle Gordon, and Aunt Brenda. And we went to the meetings, where we learned about the program. The goal was to raise our calves into sellable steers that were tame, groomed, and ready to show on Achievement Day, the annual 4-H event. I conquered my shyness with their excellent public speaking programs, coached by our kind and patient club leader, Mrs. Janet Dechaine. I won my first provincial public speaking award at twelve years old and this continued to feed my need to win at everything that I tried.

On Achievement Day, all the 4-H participants brought their groomed and readied animals that they'd raised all year to a show, where the animals were paraded around and then auctioned off. The payoff was the big check from whoever bought your steer. You could make up to a couple thousand dollars, depending on how the auction went. And that's how you were paid for raising the animal.

I wanted Blackie to be the tamest animal on Achievement Day because that would make me the best animal showman. Always a competitor, I wanted to be better than all my 4-H team members. So, I put a lot of work into Blackie, getting him used to me, spending time with him, reading books to him, telling him how wonderful he was. Auntie Brenda spent a whole weekend with me, teaching me how to bathe Blackie to get him ready for the show, trimming and blow-drying him, fluffing the hair at the end of his tail-tip into a ball and spraying it so it would stay in a perfect orb of teased hair. Black angus steer are gleaming black from tip to tail, like a panther, and I knew if I made him look perfect that the buyers would pay more for him. When I had him all shined up and beautiful, I took him to Achievement Day, like all of my other friends and their animals, and I paraded him around the arena. After Blackie's auction, I tried to reimburse my dad for the calf and feed, but he wanted me to keep it all. I had more money than I'd ever seen before. And Blackie left with the nice people who bought him for meat.

The following Thursday, when I arrived at the butcher shop after school, I put my bag in mom's office like always before joining in the work in the back. It was busy that day, and Mom was pacing in front of her desk, her cordless phone to her ear and held with her shoulder. When she saw me, she cupped her hand over the mouthpiece and said, "They don't need you back there today. Stay up here." Then the phone rang on the other line, and I slipped out when she answered it. I avoided conversation with her as much as possible.

I suited up in my rubber boots and waterproof apron like usual. But when I got to the kill floor and opened the door, I saw why she'd tried to keep me up front. Blackie, what was left of him, was laid out on the table getting skinned. He was dead now. Bled out at the throat. Lying on his back, hooves knocked off, and half his hide was peeled away from his body.

I was shocked, and as soon as the butchers realized it was my 4-H animal they were processing, they stopped. I had been so blinded by earning that check that I hadn't ever considered where Blackie was headed. Every buyer got to choose what they did with their animals, and my mom's was the only meatpacking plant within a two-hour radius. I had always been comfortable with the cycle of life. I knew that farm animals are raised for human consumption. I was fine with all that, but seeing the animal I'd loved and raised all year took me completely off guard.

I started crying, and the butchers lined up to shield me from the view. But I had to leave and close the door. I made my way to the break room and sat with my head in my hands. That day, when all the butchers and Vivianne, the meat inspector, came and sat with me, still bloody in their kill floor clothes, they all talked about how proud they were of me, and they cried with me too.

I still managed to do 4-H for the next three years, but I never went to the meatpacking plant on the days that prize-winning 4-H animals came for slaughter. I empathized with all those animals. Those animals knew a different kind of love by whichever kid had raised them in the program. My fault had been getting attached in the first place. I would never love another animal again, not if it meant hurting like that.

5

BOOM AND BUST

"If adventures will not befall a lady in her own village,
she must seek them abroad."
—JANE AUSTEN

RENOVATING OUR NEW HOUSE—TRANSFORMING IT from a rough shell to the home of our dreams—brought a wave of hopefulness to everyone. The man Mom hired to finish the house, Gilles, was a carpenter who lived down Lessard Road, our road. When we moved in, the kitchen was done and flooring had been laid. But the walls didn't have drywall, so we could pass from room to room through the 2x4s. Gilles, who worked on our house between his other projects, blocked off all the bedroom walls first, then chipped away at the rest of the renovations. And all the small decisions and work that went into the project seemed to give Maurice and me something to look forward to—a promise of a better life, filled with love.

I could see my mom trying to be good to us. When I was thirteen, I told her that I wanted to move my bedroom downstairs, where I had more space to practice ballet. I was sure she'd never go for it, but she said yes. She talked to Gilles about building me a suite, and she let me dream up an amazing room. I chose the trendy peach and forest green colour combination, and Mom and I bonded over the plans. She wanted my opinion on the finishing touches, and it felt like she cared. Soon enough, I had a custom ballet studio bedroom complete with an entire wall of mirror and a ballet bar.

Around this time, I started noticing stolen glances between Mom and Gilles, who was around all the time working on the house. Then, when they were talking about flooring for the hall, I saw him touch her hand. Then she kissed him goodbye one evening as he was heading home. I hadn't ever given it much thought, but Maurice and I were old enough now and spent a lot more time by ourselves, giving Mom plenty of time to go out on dates with the carpenter. Maurice and I, through conversations had when she wasn't around, gathered that Gilles was Mom's boyfriend. This was positive development; we liked Gilles and he seemed to make mom happy. He was ten or fifteen years older than her, and seemed to let her hot temper roll off his back. When they came out and told us they were together and loved each other, I felt happy.

But that better life we were all hoping for, even though I saw glimpses of it, always seemed to have a dark thread running through it.

§

Money helped build the façade. Mom took her role as provider seriously, buying us name-brand clothes and herself a new Chevy Blazer SUV, fitting of the success she'd built. This was a boom time, not only for Mom, but for everyone in the area. The whole town of Bonnyville brightened and bustled: beef, pork, and grains were a healthy price, BP and Esso couldn't hire enough people, and we welcomed hundreds of domestic migrant workers to the area. They came from clear across the country from places like Newfoundland, where their entire fishing industry had recently collapsed. High commodities pricing brought high spirits for everyone in town. My grandfather's operation was making lots of money. And filling all the meat orders from the work camps and everyone else kept Mom busy. She was flush, but she was also busy and stressed as a result. And this kept her from fully understanding us and fed the conflict.

Every night for dinner, we had meat—a steak or a roast, always choice cuts, which were readily available through her work. But we got sick of it sometimes. When Maurice and I asked for Kraft Dinner or even meatloaf, she turned up her nose in disdain. But we'd heard how simple and delicious those types of suppers were from our friends at school.

"You kids should feel lucky you don't have to eat that disgusting junk," she said.

We put our faces down in our plates and ate. Maybe she was right; maybe we were lucky. But it also felt like we were a little deprived of the simple childhood pleasures that other kids seemed to get. And I started seeing how desperate we were for a parental bond and a normal childhood away from places like the butcher shop.

§

Gilles had a woodworking shop at his house, where he worked on ornate, detailed millwork. He was an extremely talented finishing carpenter. When Maurice got a science assignment to build a boat, Gilles took him there to help him work on it after school. The class was testing physical properties like buoyancy and propulsion. The boat could be any shape or from any material, but it had to be made from scratch. And then everyone would participate in a boat race at the end. This was the kind of school project that we'd normally shy away from and fail because it required so much innovation and help from adults. I couldn't really help him the way I often did with projects like this because it was too complicated. Mom was always working, so she never helped with school work. But Gilles took ownership over helping him get it done in a way that neither my mom nor I could do.

One night when we were picking Maurice up from boat-building at Gilles's shop, we went into his workshop to see their progress. The shop had a crisp fresh-cut smell, and fine sawdust on almost every surface, even after it had been swept. It was a wonderland of smooth, intricate wood pieces and elaborate machinery. Gilles and Maurice were sanding and finishing the hull, getting ready to seal it. The boat, even unfinished, was the work of a professional, and Maurice was so excited and confident his would be the best in the class. He beamed, running his hands over the smooth wood and passing it to me as if he were passing a puppy. The model sailboat was over a foot long with a central mast, like something capable of crossing the Atlantic.

An intense, warm feeling came over me then. In lieu of our real father in moments like these, Gilles seemed like a perfect fit. Mom was happier than she'd ever been with Dad, and spending time with Gilles was a window into a family life less lonely and cold.

I passed the boat back to Gilles, who smiled at Maurice and started sanding off a rough edge they'd missed. He was happily taking on the boyfriend/father-figure role. And I felt so elated for my brother that I said, "Gilles, are we supposed to call you dad?"

He was caught off-guard, but didn't flinch or stop sanding. After a thoughtful moment, he said, "How about we say that we're really good friends for now. But I might have a surprise for your mom and you guys coming up."

He winked, and kept working on the boat. Maurice and I looked at each other, knowing that meant he would propose soon. He did a few months later. Gilles's presence eased the tension in our lives. He made each of us a custom-crafted desk, so we had a place to do homework in our new rooms. He must have spent days making each one. Inside one of the drawers on mine, he tucked a dictionary, inscribed: "For someone with such a giant aptitude to read, I hope this dictionary proves useful for you. Love always, your friend, Gilles." He was such a warm and thoughtful person, and seeing our mom through his kind and loving eyes made us see her a different way as well. And Mom put her best foot forward for Gilles. She was still a strong, dominant personality, but she wasn't as harsh or abusive in front of him. I don't think he had any idea what Mom was like when the door closed.

§

One weekend that spring, when Grandma Anita and I finished our work for the morning, we had plans to go shopping in St. Paul. She had received a brand-new, red Toyota Corolla the previous Christmas with a big red present bow on top. It was the most adorable sporty little car, and although she was a no-frills woman who never wore makeup or anything noticeable, she loved the way the red stood out in parking lots filled with dirty farm trucks.

"Now, Carmen, you're going to be fourteen soon," Mémère said when we went to get in the car. "You'll need to know how to drive if you want to get your learner's permit. How about if you drive us to St. Paul?"

I'd driven before; not as far as St. Paul, but around the farm. The challenge with driving Mémère's Corolla was the standard shift. This was something I had no idea how to do. But she put me in the driver's seat of her shiny new car, and at the top of their mile-long estate driveway, explained how to ease off the clutch while slowly pushing the gas. I listened, with the clutch pressed firmly down under my shaking leg. Their yard and forested property spread out below us.

"Let it off slow until you feel the engine catch," she said. "Whenever you're ready."

The stick shift between us felt cool in my hand as I slid it into first. The engine purred, barely audible. I followed her directions, but went too hard on the gas. The engine whined as the car lurched forward, then stalled out with a clunk.

"Sorry, Mémère," I said, cringing as I looked at her. Whatever I'd done, I thought for sure I'd damaged her car.

"It's okay, Carmen. Just try it again. Press the clutch and slip it back to neutral." She guided me through each step. I stalled out again the second time. But the third time, the car slipped forward without complaint, and we started down the drive.

When the engine started to sound tight, she said, "Now press the clutch and move the stick to second."

I pressed the clutch with my foot, awkwardly found second gear, and then released my foot. "That time was much easier," I said, delighted that we were still moving.

"Once you get going, it's easy," she beamed. At the end of the driveway, I stalled out once. And on the drive to St. Paul, I stalled at a few more stops. But we made it there, and she sang my praises the whole time.

"Want to see a trick?" she asked from the passenger seat on the drive back. She pulled out a cigarette and lit it, breaking her steadfast rule about smoking in the car with children. Then she cracked her window only enough to suck the smoke from the car. That was the trick. She smiled at me and smoked, and I felt like I'd been fully initiated into an adult club.

When I pulled back in the driveway of the estate, Anita glowed with pride. I was a natural, and she'd had such a wonderful time. Then, wistfully, almost as if she were talking to a friend, she said, "Wouldn't it be great if you lived here all the time?"

That was how the conversation started about me and possibly Maurice too going to live with Anita and Pierre in St. Vincent. And Mémère felt it would be wonderful for everyone. My mom could get a break. Then we could go to the French Catholic school in Mallaig. She knew I didn't get along with my mom, and she knew my mom could be difficult. And she liked having us around.

Most weekends and breaks from school, Maurice and I spent with Pierre and Anita. I babysat for my cousins, and had grown into a capable assistant for Anita when it came to housework. Pierre liked everything neat and tidy, insisting that Mémère iron everything down to his pocket hanky. Keeping the house clean, doing laundry, and cooking all the meals was a tremendous amount of work, but with me around, we could get it all done before lunch. Every morning at ten, Anita's friends met for coffee in the nearby Village of Glendon or at Beacon Corner gas and coffee shop.

For all the fifty-five-plus local farm wives, most of whom had known each other since elementary school, the Glendon Confectionary was the central hub. They gathered in this small-town café where coffee served in white truck-stop style mugs was on all day long. They played drop-in games of cards, gossiped, and caught up. Anita was well-loved by her friends, and they welcomed me into their social circle. Their grandchildren were toddlers, so spending time with me was like glimpsing their future. They enjoyed having a maturing young woman's company. And Anita was held in high regard, even though she was one of the quieter ones in the group. I could play card games and crib. I was funny and a little loud. So Mémère and I contrasted in a way that everyone loved to be around. When I was with her, her friends lit up. I loved to make them laugh and accuse them of looking too young.

During those morning social hours, I met a few kids my age and made some friends. By this time, I had learned how to tweeze my eyebrows. I had new breasts and a tight dancer's body that was hard to conceal under anything I wore. I was approachable, friendly, and not shy, introducing myself to everyone. And they'd heard of me. Glendon was a small community outside Bonnyville where the Kissels came from too, and everyone—even the kids—had heard of my Grandpa Pierre. They knew he lived in the nicest home in the area, and they knew he had a helicopter. And I didn't look like a boy anymore; I was a pretty, young girl. The epitome of Glendon blended families of Kissels and Dargises. Glendon was the epicentre of my bloodlines.

I had fully rejected the tight perms my mom always got me to match hers and had started experimenting with my hair and makeup, with the help of my aunties and whatever fashion magazines I could get my hands on. My mom didn't wear makeup or even have her ears pierced, so I was becoming a girl all on my own. At thirteen, after so much begging, I convinced Anita to take me to get my ears pierced in St. Paul. But this seemed to trouble my mom, who was physically my complete opposite. I had dark hair and eyes; she had blonde and blue. I was petite and athletic; she was large and overweight. Although I didn't realize it at first, because I was just a kid, I was becoming, in Mom's eyes, more like her sisters.

§

Despite everything we had stacked against us, Maurice and I had grown into charming young people. We were always with Mom's family—my grandparents and aunts and uncle—and they complimented me on my athleticism and blossoming capabilities. And as much as Mom needed her family's support to raise us, she seemed a bit jealous of the relationships we had with them. I was so well-received and everybody in her family, her mother, her father, her sisters, and brothers all really adored my brother and me.

This started to get under my mom's skin. But it bolstered my confidence in the face of her abusive talk. I knew what love looked like and felt like. I knew from the Kissels. I knew from Anita. I knew from Jean and Joanne, Joe and Cheryl and Martine. I got it from everyone but her. And when she came after me, telling me I wasn't good enough or that I was stupid, I started backtalking her, which only made it worse. And it made living with my grandparents seem like a viable, sensible idea.

I loved being in the big house, at the heart of the huge Dargis family. Grandpa Pierre was one of eight children, and Mom was one of fifty-something first cousins, so the Dargises covered the area. Within that empire, we felt like we had a powerful tribe. And anytime I was around them, I loved it. But I didn't know if I wanted to stay with my grandparents full-time because that meant changing schools, playing for different teams, and being away from everything I knew in Bonnyville.

I had met a girl named Danielle at a coffeeshop visit with Mémère in Glendon and late in the school year, I went to school with her in Mallaig, to shadow her for the day and see if I might like to go there. I spent that day getting to know Danielle and meeting everyone at the small Mallaig school, many of whom I also recognized from school sports. It was amazing. No one knew me as the dirty butcher shop girl or for my old unibrow. And my Dargis reputation preceded me.

When my school year finished, I was still undecided. Like all the others before, I spent that summer with my grandparents, going back and forth between their house and Jean and Joanne's farm next door, where I watched their three blonde-topped daughters. Maurice spent the summer tagging along with Pépère or Uncle Jean, his godfather, who with three little girls in the house was happy to spend time with him, too. And that was when my brother and I fell in love with the idea of being part of a real family. All my aunts and uncles had grown up on the farm, gone to college, then came back and started their own families. That was what life was all about. We never experienced that firsthand because Mom didn't choose the person she wanted to make a life with; she seemed to have gotten stuck by a teenage pregnancy. So, we got to see up close the beauty and love of a family when done this way, but this time there was a promise that we could be a part of it.

This summer was also different from previous ones because now I had a social circle in the Glendon-Mallaig area. Between helping Anita and watching my cousins, I had the phone cord stretched to the max, around the corner and into the bathroom for privacy, talking to all my new friends. For the first time in my life, I was popular. And I was enjoying coming into my own—so much so that it became my undoing.

Not long into the summer, on one of those phone-cord-stretching conversations, Danielle asked me to go to a bush party.

"Everyone gets together in the field; they'll build a fire," she said. "It will be fun."

"I don't know," I hesitated. These parties didn't start until the sun went down. Darkness that time of year only lasted from eleven at night to four in the morning, and I knew my grandparents would never allow me out so late. "I'll have to sneak out."

I was staying in my Aunt Martine's old princess room upstairs and switched to one of the bedrooms downstairs, because the wide windows opened onto the yard. A few nights later, when Mémère and Pépère went to sleep after watching Friday night *Dallas*, and the sun went down, I got up, opened the window, and slipped out. As the stars came out, I walked down the mile-long driveway to the road, where Danielle and one of her friends with a truck came by and picked me up.

That night, and many nights after, we sat on the tailgate, listening to music blaring from someone's truck stereo. Bush parties were the summer social scene for high school kids. I tried my first beer at one of these parties, where anywhere from twenty to a hundred people might pass through throughout the night. I met people from all around the area. And everyone loved me and wanted to get to know me. Then, after a few hours of fun, someone would drop me off at the end of my grandparents' driveway, and I'd sneak back inside and go to bed with sunrise to catch two-three hours of sleep. I never developed the courage to ask my mémère if I could go to these parties. I doubted they'd even consider it as they were from a different generation. And I didn't want to be a bother.

I planned on doing the same thing on the night of the upcoming local Yukaflux. This communal drinking event featured vats of vodka and rum and whiskey-soaked fruit, and everyone in Glendon—everyone except the Dargises—went and got social together with music. It was being held at the local hockey rink, and all my new girlfriends were going. I wanted to go so bad that I couldn't risk asking permission.

When the night of the Yukaflux arrived, I snuck out the window and had a wonderful time, meeting all my friends' parents, who were there dancing and drinking too. Then I snuck back into the house and went to bed, as I had so many nights before.

The day unfolded as normal until afternoon, when Anita came and found me in my room downstairs. She looked stricken.

"I just came from coffee, Carmen," she said. "And when everyone was talking about the Yukaflux last night, my friend told me she was surprised to see you there. She said she didn't think she'd ever see Pierre's teenaged granddaughter at a party like that."

Her face flushed with shock, and I felt sick with guilt that I'd disappointed her. She sat on my bed, her eyes searched my face. I looked away from her; I wanted to jump out the window and run as fast as I could down that long driveway to get away from the hurt I caused. But I couldn't lie to her, even though that was my first instinct. So, I told the truth.

I told her about the window and the ride from the end of the driveway and everything about that night. And I told her how sorry I was that she'd found out from a friend in town. The last thing I wanted to do was humiliate her, I promised her that. And then I begged her, pleading, not to tell Pépère Pierre or Mom.

"Thank you for your honesty," she said, folding her hands in her lap. "And since it won't happen again, we can keep it between us."

"Thank you," I said, shame prickling my skin.

She got up and went back to her work upstairs, and that was it. Mémère kept her promise; she didn't tell anyone. And she didn't bring it up again.

§

For a bit, I stopped sneaking out to let the dust settle and avoid scrutiny and to catch up on sleep. But I was more concerned about becoming better at getting out undetected, which both shamed and excited me.

A couple weeks later, Pierre and Anita were going out of town for a few days, and they made arrangements for me to stay with Uncle Jean and Aunt Joanne. My second night there, after everyone went to bed, I slipped out and ran across the grassy mosquito filled quarter section of land to my grandparents' house. I let myself in, went straight to the garage, and left a few minutes later in Mémère's Corolla. Beep, beep! I'd practiced a few more times since that trip to St. Paul, and had no trouble making it into Mallaig, where I parked the car outside the bar and left to go to a bush party with one of my new boy friends who had a truck. Country boys are indeed very good looking, physically fit and capable. I hopped in and Garth Brooks

"Ain't Goin' Down ('Til the Sun Comes Up)" blared just as loud as my pal Aime's truck exhaust. Never met a man named Aime before; it's French too.

At some point during my absence, my Uncle Jean got up to check on me, and found me missing. He walked over to his parents, thinking I may have gone there, and realized the car was gone. He called his brother, my Uncle Joe, who lived not far down the road, and together, they went looking for me. And they were young men of the area, both of them just over thirty, so they knew where to look. It didn't take them long to find the car parked (though left in gear with the E-brake on because I didn't really know what I was doing) outside the bar. When they didn't find me inside, they went home, knowing that I'd likely turn up before dawn.

Just before sunrise, my friend dropped me back off at Mémère's car in Mallaig, and I drove back to their house. I parked it, unharmed, in the garage where I'd found it. Then I hurried back across the field and went to bed. When I woke up a few hours later, both my uncles were sitting at Uncle Jean's kitchen table, waiting for me to emerge from my room.

While I'd been having a fun summer as the Glendon/Mallaig It-Girl, getting to know my future schoolmates and myself as an amazing new person, my family saw my behaviour a different way. My uncles, who I loved and respected so much, told me *no way*.

"Carmen, you can't disrespect your grandparents, my parents, like that. I won't allow it," Uncle Jean said. "You're too young."

"I promise I'll never do it again," I pleaded, the same way I'd done with Mémère. "Just please don't tell on me."

Uncle Jean shook his head. "We're worried about you," he said. "We have to tell, we also know about Yukaflux night."

I went back to my room while they called my grandparents, who sat me down as soon as they came back home. Pierre, seated across the kitchen table from me, told me how *embarrassed* he was, how completely *disappointed* in me he was. In his deep, unwavering, piercing seriousness, he looked me in the eyes and said, "What kind of person are you *becoming?*"

I didn't know. But I assured Pépère that I would never do it again. Anita was working in the kitchen, listening to everything but not interfering. She couldn't help me now.

"You can't stay here, Carmen," Pierre said to finalize the matter. "I can't have this behaviour in my house. You'll have to go home."

By this point, living away from my mom and being the popular new girl was like my dream come true. I didn't fully understand Anita's rescue plan for me. Anita wasn't in control, and she knew that. The whole time she'd been working on my grandfather to make this situation a possibility for me, subtly influencing him the way wives do so it seemed like his idea and won his approval. But I'd completely blown it.

When he'd finished with me, I went to my room feeling worse than I'd ever felt before—more foolish, more ashamed. Foolishness and shame were starting to become my best friends. I didn't come out for hours. Then, later that night, I felt hungry and left my room to go upstairs. On the stairwell, I heard voices and stopped to listen. Pierre and Anita were upstairs, arguing.

"This is our last chance to help her," Anita pleaded. "She never had a decent mother."

"There's no way she can stay here," Pierre boomed back at her. I sat there listening for a few minutes, to my grandma defending me and my grandpa writing me off.

"She's a *lost cause*, Anita," he said in his French accent drawing out her name for finality, A-ni-TA. "I don't want that in my life." My grandfather wrote me off at near fourteen years old, and I can't say that I didn't help it along. I hoped it wasn't because I was half Kissel because I loved this set of grandparents so much. I knew that my presence would make life hard for Anita. There was no way that I'd contribute to her already hard life any longer. Who was I though? I was Carmen *Anita* Kissel and I was a bit lost and drunk on having a good time. Seriousness? I'd had enough of that for a while, thank you.

§

I turned fourteen that August, and school started with me back in Bonnyville, back at Mom's. My mom, who knew all about my wild nights out, kept a closer eye on me than she did before and looked at me with more suspicion. But she let me get my learner's permit and whenever we had anywhere to go, she let me drive her brand-new Chevy Blazer for practice. This was the first new car Mom had ever owned, and it was an SUV, which was the car to have at that time.

Early one frosty Saturday morning, Mom and I left the house to go to work at the butcher shop. The new car warmed up fast, and I drove from our house into town, the same road we travelled every day. We were about halfway there when Mom started messing with the buttons on the radio, trying to change the station, annoyed.

"How do you work this stupid radio?" she muttered more to herself than to me.

I looked away from the road, down at what she was doing on the radio. In that instant, with my gaze pulled down, I let the wheel follow and the car veered *slightly* to the right.

Mom looked up and, as if I'd lost control, and panicked. She flung her thick arm across me, grabbed the wheel, and pushed it back toward the left. The Blazer jerked at her overcorrection, then flipped over into a somersault after catching the sharp roadside edge. Fear clenched me as I watched the sky pass and disappear through the window. We flew through the air in a smooth arc, bounced off an embankment, flipped again, spun in the air and landed, upside down on its roof, on the opposite side of the road. We had rolled, end over end, three times.

When the SUV stopped moving, the radio still played, and the engine still ran. The seatbelt dug into my waist and shoulder as I was suspended upside down. I looked at Mom, who was hanging by her seatbelt in the passenger seat unconscious. Blood covered her face and dripped down all over me.

"Mom," I yelled. She didn't respond, and panic overcame me. I unhooked my seatbelt and fell down onto the roof of the car. The windshield was smashed, but the glass in my driver door wasn't. I pressed the button to open it.

"Mom, wake up," I screamed. But she still didn't move. Blood dripped off her face down onto me some more. I didn't feel hurt; I felt adrenaline pumping through me. Smelling fuel and fearing the engine would explode, my immediate impulse was to get her out of there. I unhooked my mom's belt, and she fell on top of me completely limp. Her dead-weight pinned me, but the shock and panic must have accessed all my strength. I heaved her off to the side, then slid out the window onto the grass. I grabbed Mom under her arms and pulled her through the window, dragging her away from the car. I left her on the grass while I ran to the house across the range road.

I pounded on the door in the dim morning light. We passed this house every day, but I didn't know who lived there. The woman who answered looked at me all bloody and then past me to the overturned wreck. She said she'd call the ambulance and disappeared back in the house.

I ran back to the ditch, where I was sure I'd find my mother dead. There was blood everywhere—covering her face and hands, covering me. But she started groaning and coming to. Then a man—maybe the woman's son or the man who lived next door—came across the road, turned off the Blazer's engine, and said he'd give us a ride to the hospital, it would be faster than waiting for the ambulance to arrive.

He lifted Mom and put her in his truck, and the whole drive I held her and cried. I told her over and over and over how sorry I was and that she'd be okay. When we pulled up to the emergency room, a whirlwind of activity ensued. They put Mom on a stretcher and started checking her over as they wheeled her into the hospital. They cut off her clothes, checked her vital signs, and asked her questions. At the same time, the nurses and doctors checked me for injuries. I didn't have a scratch on me, and they told me how lucky we were that we'd been wearing our seatbelts.

When the doctors had determined I was okay, the police questioned me about what happened, and I explained everything, certain that I'd be in more trouble than I ever imagined possible. There was no time for lying anymore! I was just a kid with a learner's permit; I thought for sure I would go to jail for wrecking my mom's new car and nearly killing her. But they assured me mom would be fine, there were no other cars involved, and that by my explanation, my mother was partly to blame because you should never grab the wheel the way she did. I was so relieved that we would both be okay, but I knew somehow that my life would never be the same after that. I felt fourteen going on twenty-four.

Mom was in the hospital for a few days. She had whiplash and a concussion. The window on her side of the car shattered, and the glass cut and embedded in her face and arm. They had to pick each piece out of her flesh and stitch up all the little cuts. Afterwards, her lacerated skin was glazed in a gobby thick layer of clear, sterilized goo.

When Mom came home, we learned that she didn't have full coverage to allow a minor to drive the new car, so she had to pay for it. This very expensive vehicle was a total fiscal loss. If there had been any sort of positive relationship building between my mom and me—it died in the crash. She quietly blamed me for everything that happened; I was a good-for-nothing kid. A Kissel. She worked me harder at the butcher shop and berated me nonstop when she was stressed, which was always. And after everything that had happened—getting kicked out of my grandparents' house, smashing my mom's new car, and causing her so much pain and expense—I believed everything she said about me. And I hated myself. And I hated *her*. When I saw those cuts on her face, I thought about how her words had been cutting at me all those years, too.

Now that I was fourteen, I was old enough to legally choose to live with whichever parent I wanted. And I was sure I wanted to go live with my father. My brother, who was only twelve at the time, couldn't go with me. This was my only hesitation—if I left him behind, then I wouldn't be able to protect him.

When Maurice and I were waiting for the school bus one morning, I told him that I was thinking about leaving. "I just don't think I can stay here anymore," I said. "Mom and I just don't get along, and I've been miserable for long enough."

"Maybe Mom will let me go too," he said with desperation mounting in his voice, but we both knew that was doubtful. She would take us both leaving *personally* because we were just *things* that she owned. And not only would she be losing some of her things, it would also make her look like a terrible mother. Then, as the reality of our situation sank in, Maurice got really upset. "You know, if you didn't talk back to her so much, maybe she'd be nicer to you. You could try that," he begged.

In that moment, I felt like I grew up. I truly agonized about leaving him there. He had been like a shadow my whole life, and I wanted nothing more than to take him with me. But I knew that would just cause more trouble for my dad because he'd have to stand up to Mom and fight to keep Maurice with him. I didn't have confidence that he would do that. And I didn't want to mess up my own chance to go to the farm. She couldn't stop me, but she could still legally stop my brother. And if she was upset, she'd take it out on Maurice. No one would win in that situation. I grabbed my brother's thin and narrow shoulders and looked at him hard with so much love. "It's just not in my nature to take it," I said. "But Mom is always mad at me, so maybe after I leave, it will be better for you."

That's when I started plotting my escape. I didn't want to give my mom the dignity or respect of a conversation. I wanted her to find me missing, make a painful discovery that I was gone forever. Only then would she know the price she had to pay for the way she'd treated me, and both of us.

I wrote two letters. The one to my mom went on and on about how we'd never had a relationship, how she was a horrible person, and how I wanted nothing to do with her. And I warned her that I'd be keeping an eye on Maurice at school, and if I ever found out that she'd hurt him, that I was much smarter now and that I would make her life hell. I left the letter for her on her bed. The second letter explained to Maurice how much I loved him and would still be there for him, and how in a few months, when he was old enough to leave, I would come get him. I left it for him in his room, tucked under his pillow, but he never got it. I learned later that Mom found his letter first and destroyed it.

Then I packed my clothes in a garbage bag and asked my school friend, Eldon, to come pick me up. Eldon wanted to be my boyfriend, and I really liked him too. But I was more concerned about my own life and setting up at the farm than romance. He would have helped me with anything. Eldon helped me load my bags into the back of his truck, then waited in the cab while I ran in one last time. I left all my ballet gear, books, and scrapbooks—if I never saw any of it again, I didn't care. As we pulled away from Mom's, and the house shrank and disappeared in the rearview mirror, I vowed I would never go back to that house again.

6

BACK ON THE FARM

*"Be master of your petty annoyances and conserve your
energies for the big worthwhile things.
It isn't the mountain ahead that wears you out—
it's the grain of sand in your shoe."*
—Robert W. Service

WHEN ELDON DROPPED ME OFF at Dad's house on Hill and Valley Ranch,
where he lived with his wife, Doris, I felt completely free and hopeful. It
was the same house I'd lived in before the divorce, and after being whisked
away in the night all those years ago, it felt like I was finally coming home.
The house was smaller than I remembered. I carried my garbage bags of
clothes inside the back door. The utility room smelled of pig farming.
And among the coveralls and muddy boots, I noticed a pair of old-school
high-top Converse sneakers sitting among the other shoes at the door.
They were too big to belong to Doris, and not anything like I'd ever seen
my dad wear before.

Dad knew I was coming and met me at the door. Doris wasn't back from
work yet. She was a hairdresser at a salon she owned in Bonnyville.

"Hi Dad," I smiled. I was so relieved to be there, finally.

Dad smiled and took my bag and I crashed into his arms. I followed him inside. Doris had a makeshift hair salon set up off the utility entrance to do the local ladies' hair. But otherwise the place was like a time capsule. The house had the same dark blue shag carpet in the living room and brown and taupe vinyl kitchen flooring that they'd put in when they built the place in 1979. The living room window still had the light blue curtains that my Great-Aunty Mary (Lloyd's sister) sewed for Mom and Dad when they moved in.

"Whose shoes were those by the door?" I asked, following him up the stairs to my old room.

"Well, those are Kirk's," Dad said.

"Who's Kirk?"

"One of Doris's sons. He must have left them here when he stayed with us a while back."

I didn't ask any more questions, but it occurred to me, as I settled back into my old room and sat on the bed which I hadn't slept in in ages, that I didn't know Doris very well. She was about ten years older than my dad and had four grown kids. When she wasn't working—either making women look beautiful or getting dirty in her coveralls around the farm—she had a cigarette pinched between her fingers. I'd gathered from my other family members that she'd had a terrible life with her previous husband. But her strong personality and the way she told my dad how things were going to be reminded me of my mom's strong personality overpowering my father's weaker one. He'd been raised by an alcoholic father, so he wasn't the kind of person who piped up. Doris seemed in charge, her stuff was everywhere, but she made Dad happy.

Aside from Doris, I had my dad to myself. And it felt good to be back with Grandpa Lloyd and Grandma Betty and Porky right next door on the farm. The same path I'd worn running back and forth between the two houses as a preschooler was still there, but other aspects of the farm had transformed.

While I'd been away at Mom's, Lloyd quit drinking! Like cold turkey. In addition to several DUIs and the threat of losing his license for years, my dad's siblings, Uncle Gordon and Aunt Brenda, both returned home after university and took a hardline stance with Lloyd. My aunt and uncle at the time were both newly married and ready to have their own families, and they told Lloyd that if he didn't stop drinking, they wouldn't be coming around very much. They'd seen him with Maurice and me, as a drinker and as a grandfather, making us fight in boxing matches for entertainment and asking us to bring him drinks. They didn't want any part of it. And I think this, more than anything, scared Lloyd straight. He valued nothing more than his family, and when my cousins Jamison and Brett and Carter were born, he put the bottle on the shelf and *never took it down again*. I was completely shocked. Lloyd Kissel had been a high-functioning alcoholic for at least forty years.

Lloyd was still Lloyd, but he was also a different person sober. Everyone noticed the change, and when I got there, I saw it for myself. Sobriety brought more mental focus and clarity. He was a little less silly and a bit more serious. He wrote in a diary every day now. And his stories were still funny and animated. But he never stopped loving the social and communal atmosphere of a good honky-tonk bar.

One night, not long after I came back, we all went into town for dinner at the Lakelander Inn for Lloyd and Betty's anniversary. We were all gathered in the lobby, slipping off our coats and waiting for the host to seat us, when I saw Grandpa veer away from our group and head for the lounge.

"Grandma, where's Grandpa going?" I asked, touching her arm. I was worried he was going for a drink.

Grandpa, who overheard me, turned back and said, "It's okay, Dolly Girl. I'm just going to look at the *shiny bottles*." I knew what that meant. I became panicked.

A few minutes later, he joined us at the table. No one ever questioned it after that, and he did it every time we went out. I often wondered how he could abstain from drinking in such a triggering environment, but I think Lloyd needed to face his addiction head-on. Beating it through exposure gave Lloyd the courage to continue to stay sober. Lloyd Kissel was still my hero. He was strong.

We all sat around the table that night, eating our food and celebrating my grandparents' many years together. My grandmother was now fully retired from teaching and free to create all day long in her sewing room the next round of blue-ribbon-winning goods for upcoming trade shows and fairs or quilting guilds. And Betty was visibly relieved that Lloyd had quit drinking. She looked at Lloyd differently and laughed at more of his jokes. She made his tea just the way he liked and gave him razor shaves while he sat on the closed toilet seat at night.

Swept up in the moment, I asked, "Grandma and Grandpa, what are you most grateful for after all these years?"

Lloyd, without hesitation, said, "Ma and my family." He was ever-proud of his family, and so proud that it was growing, and that it had new grandchildren.

When I looked at Betty to indicate it was her turn, she said, without hesitation, "I'm most thankful that Lloyd quit drinking." We laughed together and carried on. That's what Kissels did with adversity. Once through it, they laughed together and carried on, together.

A lot of good came from Lloyd sobering up. Maurice and I couldn't have been more delighted to share the spotlight as grandkids with our cousins. We were ten years older than them, so they never knew Lloyd as a drinker. No one goaded them into fights the way he used to with Maurice and me; no one drove around drunk with them in the car. And Maurice and I were thankful for that for them, but it created a painful contrast to our own experiences. We had young grandparents who were in their late forties and still working full time and figuring out their own lives. So, while I prized that we got extra time with them, I still can't help but feel and notice that it's a bit sad when you don't get the chance to live a normal life, with grandparents that are already older, and have a normal mom and dad that have kids after they're married. My cousins had something I didn't. Seeing this and how glorious my little cousins were, how happy they were in thriving and stable little environments because their parents had their shit together and did things the right way, stung a little. I vowed I would never, ever have a teenage pregnancy. That was the biggest hindrance to me having a sweet, charming, stable life like they had. I promised myself it would never happen to me.

Everyone laughed and talked farm business over dinner. And as we finished and got ready to go, I felt so lucky that I could be there. If I were still at my mom's, I wouldn't be. Maurice wasn't there and I missed him so much. I didn't see my brother much now that I was back on the farm. When I saw him at school, he always assured me that everything with Mom was fine. I could never tell if he was covering for her or if their relationship was just different, that she was a better mom with him. I liked to imagine that my mom learned her lesson when I left, that she had looked at herself and realized she should be better to her one remaining child. And my brother, being a boy and a son, was far less trouble to her than I ever was. He didn't talk back. He was smarter that way. He was also more like a Dargis with his blonde hair and blue eyes, always a complete contrast to me. While I looked a lot like my dad, he took after my Uncle Jean. I didn't worry too much about him, but I always talked up how great it would be once he could come to the farm too. How Grandpa Lloyd quit drinking, how Dad was growing the farm operation, and it was just like when we were kids, with Grandma and Grandpa and Porky around. We were all back on top at the farm!

But I also didn't mind being the only kid. Now that I was older, the adults didn't watch what they said as closely as they had when I was little. Or maybe now I was just old enough to understand what they were saying. The long wooden kitchen table at my grandparents' house was where we ate, but also where information was shared by the adults and gleaned by my teenage ears. I learned through my grandparents, sitting at the kitchen table and chit-chatting without my dad around, that Kirk was, as Grandpa Lloyd called him, a *jailbird*. He was in and out of jail all the time, and when he was out, he used my dad's house as a transitional place to crash. This explained the prison-issued Converse shoes. Everything I knew from Doris about her kids was how wonderful she thought they were, so I was shocked to hear this more sinister description of Kirk. I'd never known anyone who went to jail like that. I didn't even know Kirk, but I was afraid of him. I was a little afraid of Doris too. She was nice, but I suspected she called the shots with my Dad. I knew that I needed her to like me to stay. I could see that I needed to win her over.

My dad shied away from all confrontation and didn't like it when Doris was occasionally upset with him. She cut hair at home to make money to go to bingo every single night. She loved quick cash to hit the VLTs and to go to bingo.

And I knew if my mom found out that my new living arrangement put me in association with jailbird types of people, she'd use that to get me away from the farm.

§

Work started early, and being back on Hill and Valley Ranch meant rolling up my sleeves. Doris cooked breakfast every morning, something fast like bacon and eggs, and then we threw on our dirty clothes, headed over to the farm, and fed the two thousand head of cattle on our feedlot. Dad had grown the operation considerably since I was a kid. And he'd matured into a confident, capable, and sober man who could put on a big cowboy hat and go into my other grandfather's auction mart to sell his steers by the hundreds. I had never seen my dad in a cowboy hat, let alone dressed in full Western wear. I'd only seen old rodeo days pics of my dad as a saddle-bronc rider. But he got dressed up to take his steers to the auction.

Hill and Valley Ranch sewed approximately 1,500 acres of crop product on various quarter sections of land. Some of that cropland was Kissel property, but lots was leased from neighbours. Grandpa Lloyd, being a social butterfly, maintained the relationships that went into getting and keeping the leasing agreements, like with his pal, Ross Maclean. Leasing from neighbours is ideal because that means your equipment is close by. Transporting it any distance means extra time, wear and tear, fuel, and other expenses that make it less profitable. These landowners weren't farmers, but they were holding onto and profiting from their assets by leasing it to their favourite farmers. My dad, not one to cozy up with the neighbours, took a secondary or offstage role in these negotiations. But he was the successor to the family farm. And he counted on Lloyd to secure five- to ten- to fifteen-year lease deals with the neighbours. Lloyd. Wheeler. Dealer.

That first winter, I was out there in temperatures of minus 30 or 40 degrees Celsius. When my warm breath escaped from the scarf I wound tight around my neck and face, the vapour condensed and froze on my eyelashes and eyebrows. I learned to appreciate how hard farm life was; rain or shine, no matter how cold, the cattle had to be fed first thing in the morning, every single day. We used the front-end loader with the grapple to grab a round hay bale from the stack, chop it up, and place the loose hay in the trough. Then we added the grains and other vitamins and nutrients that go into a quality feedlot diet to the hay. In Canada, we fed grains, instead of corn, because we didn't have the long and hot growing season required for corn, and grain-fed beef has a higher amount of fat marbling through the meat and it makes the meat taste better. We were so happy to be producing this great Canadian AAA-grade beef out of our feedlot. And so were all the other farmers in our area. After the steers were eating, they were so happy, mooing and swishing their tails, chewing and chewing. Winter meant we were finishing the steers. They'd been born during the spring, spent summer in the pasture with their mothers, feeding on milk and foraging on fresh greens, and then were fattened up and finished through the winter in the smaller pens where they couldn't move around as much, in our feedlot.

Then after feeding, we attached the bale buster to the tractor and spread straw bedding in the steer finishing pens. Dad had a bad hip, so my job was to climb down from the tractor at each pen, open it, cut the binding twine off the giant bale so it didn't get tangled in the rotating mechanism on the machine, hold the gate while he drove the tractor in to spread the hay, and close it after he backed the tractor out. Even when the temperatures dipped to thirty below, I was in and out of the tractor for about two and a half hours before school. I'd run from the farmyard to the house, where I showered, dressed, and caught the bus at the end of the driveway.

Even though I didn't stay with Anita and Pierre, I did change high schools. I'd struggled so much in my Math 10 class at the French Catholic High School that I had to retake the class at the public school. That semester, I liked it so much that I changed over full time to the public high school, Bonnyville Centralized High School, BCHS. This was where my dad, Auntie Brenda, and Uncle Gordon went to school. I found all their faces on the dusty old grad class group photos in the main entrance hall. And I had a new identity there. Because BCHS was the public school, I thought I could totally ditch the confines of my French Catholic high school, which meant, really, saying goodbye to my mom, her ideals, and the whole Dargis family altogether. I made a pile of new friends who had no knowledge of my butcher shop upbringing or would guess that I spoke perfect French, accent free. They just knew me as me, a blossomed, attractive girl who was bubbly and fun and aced A-team tryouts for sports teams. And I had clout, coming from a full-time farm and ranch. Most farms were hobby farms, where they needed outside or supplemental income to make ends meet. We no longer needed that on Hill and Valley Ranch. Kissels were full-time farmers, so I felt legitimate. A lot of gravitas came with my father having two thousand head of cattle.

I wore Wranglers that hugged my tight, ballerina body, and Roper boots with kiltie plates. Only the bad-ass farm girls like my friends, Marina and Tanya, had kiltie plates, and that's who I was. And I wore it proudly because I was not a hobby-farm farm girl. I did chores in the morning, came to school, and then went home after school to do chores again.

With this new identity at my new high school, I was starting to get a lot more popular and started smoking in the BCHS smokers' alleyway. And with that came a lot of friends, a lot of invitations to parties, and a lot of skipping school. We used to skip school and meet in the morning at the Nut 'n Honey Bakery. This small, corner bakery was popular because it was so close to the school. Kids came in for coffee and doughnuts and to sit and chit-chat, just like adults. Then they'd either go off to school or find something else to do all day. I got good marks when I paid attention and submitted assignments. I never had a problem with school work, especially since I had a new math teacher, Mr. Sadlowski. But I didn't value school, so most days I'd hit the morning classes and skip the afternoon ones.

Aside from the daily chores, winter meant a slow season on the farm. After feeding and bedding the animals, because everything was frozen solid, my father spent most of his time planning for the upcoming crop year and doing paperwork in his office. We'd be reviewing land maps for seeding, choosing the crops we were going to put down and where, weighing different possibilities. If we invested in canola, the seeds and fertilizer were expensive, but it brought the highest price. Or maybe we should be barley kings? Or maybe we should try something different, like peas or risky corn. But it was always great fun to decide what we were going to put where, and what we were going to take a risk on in terms of purchase and nurturing to get that better crop price. So once we got all our seeding done, we then prayed for rain. The climate in our area of Canada usually had wet springs, which was great for seed germination. We had our cash crops that we were growing for sale, the wheat, oats, barley, and canola. And we always kept some fields designated just for hay, because we need to chop it down, roll it into big bales, and bring it back to the feedlot to feed and straw to bed the animals.

When spring break up started, the days were warm enough and long enough to thaw out the ground, which meant all the manure that had been frozen solid all winter now stunk. That was when we started getting busy again—cleaning out pens, making repairs, getting ready. And when it warmed up, fields were planted.

The existing feedlot had big cement troughs, but needed a barrier for the cattle to stick their heads through and then access the cement trough to eat. Dad designed this fantastic system using thousands of pieces of salvaged oilfield pipe and polish rod welded together to create the barrier that the cattle would come and stick their heads through to get to the food. Every afternoon for months my father spent welding. He wasn't a master, but like any good farmer, he was a jack of all trades. And stick welding is easy enough if you've got a little finesse and practice.

One late spring weekend when I was helping him, he had me hold the pieces of pipe so he could tack-weld them together. Tack welding required an extra set of hands to hold the pieces in place. On the farm, it was old jeans and work boots and ponytail and grab your leather work gloves as you head out the door. We started at six in the morning, the sun already bright and shining on the dewy grass.

"Now don't look directly at the weld when I start, Dolly Girl," he warned me. He was wearing a helmet so he could look at the live welding and see what he was doing without burning his eyes. I didn't have a welding helmet, so knowing how damaging it could be to my eyes, I looked away. I imagined something like a laser beam hitting my eyeballs and turned away every time, well before he sparked up again.

We listened to the blue jays and robins sing with 790 CFW country radio station playing on our portable radio. I loved being outside and this was my second favourite time of the year as by noon I could peel off the plaid coat to sweat it out in a tank top as we worked. The feedlot yard was empty because the cattle were out to pasture in fields away from our farm on the big quarter sections of land down by Kissel Lake. The feedlot yard, with twenty pens, was like a small town with big squares of pens, five deep and three wide, and enough room for a feed tractor to maneuver in between. With the cattle out to pasture, we could reconstruct the facades of the feed areas in each pen. We took out the old roughed up wood and replaced them with steel pipe that would last forever and need less maintenance. Beads of sweat rolled down my hair, and I wiped it away with my gloved forearm. We drank water from the canteens Grandma had packed for us.

We did a full day of hot work in the sun, welding so close to the grass that we had to trim it and keep a bucket of water close in case any sparks ignited. We were super productive and got so many tack welds up. Our feedlot was starting to really take shape, and we could see how much of a beautiful, shining improvement this was going to be. We were going to paint it all bright farmyard red afterwards! Dad talked all day long about how he would plan a farm tour when we were finished so people could come and see how he'd salvaged oilfield material and created these beautiful improvements to our feedlots. He fancied himself an innovator. And I did, too; I was so proud of him. We'd had a great day working on the project together, and we were at Grandma's dinner table that evening relishing all of Lloyd's praise.

Had Dad been a professional welder, he would have learned that peripheral exposure to the arc of light can still cause welding flash. Worse so, if it's coming at your eyeballs sideways. When I woke up in the middle of the night that night, I felt like my eyes were filled with gravel and sand. It was so painful, I screamed and ran upstairs to my dad's room. He knew immediately what had happened and took me to the emergency room, where the doctor explained this could happen even though I'd turned away from the light. The doctor dropped these glorious, numbing drops into my eyes. The second they touched my eyeballs, relief washed over me. I would be okay, he said, but the blisters on my eyes were some of the worst he'd seen. I went home with drops I could use as needed to ease the blinding pain, and for the next two days, I had to stay in my dark room with cold steeped tea bags over my eyes.

My dad felt horrible that we'd been out there doing such dangerous work without really knowing what we were doing. But a lot of farm work was like that. A loose sleeve or a strand of hair could get caught in a rotating PTO driveshaft and you'd be a goner. And, as strange as it sounds, my dad and I bonded, not only through the shared traumatic experience of me getting hurt, but through our day-to-day work. It was always him and me, side by side. He got me my own welding helmet and we got back to work. When the welding was finished, we painted the steel. It took months, but by the end of that summer, our feedlot looked amazing, modern, and quite improved.

Haying season was about beating the rain because we couldn't bale and bind damp hay. Between rain spells, we tested the humidity by cutting a strip of hay and seeing if we could bale it. When it was good to go, we worked almost twenty-four hours a day to get it all in before the rain started again. My dad hired extra seasonal farmhands to help us run the equipment and get as much hay in as short amount of time as possible. As they say, you've got to make hay when the sun shines. That statement means near round-the-clock work.

These were the long summer days, when it wasn't dark until midnight. After baling hay all day, Dad and I drove over to check the cash crop field. We parked the truck on a ridge between two quarter section fields. The flat prairie landscape spread out all around us as far as we could see, and the grains, golden with dusk's warm light, swayed in the breeze. We had a bumper crop that year, dense, with many husks on every stem. Those were the most satisfying times, looking out over all the work we'd done all summer, all the money that would come as long as Mother Nature continued to do her part. Dad pulled a few husks and felt them in his hand to see how they were coming along, thinking about the coming weeks and assessing when the perfect time to harvest it would be.

I ran my fingers across the tops of the soft fuzzy barley plants, plucked a stem, and put it in my mouth. When I looked at Dad, he was smiling and the sun enveloped him like an angel halo. We were both so proud, so in love with the prospect and opportunity of turning it all into money and success. And he was always willing to share the credit with me.

When we got back in the truck and headed home, he said, "You know, Dolly Girl, we did this. We planted this. And isn't Mother Nature great this year?"

He was forever grateful for the simple things, and it was infectious. I loved his positivity within his quiet way.

§

If you want your kids to learn a lot about life and how people work, make them ride the bus to school. Over many years riding the school bus I mingled with older kids and studied them with great curiosity. The older girls in grade ten, eleven, and twelve were my favourite creatures to silently observe. When I was little on the school bus, these older girls had long permed hair and wore the tightest acid wash jeans with high waists and tight ankles. Every girl had their best bodies that peaked at about sixteen years old, from what I could tell from the school bus and from ballet class. Gobs of mascara with shimmery hue eyeshadow and frosty lips and boy band sweaters and high-top sneakers was the go-to mid-80s look. I loved when the older girls stepped onto the bus in the early morning because when they walked past me, I could smell them as if they just walked out of the shower. Amongst the diesel and stale vinyl smells of the bus, they stood out by scent. EXCLAMATION! and Baby Soft perfume were usually the top fragrance selections. There's always a hierarchy of school bus seating with the oldest, coolest kids seated in the very back, and the youngest at the very front, behind the driver.

When I moved to the farm, I had to take the bus too because I wasn't old enough to drive myself. Stepping on the same bus route that took me from the farm to school all those years ago was terrifying. It had been many years since I'd last seen this set of country community kids. Some remembered me, some didn't. I had to choose my seat wisely. If I sat in the wrong seat before a favourite kid boarded, then I'd be judged for it. If I selected a safe upfront seat next to middle school kids, I'd be judged again. It's agonizing to understand what to *pick* or where to *be* on a new school bus. For the first few weeks, I sat by myself closer to the little kids to play it safe.

But since I was in high school now, I wanted to move closer to the back and get to know the older kids who lived around our farm. Stephanie Harnum was queen bee of our bus. Next to her in ranking was Tannis. Stephanie had kind eyes and was gorgeous to look at. Tannis was not attractive and rude for sport. I learned this the hard way.

After a bland school day, I hopped on the bus ride home to find Tannis was not riding home that day. So, I sat in her seat and started gabbing with Stephanie. We were having the best conversation when all of a sudden Tannis stepped on and headed straight for her seat.

"You're in my seat, MOVE," she barked. Stephanie even tried to interject and offered that we sit together. But Tannis wasn't having that. I could tell that over the past few weeks that Tannis had no interest in getting to know me better. Our dads were even old truck driver friends who used to work together.

"Well, sorry, Tannis, but we don't have official assigned seats, so I was here first today," I replied coolly. I stood up from my seat to match her height and to show that I wasn't backing down. All of a sudden, Tannis wound up a scrawny fist and punched me right in the cheek. Hard, too. For a few moments I was completely stunned as to what just happened. Immediately conceding to her violence, I stepped aside and moved to the seat in front of her. The other kids on the bus all stopped to stare and watch. I felt their burning stares and saw the little kids' faces, mouths gaping wide at what had just transpired. A *girl fight* on the school bus. They were scared of Tannis too.

I shrunk down with my knees on the back of the seat in front of me. Terror and shame and embarrassment flashed over me. I had never been struck by a girl or a kid my age before. It was so quiet on the bus. Everyone held their breath and watched some more. Suddenly, I replaced embarrassment with rage. My rage morphed into action. I was not going to take this from Tannis, not from anyone. For the first time in my life, I was going to fight back against bullies like my mom and Tannis. With full autonomy and little recollection of that precise moment, I stood up from my seat, reached over to Tannis's seat and grabbed her hair by the back of her head. My left fistful of hair pulled her to stand up and with my right fist cocked, I clocked her back in the face, repeatedly. Over and over again I threw my shoulder into every punch with zealousness. Tannis recoiled deeply down into her seat but I still held onto her head by her hair and continued to strike her with vehemence. By this time the kids were cheering and egging on the show as they looked on with energy that fed my blows. Her one-shot to me resulted in countless repayment for her. The bus driver pulled us apart and Tannis's face was complete hamburger. Bloodied nose and eyes swollen and her smile was now missing a front tooth.

Tannis was left bewildered and shocked and darted off the bus to all the kids cheering for my victory. I was left unscathed and sat right back down in Tannis's seat, and everyone gushed about the show and how tough I was. Slaps on the back came with their stories of how Tannis had terrorized each and every one of them in the past. I couldn't believe myself, what just happened, or more so that I had responded as such. I knew how to take physical abuse, but fighting back with my fists was an all-new territory. Even more shocking to me was how others would cheer for you when taking down a known POS. I resolved in that glorious moment that I would never be the victim of physical violence again. I would not throw the first punch, but I would make my opponent pay dearly if they came at me. Once the bus driver had everyone settled and high excitement was waning, she proceeded to drive us all home. That was it. It was over.

I was home for about half an hour when a Suburban flew into our farm-yard. Tannis's mother demanded to speak to my father outside.

"Your daughter is an *animal*," she screamed to my dad and Porky, who was standing next to him. "Tannis even has a broken *tooth*. *Who* is going to pay for that?" she screamed some more. My dad had no idea what his neighbour was screaming about. I hadn't told him a thing about the school bus fight because I didn't want him to judge me poorly or assume that I'd started it. She yelled that she was going to *press charges* and that the RCMP was her next call. I was going to be charged with *assault*. Tannis's mother became so distraught with her own outrage that she hopped back into her SUV and stormed out of the farmyard.

Sure enough, the RCMP called to inform my dad that they would be investigating the assault claim. They were going to call some of the other kids on the bus and learn from their eye-witness accounts. My dad was incredibly upset with me, I could tell. I had shamed him before I could explain. He regarded Tannis's family as relatively close friends and good neighbours. And I was disrupting his peace and he was embarrassed over me.

"Dad, she hit me first, and hard. I don't know what came over me, but I wasn't going to take it, I've never fought anyone before," I pleaded back to his growing disappointment. The last thing I wanted was to bring him this kind of shame. It had all happened so quickly.

Porky, who had stayed silent when Tannis's mother unloaded her senti-ments, grew giddy with glee at what he'd just learned. After I'd begged my dad to see my side and he walked away in a huff to process it all, Porky slapped me on my back and reminded me to hold my head up high.

"Dolly Girl, you make me proud! For too many years, we Kissels get the short end of the stick, but not today! That girl hit you first and you broke her teeth and blackened her eyes! She doesn't know who she's *messing* with," he lauded. "Those must be some great *fisticuffs* that you got there."

While I appreciated Porky's support, I was more concerned about my dad and what he thought of me. I was new to the farm, all was going so well, and I didn't need or want to seek out this kind of trouble or attention. In the late evening of that same day the RCMP officer handling the assault complaint reported back to my dad. He said that after fielding eight other bus children, he learned that Tannis was in fact the aggressor who threw the first punch. There would be no charges laid, the matter was dropped as far as they were concerned. I felt shame and pride, simultaneously.

I had escaped serious and legal trouble by telling the truth. While that earned me points, the revelation that I could become as savage as such was another matter. I knew that I went too hard on Tannis. There was a secret moment during my fit of rage when I knew that I should stop. I kept going because Tannis was *my mother*. Of course she wasn't my mother, but I saw my mother's face as I kept going to work on Tannis.

§

Being on the farm full time meant I got to see my second cousin, Candace Kissel, who lived near Glendon where all the original Kissels settled. She was my dad's cousin's daughter and about my age. Her dad and my dad were near the same age and were close growing up. Candace's mom was a school teacher and her dad worked in the school's maintenance department. They had a small hobby farm near Glendon and often came over to borrow a bale of hay or a piece of equipment from Hill and Valley Ranch.

Porky, who still spent most of his time with Lloyd, thought Candace and I were the best-looking fresh crop of Kissel girls, and jokingly floated the idea of selling us to a rich man in Bangladesh, noting that he had heard of these sorts of harem-collecting men from listening to our national broadcast radio programming on CBC. He recalled the story in great detail, amused at the concept, and scooped out the latest dip of chewing tobacco protruding from his bottom lip, and tucked it back into the Copenhagen tin.

Porky played the role of lovable uncle well, but the poor man only showered a few times a year. He changed his clothes weekly, but they weren't ever clean, despite my grandmother's repeated offers to do his laundry. Eventually she stopped asking. He had a head full of salt and pepper hair, so greasy from sweat and never washing that he combed back like Elvis. And he smelled like a ripe mixture of the pig barn and body odor. Everyone stood a few feet away from him when they spoke to him because of the smell and the tobacco spittle that flew from his mouth when he talked. I don't know why he never cleaned himself up, but he was also ashamed of it. Grandpa suggested once that the running water at Porky's was not reliable. He never sat at the table during dinner because he said his clothes were too dirty; he sat at a nearby counter where he could still join in the conversation. When I was a kid and asked him to come join us at the table, he said, "Oh, no, Dolly girl. I need to change my clothes." Porky kept a denim bag with a Crown Royal whiskey tassel that Grandma fashioned for him filled with loonies. Loonies were newly minted Canadian dollar coins, which had the queen of England on one side and the Canadian loon on the other. He kept this pouch strung on his baling twine belt.

Every time Porky saw me or one of the other kids, he gave us each a loonie. Jamison and Brett were Uncle Gordon's sons, and Aunt Brenda's sons were Carter and Thomas. Four boys who all loved the farm. I loved seeing the boys holding soft pink baby piglets or watching Brett pick on his new Fisher-Price guitar. Grandma Betty always pulled them up on her piano bench to show them the "bears" and the "birds" on the keys. Brenda, when she left the farm, went to university and became a dental hygienist. She worked in a dental clinic, and her husband worked for the power line company, so they weren't farm kids anymore. They lived in town, but always came out to the farm on weekends.

So, Porky gave us each a loonie, and then he started joking about how expensive it was becoming to give me a loonie every time he saw me because I was living on the farm full time. I always insisted he save his money for the little kids. But he still gave me a loonie every time. And if he didn't have a loonie, he gave me a five-dollar bill. He was endlessly proud of Candace and all my other cousins, and he was always proud of me. Being in the full embrace of an unconditionally loving family felt bittersweet, even if it was off to a bumpy start with my bus fight.

One day I was visiting Candace at her house, and she showed me this dresser that she'd had in her room since she was born. She and her mom had recently refinished it. They'd sanded the wood and repainted it, and Candace was so proud of how it turned out. It was beautiful. Marilyn, her mother, used big words and was elegant and poised. And I was so happy for her, but standing there looking at it and listening to her talk enthusiastically about the project, it hit me how incredible her mom must be to help her with it. I couldn't recall a single instance when Françoise helped me with a project. I couldn't even imagine recounting a story to someone else with glee, about a project accomplished with my mom. These little painful examples of what a stable, loving, and encouraging mother-child relationship looked like were all around me. A few minutes later her mom called us down for a snack that she'd lovingly prepared for us, which was something I never had.

§

Mom often called me at my dad's or my grandparents' to check up on me. Of course I told her everything was going well. I didn't elaborate or ask her how things were going for her, because I only wanted to give her the basic level of respect that I'd been raised to give. I also didn't care very much about her life. But I thought I could hear a mounting sense of guilt in her niceness. She sounded like she was genuinely interested in how I was doing. But I resented her efforts at controlling me, which was how I took everything she said. And I got off those phone calls and went back to the dinner table, griping about my mom this and my mom that. And my dad, of course, always smiled like a Cheshire Cat because he knew what I said was true. He was divorced from her. My mom was certainly not his favourite person, and he resented the many ways that she tried to power over him with us kids.

Porky, who didn't like mom much either, loved throwing a jab at mom. He once said, "She's like a wolverine. When she gets you backed in a corner, she'll attack." They all remembered my mom from when she was married to my dad and living there, and nobody could deny the comparison with

Canada's most vicious animals. Whenever she called and I wasn't around, Porky would tell me, "The wolverine called for you."

My grandma never had a negative word to say, being the polite, quiet schoolmarm that she was. But if it went on for too long, my grandpa would slam his hand down on the table, and say, "That's enough. That's your mother. You will always respect her, and you will always talk of her with respect if you're sitting at my table."

I was shocked the first time Lloyd said that. But he insisted on maternal respect, and family was family.

"She's still my daughter, too," Grandpa said.

"Well, I don't think your 'daughter' cares very much for you," I said. My mother's abuse certainly targeted Lloyd. For all the years I'd lived with Françoise, she called him a good-for-nothing drunk to anyone who'd listen. She ran Lloyd Kissel's name through the mud all over town, and I never told my grandfather this, until now.

"Well, that may be. But you know what?" Lloyd looked at me hard from his spot at the head of the table. "That's a reflection of her. And a reflection of me is that I still care for her, and I'm not afraid to say so. And I wish her well." Lloyd was still my hero, always giving me a new perspective to think from, even if it was from the 1940s.

§

When I was fifteen, Dad and Doris went out to Vegas for four days; they were leaving Thursday and coming back Sunday morning. And they let me stay at the house because Lloyd and Betty were right next door. The day they left, I asked my dad if I could have a couple friends over on Friday night for a sleepover. Of course, he said. I was always having sleepovers at the farm, and we'd be running on the tops of hay bales and riding the ATVs and having farm girl fun all night. That was all I had planned for Friday. But my friends told a few other friends about how my parents were out of town and I was having people over. And those friends told a few more friends. And so on. Friday night, a few of my friends came over. Then a few more friends came over. Then a few more. And they—just—kept—coming. The more people who came, the crazier and more out of hand everything became. I had tried beer at bush parties when I was sneaking out of Pierre and Anita's, but that night, I had way too much to drink. I remember being completely confused and overwhelmed while everything spiraled out of control. Cars lined up from the house to the end of the driveway, and when that filled up, they parked along the side of the busy Highway 28. There had to have been over two hundred people in and out of there all night. The evening's events blurred, but even as it was happening, I knew there was damage that I couldn't keep up with. But there was no way I could stop it. Drunken testosterone boys fighting over here, big sticky booze spills over there.

In the morning, when everyone had dispersed, my couple of girlfriends and I found a giant mess. There had been so many people, and so much going on, that every inch of the house was compromised. Liquor spills on the carpeting made the air smell like an old bar. Snacks and drinks and beer cans littered every surface. Pictures were crooked on the walls. We went outside, and the barbecue was stuck upside down in a bush. Someone must have picked it up and tossed it in there. Maybe that was what the chanting was all about earlier? My dad's new truck was parked in the garage, but a drunken fight had broken out, and one kid smashed another kid's head into the side and dented it. Destruction and Molson Canadian beer cans were everywhere we looked.

Dad and Doris were coming back the next morning, so for the rest of the day Saturday, my girlfriends and I scrambled and cleaned and cleaned and cleaned. Desperate to hide as much as we could, we soaked and scrubbed the stains on the carpets. Wetting the carpets only made bigger stains, so we scrubbed again. Then the carpets were so wet we used hair dryers to dry them. When we went to fetch Doris' home salon hair dryers, we noticed that a few kids must have given themselves buzz cuts too. Hair of every colour was on the floor—it was probably the Junior A hockey team kids in attendance, spotted hanging around there. We cleaned up all the empty drinks, sprayed the rooms with air freshener, and put everything back where it belonged. It took us all day. When we were done, my friends went home, and I sat down in the living room, running my eyes over the whole place one last time to make sure we didn't forget anything. I emptied two cans of room freshener and felt satisfied that it might be meadow-fresh now. I wasn't sure what to say about the truck yet, but I thought for sure the house would pass inspection. Depending on how much traffic my grandparents saw coming and going, I thought I might get away with it. But I knew that they were smarter than that.

When Dad and Doris got home, I played it cool. "How was your trip?" I asked, fixing the halo over the top of my head.

They eyed me and looked around the house, carrying bags and telling me about the plane ride and the casinos and the shows. They seemed suspicious; maybe they sensed my anxiety, or maybe they could smell the cleaning products in the air. But after bringing in all the bags and getting settled in, everything seemed to be going okay. Then Dad went to sit in his recliner.

As soon as he let the weight off his feet and eased back into it, a crunch sound came from underneath the chair. Everyone heard it, but ignored it, as they kept going on about the gambling and the heat. I smiled and nodded from my seat on the couch. A minute later, Dad shifted the recliner and it crunched again.

"What in the world . . ." Dad bent over and looked under the chair. He reached down under it, grabbed something I couldn't see, and sat back up. He had a squashed beer can in his hand. "What's this doing here?"

I shrugged, played it cool as panicked flooded my face.

"You know, it smells in here." He stood up from his chair and started walking around the house, scrutinizing it more carefully. "It smells like booze."

While I stood by, firm in my denial, they looked the place over from top to bottom, found the dented truck, the broken barbecue, and a gutter that someone had pulled down off the side of the house. Dad's liquor collection was gone or topped off with water. And all our dismal attempts to hide the ginormous party exposed us.

He called my grandparents and asked if I'd had a party.

"Oh, no, it was just a few people," Betty said. "It didn't seem like that big of a deal," Lloyd added. Whether they knowingly lied for me, or I'd truly gotten away with it, I don't know. But it seemed like I was going to get away with it, until Doris went in to work at the hair salon. That place was a beehive of gossip, and everyone in town was talking about the Kissel girl's wild party. Over the next few days, additional details of my party began to emerge. Everyone in town had been there. The more Doris heard, the more embarrassed she became. Some of her jewelry turned up missing, and I felt horrible about it. In classic teenager fashion, I said, "But, Dad, it was only supposed to be a few friends. It got out of control, and I'm sorry."

My dad was understanding and forgiving about everything at first; he'd had his wild youthful days. I'd heard all the stories of him and Uncle Gordon pushing Lloyd's red Ford out the driveway after he passed out, like stealthy ninjas, to go party in their day. But Doris, who I suspected was jealous of my dad's new relationship with me, was really mad. They didn't fight it out in front of me, but not long after the party, Dad sat me down at the kitchen table in our house and told me about the conflict my actions had brought.

"Doris feels that it's not a good idea that you continue to live with us any longer," he said with a deep, defeated sigh.

"Well, how do you feel about it?"

"She's my wife, and I don't want to upset her."

"But I'm your daughter." My voice raised at the unfairness of what he was telling me. I believed that he would fight a bit for me, and was angry that he wasn't. I saw it as pathetic, as if I was tougher or braver than him. I didn't like to see men weaker than women. I was raised by a woman who wasn't afraid of anything; I expected him to be more like that. Seeing that he wasn't was frustrating. "And I finally get a chance to be with you, and you're going to let her boss you around, like mom does?"

"Well, you know, Carmen, it's not easy for a man. I'm kind of stuck between two positions that I don't want to be in."

"Fine," I yelled, flushed with anger and the sting of another rejection. "You don't have to choose. I'll make it for you. I'm going to go live at Lloyd and Betty's."

"Well," he said hopefully. "Maybe that's the answer." Of course he thought it was a great idea because then he didn't have to confront his wife, me or *anything*. She won, but he didn't exactly lose either. I would still be on the farm, just at the next house, and everything would be fine. That night, I ran across that same little stretch of field that I used to run across as a little kid. Like in a Crystal Gayle song, I ran to my grandparents' house, crying, feeling rejected from another place again. Of course I resented Doris, blamed her for running me out of my own house. Who was she anyway? A mom to a jailbird? I blamed it all on her. And I felt like nobody wanted me anymore. I couldn't live at my mom's, and now because of Doris I couldn't live with my dad. Even if my dad wanted me, he wasn't going to do anything about it. He would never stand up to Doris. I couldn't depend on anyone; I had to take care of myself. And in this case, "taking care of it" meant running to my grandparents and begging them to let me live with them.

7

YOUNG ANARCHIST

"Tyranny and anarchy are never far apart."
—JEREMY BENTHAM

LLOYD AND BETTY, WITH OPEN arms, welcomed me into their home and shifted to make room. They gave me Aunt Brenda's old room downstairs, right next to Grandma's sewing room. Grandma helped me make new pillows and a quilt for my bed. Porky, who didn't like Doris anyways, winked and told me she wasn't so great. And Grandpa had a second bathroom put in downstairs for me to use. I was always bathing for hours and using Grandma's hairspray, and Grandpa said he'd always wanted a bathroom down there anyway. Many nights I read myself to sleep next door to the soothing whir-sound of Grandma Betty working with her serger machine. There was an old chest in my room that held all of Porky's CN Rail steward uniforms from when he worked on the railway during his teens. I used to love to look at them and imagine Uncle Ray shined up in this official and important uniform.

"Now that Dolly Girl's here," he said, "it's time. She's a teenaged girl; she needs her own bathroom." Lloyd found a Newfie guy with a tool belt to put walls up around where the bathroom plumbing was already roughed in. They popped up this crude, bare bones shower stall, like something you'd see in an industrial work camp, and put in a toilet, a tiny vanity, and a mirror. It was so plain, with a concrete floor and unpainted drywall, but it was the best bathroom I could ever imagine. My grandma made a cheerful shower curtain, and I had my own space.

Even if I was working on the farm all day, I came in in time to help Grandma with dinner. She didn't have a dishwasher and her kitchen wasn't fancy. But she was always cooking the most delicious, hearty food. Plenty of it, too, because she never knew how many people would turn up for dinner. My first evening there as a full-time resident, I set Porky's plate at the dinner table, right beside me, instead of at the end of the radio counter. I arranged his plate, fork, knife, spoon, and teacup on the long wooden table.

At dinner time, Grandpa and Dad came in from the field first. They hung their coats and washed up with Irish Springs bar soap, then converged on the table. A minute later Porky came in from the barn. As soon as he saw his plate wasn't on the counter, he said, "No, Dolly Girl. I'm not sitting at the table. My clothes are too dirty."

"Porky," I said. "You're sitting next to me at the table tonight, and every night from now on."

"Oh, no, now . . ." he started to protest.

"Yes, you are." I pulled out the chair at the place I'd set for him. "I won't have anything of it."

He hung his head and shrugged, then sat down at the table, that night, and every night after. He had been so supportive and kind to me, looking past all my mistakes, that I didn't care how bad he smelled. I wanted him to be included. And no one cared. We were all happy to see him at the table, even though we had to choke down every bite of food with his strong body odour. We were all able to put our grievances behind us and enjoy each other's company. While Doris and the Dargis family made it seem like I was going to hell in a hand basket, the Kissels, who knew the very same stories, didn't care. Especially Porky, who chalked up my many indiscretions to kids being kids—he thought I was a "firecracker." I wanted to make him feel just as welcome as he, and Grandma and Grandpa, made me feel.

On the day of the written part of my driver's test, Porky, who'd gone to the bank ahead of time, pulled a ten-dollar bill from his pocket and placed it on the table at lunch. "I've got ten dollars says Dolly Girl fails her test today."

I laughed and looked at him like he was crazy. "I'll take that bet," I said. "I bet ten dollars I pass."

Lloyd and Betty and Dad all bet that I'd pass too. I'd been driving around the farm and around town for years by this point to fetch parts or medicine for the animals; but now that I was sixteen, I could make it official. Sure enough, I passed the test on the first try, and Porky happily handed me the ten dollars, probably his last ten dollars until his next government check. He'd known the whole time that I'd pass it; the only reason he'd said any different was because that meant he got to give me his money. In that way he was always in my corner, always that fun, weird uncle. No one retold the story of *The Three Billy Goats Gruff* quite like he did; bangin' his fist on Grandma's solid wood, creaky table to simulate the billy goats crossing the troll bridge. And he was always willing to take my fifteen or twenty bucks to the store in town and bring me back a pack of beer or wine coolers. We had a secret spot in the barn where he always tucked it for me. Porky and I kept many secrets.

Maurice came around every other weekend because we still kept our 4-H steers on the Kissel farm. But he and I weren't as close as we had been. I was in high school now, and popular, in a whole new world of adult themes and interests. But I could see that he was okay. He never had any bruises on him, and he was always smiling. And I always spent time with his steer as part of my daily chores, so Maurice's 4-H animal was doing well too. It had to be fairly tame. If you had a wild animal in the ring, you wouldn't get as much money for it, so I loved my brother's steer too and played with it and groomed it. And I kind of felt like that was taking care of my brother still, handling his responsibilities until he could.

As soon as I could drive, life just started taking over. Dad let me take the farm truck to school on days I had practice, which meant I had it all day. I skipped school like crazy, and started skipping ballet class on Saturdays. The teacher called my mom to tell her I'd stopped showing up, so she quit paying for it. I still made it to volleyball, basketball, badminton, synchronized swimming, and track and field practice for the social elements. But my

sporty girlfriends were "academics'" and I was fast becoming more "arcade."
And my grades started circling the drain pretty quickly.

At the end of one term, when I knew I was failing biology with a 22
percent grade point average, I started watching my dad's mailbox for the
report card. When it came, I steamed open the envelope and took it to
the computer lab at school the next day. Replicating the format, I created
a fake report card. Giving myself nineties would have been taking it too
far, so I gave myself strong seventies and eighties. Then I printed it out
and popped it in the envelope from the school. I got the mail from the
box that afternoon and stuck my report card in the stack. And it worked;
it worked all day long. They did nothing but sing my praises. Grandma
and Grandpa, even Porky, went on and on about how smart I was. And
I felt so guilty, knowing I was turning into such a liar and a cheat. But at
the same time, I didn't want to give up doing whatever I wanted with my
friends all day long.

On a hot, early-June day, in the final weeks of the school year, the sun
was shining outside and we were all wearing shorts and ready for summer
to begin. I had my dad's truck, and a few friends and the boys we liked
skipped school to go swimming at the La Corey bridge a few miles outside
of town. I was supposed to meet my mom after school that day. The 4-H
Achievement Day was coming up, so as part of the program, Mom was
taking me around to local businesses to personally invite them to attend
our auction. Lots of businesses bought animals, and the 4-H organization
felt like the personal invites kept us connected to the community and the
market strong. Mom and I made the plans weeks in advance, but when I
parked the truck under the bridge and jumped into the cold water, spending
time with her felt a million hours away. And when I smoked a joint—trying
marijuana for the first time—I never gave it a second thought. The ripe
smoke billowed around me as I passed the joint to my friends, and we
giggled and sat in the glow of early summer on all the dropped tailgates.
I drove back to the school in time for them to catch the school bus. Then
I drove myself home to the farm, walked through the door, said hello to
Grandma, went downstairs to my basement room, and collapsed on the
bed. The heat, the thrill of seasons changing, the extra farm work, the

weed—it all caught up to me. I slept from 3:30 to 5:30 p.m., when I awoke to my mom shaking my arm.

"Carmen," she said. "Get up. We made these arrangements weeks ago."

"I forgot," I said, still groggy and stoned, cursing the terrible timing.

"Why are you so tired?" Her frustration at the inconvenience of having to wake me became suspicion. "What's wrong with you?"

"Nothing," I said. "I just had a really hard day. I'm getting up."

Ten minutes later, we were heading into town. One by one, we visited all the most powerful business owners in Bonnyville. I cursed my own terrible timing with this set-up. And it became clear, in the way my mom smiled and showed me off, that she had it all planned in her mind. This was not only about fulfilling a 4-H duty, it was an opportunity for her. She got to introduce her daughter to all the people she cared about impressing, only adding to the purported narrative that she was an amazing mom.

At each meeting, I gave my 4-H schtick, mentioning all the public speaking awards I had won with the program, the whole time feeling high enough to float away. All I wanted to do was crawl back into bed. The whole exercise seemed insignificant and unnecessary; the people I was meeting seemed just as bored as I was. Finally, I couldn't stand it anymore. "Mom," I said weakly. "Can we be done now?"

"What do you mean?"

"I'm just too tired," I said. "I don't know what's wrong with me."

"Fine. We'll hit one last stop, and I'll take you home," she relented.

By this time, still dressed in my dirty shorts, my skin pink from the sun, and red-eyed, I can only imagine the impression I was making. But as soon as the important owner of the construction company laid eyes on us, a smile filled his face. He couldn't have been more than thirty years old and here I was talking to him in his fancy office, telling him how hard I'd worked, how much his presence at Achievement Day would mean to me, and to please join us. He looked at me, and then he looked at my mom, who was smiling and pretending everything was fine, and knew exactly what was going on. I think he thought it was all comical and amusing.

"Thank you very much, Françoise and Carmen, for coming in." He added with a professional tone. "Thank you for your presentation. I will be there."

But that night, after dragging me all around town, she drove me back to the farm.

"You know, Carmen, I just can't count on you," Mom said from the driver's seat. Annnd right on cue, here we go, I thought. Surely an endless tirade was upcoming about who I was shaping up to be. She may have bought my sick routine, but she was not happy that I was cutting the evening short. Then she escalated her routine to the bigger picture. "What are you doing with your life? And don't you know God's watching?" Ugh. Barf.

I let my head fall against the glass as we drove, the whole time wishing that the farm was closer than it was, that she would drive faster, and that she would shut up. And I was upset with myself for getting carried away earlier and not making the best choices. She was still giving me a hard time when we pulled in at the farm. I got out, shut the door on her unending verbal assault, and didn't speak to her for weeks after that.

But she started getting suspicious. She'd heard around town that I was spotted in my dad's truck doing this or that, even though she never saw me herself. When she called my dad to talk about it, he brushed her off and said I was fine.

"Well, how's she doing in school?" Mom pressed him.

"I've seen her report cards, Françoise. She's doing fine. Leave her alone."

Mom, less trusting than my dad, was unconvinced. She went straight to the school and talked to my teachers, where the truth came out. Mr. McRae from chemistry said I was a bright girl who knew what glow plugs for diesel engines were last week in class, but had been playing "pillar and the post" for quite some time. I was never there, they said, and failing just about every class. Of course, she told my dad, who told the Kissels. And everyone was disappointed in me, disappointed that I'd deceived everyone like that. But the way the Kissels handled disappointment was not by shunning me or sending me back to my mom or bashing my character. They were upset, but they didn't give up on me. They didn't even ground me or punish me. Lloyd decided it was best to pepper me with examples of what a "dumb klutz" was and how to avoid becoming one. I heard them, loud and clear.

After some time, my indiscretions became little inside jokes. Porky, for example, called me "Crash" for a bit after wrecking Mom's new car. But they didn't treat me any differently. They preferred to move on through chats about their own wild adventures. Grandpa Lloyd always had a relatable lesson to share with a story from growing up in the '40s and '50s. He and his siblings, as teens in the little Village of Glendon, tore up these little one-horse towns, walking the train tracks from place to place. They saw my youthful antics in the same vein as their own.

Mom, on the other hand, needed a heavier hand on my discipline. She started looking into elite Catholic boarding schools and talking to her parents about it. And they decided it was best for me to go to St. Angela's Finishing School for Women in Saskatchewan. Grandpa Pierre agreed to help pay for the expensive tuition, and that would straighten me out.

I told her *no way* would I ever go to St. Angela's. I couldn't go to some fancy private school for girls; I wore Wranglers, I lived on a farm. And I was popular. Leaving would be a complete disruption of my life.

Grandma Betty, having spent her career in academic advancement and education, said maybe it would be a good opportunity for me. But Grandpa Lloyd didn't like the idea. "I don't think we should let her go to that," he said. "That's not who she is, and she'd be too far away. Anything could happen to her. There's no parents there. There's no *grandparents*." Dad didn't want me to go either. But at the same time, no one really knew what to do with me, and I seemed dead set on getting in trouble.

They encouraged me to go through the process with my mom, which meant seeing a doctor and having a hearing and vision screening. No matter what, it felt like my mom was always fighting for control of my life. The thought of leaving my friends and the farm made me feel like screaming. When Mom dropped off the "welcome package" and application of prospective student materials, I looked through it—not for hope but for a way out. I quickly scanned the documents for expulsion guidelines—aha! Smoking! I didn't smoke cigarettes but what a great time to start, I mused.

When I went to the doctor for my checkup, Mom drove me and waited for me in the waiting room. I said as little to her as possible. As soon as I was alone with Dr. Mueller in the exam room, I asked him for a prescription for birth control. I figured if I had to follow along with my mom's charade, I would at least get something I wanted out of it.

"You want birth control?" He asked over his glasses. "If you end up at St. Angela's, you might need it."

He wrote me the prescription. With that, I decided I was done humouring anyone. There was no way I was going to St. Angela's.

"I'm not going," I told my mom when she pulled in the driveway at the farm to drop me off. "There's no way."

She put the car in park, turned to face me, and said like a dare, "Oh, yes you are, *girl*."

"No, I'm not." I faced her right back. "And you can't call me *girl* anymore. I'm Carmen." Nothing offended me more than that name usage. I was not her *thing*. I had read all the orientation materials from the school, so I knew the rules. They'd throw me out if I got in trouble twice. "If you make me go to that school, you'll spend all this money getting me there, and on the first day, I'll light a cigarette in the face of the first important person I see. And when they make me put it out, I'll light up another one. And I'll keep doing that until they send me back to the farm. After you've been such a crap parent to me, there's no way you can make me go anywhere. So, it's up to you! Take Pépère's money and look like a fool in the end or drop it." This seemed to speak her language, and I wagered that there was no way that she'd risk disappointing her father to embarrass herself.

As I let it all spill out, her face reddened. I thought steam would come out of her ears. But she must have known I wasn't bluffing because she backed down. I got out of the car and slammed the door. And she let it go. I had *won*.

A few weeks later, me still not speaking to her, Mom showed up at the farm with a brass mirrored vanity set.

"I saw this and thought of you," she said sheepishly. It had a glass top and a plush, lovely tufted seat. And when she pulled it out of the back of her SUV and set it down, it seemed like a last-ditch effort to apologize. I think she felt guilty for how she'd raised me, the connection that she had never forged, for the person she wished I'd be. But the gift was awkward, something you'd give a ten-year-old girl, not a troubled teenager. And it looked like it belonged in a room where a person with a different kind of life lived. It belonged in a house where a girl had a beautiful family and a kind and loving mom, like Candace's room, not in the room belonging to a person who'd had my life. And I felt sad for Mom, standing there in the driveway, looking at the vanity, wishing to rewind time.

"Thanks," I said, flat and unemotional. "I appreciate it."

There was nothing else to say, so she got in her car and left. After that, when she called, I hung up as soon as I heard her voice. I didn't care to speak to her. She'd call back and call back, and Grandma would yell, "Who's getting the phone? Carmen, get the phone."

"It's Mom," I'd say. "Just leave it." And everyone did. Eventually, Mom stopped calling.

§

But I didn't cut Mom out of my life forever, at least not yet. As I got older, I needed to make money. I wanted to buy clothes, I wanted to put gas in the farm truck. I could work all day on the farm, but no one was going to pay me to do it. That was just life on the farm. If I wanted a paycheck, I had to look elsewhere. When Maurice came around, taking care of his 4-H animals and hanging out, he told me about how Mom was paying him to work at the butcher shop. Maurice and I weren't as close now, but he seemed to be doing really well with my mom. I kind of half-resented him too, because him doing so well forced me to wonder if I really was the problem all along. And he had all this money from working for her after school. That was where I got the idea to work at the butcher shop too. I already knew the work, and Dad thought it was a good idea because it might help repair my relationship with Mom.

When I asked her for a job, she gave me one. And I started working there, cautiously, after school and on some Saturdays. At first, it went great. She gave me space, and when she didn't, I decided not to let it bother me. Like water off a duck's back, as Maurice would say. Soon, she started giving me bigger jobs and more responsibilities. I was always a good worker. And she felt like she could trust me, at least with that.

Now that I had my driver's license, I started driving the delivery truck two and three hours away, taking meat orders to universities and hospitals throughout the region, places like Lloydminster and Vermilion. I'd arrive after school, and they'd have the van loaded and waiting for me with hundred-pound boxes of meat and half sides of pork on top of poly plastic. This was adult work, very responsible, and I got to know so many people in the extended business community. And through everyone's impressions of my mom, I started to see her as a Jekyll and Hyde person. People would meet me and say, "Oh, you're Françoise's daughter. We've heard all about you. Look how grown up you are. Isn't your mom the greatest?"

I found it so nauseating. And eventually it wore on me. At the same time, Mom started getting weird about paying me. She said that since I was family and underage, and because the paperwork for the taxes was such a pain, that she'd just start giving me $1,000 a month. But she was only going to pay me every two months. I agreed to this arrangement, not having any reason to doubt her. But at the end of the second month, when I went to Mom and told her it was payday, she said, "Yeah, but you know, I'm afraid that if I give you that big check, you're just going to waste it."

Things had been amicable between us. But standing there in her office, after working all day, and hearing her say that made me feel like a child all over again. I'd been working like crazy and she wasn't going to pay me. I was so offended, and I took it as another power and control grab over me. Because playing with someone's finances is control, and it seemed that nothing I could do would ever be good enough for her.

At the same time, her withholding my pay created another problem. My friend Jael and I were hatching a plan to get an apartment together, and I'd been counting on that money to fund it. Jael came from a strict, devout Jehovah's Witness family, and in her I found a kindred spirit. We often griped about how religion had made our upbringing horrible. In my case, Mom and her parents and their devout Roman Catholic outlook on life. She and I were completely different from each other in terms of what religion was shoved down our throats. And yet, we found so many similarities in the treatment that we had experienced. She, too, at seventeen, was barely hanging on with school, struggling to make a positive difference with her family life.

When she brought up the idea of getting an apartment together, I couldn't think of a reason why not. I had $2,000 coming that we could use as a down payment. We found a place in town that wasn't fancy, but it had two bedrooms, a bathroom, a living area, and a decent kitchen for $475 a month. Jael had been working at A&W for a while now, and she could easily make enough to cover her half and still go to school. Even if Mom fired me, I could find another job. It sounded so mature and adult; we were going to shed our troubled childhoods and live the adult life the way we wanted. And we were really close to getting it, until Mom refused to pay me.

Instead of fighting her, though, I kept my mouth shut. I'd outfoxed her before, and if she wasn't going to pay me what she owed me, *I'd take it another way.* Jael covered my part of the down payment, while I went to all the stores in town where Mom had business tabs or accounts, and charged two thousand dollars' worth of food and housewares to furnish and outfit our new place. Through driving the delivery services, I'd gotten to know all the people at the stores where Mom held accounts, so no one asked questions when Françoise's daughter came in and bought hundreds of dollars' worth of dishes and appliances and cleaning supplies and furniture. They even helped me carry it out to the truck. And I didn't spend a penny more than what she owed me. When the bills came a few days later, she absolutely lost her mind, but she went and paid all of those accounts.

When I broke it to my Dad and the Kissels that I was getting my own apartment, I tried to make it sound like it was all for the best. I said, "I don't need to be here, bothering you anymore."

Lloyd and Betty were fairly understanding because they only saw the good in me. And going out on your own at seventeen wasn't unheard of or even uncommon for their generation. But Dad didn't support the idea at all.

"As soon as you get a job and start making money, Carmen, you're never going to graduate from high school," he said. "You'll regret it for the rest of your life."

Needless to say, when I asked him for one of the farm trucks, he said, "No way."

8

ADULTING

"All my life I have been hearing that the oil was going to run out. It never happens. They keep discovering new oil fields. The world is apparently floating in oil fields."
—JANE JACOBS

THE TWO-BEDROOM APARTMENT ON LAKESHORE Drive looked like a brown and taupe explosion, furnished with tired couches and coffee tables that we'd collected from friends and family. It wasn't the newest, fanciest place, but it was ours. And the bathroom counter had enough space for all our girlie potions.

Jael and I met in the smoker alley of Bonnyville Centralized High School, and we bonded over stories of our strict religious upbringings. She had it worse than I did; her Jehovah's Witness family placed even higher standards and more severe constraints on Jael. Her parents demanded a high level of decorum, but Jael was a very colorful, beautiful person who did not fit in that mold. She was the baby of seven or eight siblings and her aging parents wanted perfect grades and insisted she stay at home, and they omitted affection when she didn't meet their standards. We both struggled with realities where we had to be a certain way to get affection from our parents. And we'd both had enough of it. Our religious backgrounds, though similarly strict, felt different at the same time. Because of work, we mostly saw each other at school. But on one of our infrequent nights together in the apartment, we ordered pizza and curled up on the couch to watch television and talk. This time, talking about our families brought us to the topic of religion.

"I really don't know much about Jehovah's Witnesses except for the stereotypes and that they come to your door every Saturday when you're trying to sleep in," I said.

"Yeah, I don't know anything about Roman Catholicism either," she said.

"Can I look at your Bible?" I asked, knowing she had to have one lying around if I did, and I did, a treasured "first Bible" given to me by Anita at my First Communion.

"Sure." She didn't hesitate. "But I want to look at yours too."

We pulled the texts from our respective shelves and traded. After reading a few pages, we looked up at each other at the same time, slapped our books down, and laughed at how similar the two texts were. I had always felt our religious backgrounds were something that separated us, but we had a quiet epiphany together that we weren't that different. We were spiritual sisters in every sense. Our upbringings were ruled by different ideologies, but her and I were simpatico. And we became great friends.

Our apartment was within walking distance of the school, and I got a job waiting tables at the Midtown Motor Inn, a popular family diner close by. And at first, having our own place, finishing twelfth grade, and waiting tables—with Jael doing the same, working at the A&W—felt empowering. We didn't have any trouble paying our bills; our days fell into a comfortable pattern of school and work that made it seem like everything was going really well. But then my work started cutting my hours and scheduling me for shifts during the school day.

A husband and wife owned the Midtown Motor Inn, and the wife, who made the schedule every week, was perpetually annoyed by having to deal with the restaurant staff. I pleaded with her to only schedule me on evenings and weekends, but she didn't care.

"That's the way it is," she said. "You can either work when I put you on the schedule, or you won't have a job."

A few times I had to skip school to keep my job, which weren't always easy to find, especially without a car. That was when I started thinking I didn't need to bother with school at all. I wasn't going to university, I knew that much. I had a job and was paying my bills. My father's warning was coming to fruition, but I didn't see it that way at the time. I decided that making money was most important, so high school for me was done, and I started looking for another, better, full-time job. For better or worse, I was already living as an adult, feeling like I was twenty-five at seventeen.

§

My mother's side of the family had pretty much written me off completely by this point, or were so out of touch with what I'd been up to for quite some time. But I knew I needed to tell the Kissels about my decision to quit school. I wasn't looking forward to this conversation at all, knowing I'd be letting them down. But I'd lied to them enough already, and the next time I was there, I sat down with everyone at the kitchen table, and told them I'd dropped out.

Everyone was quiet for a minute. This had to be a disappointment. They all advocated for education, especially Grandma, who had her degree in education and spent her career as a teacher.

After an awkward silence, Grandpa said, "Well, Dolly Girl. What are you going to do?"

"I'm waitressing now," I said, trying to sound confident. I felt ashamed telling them that I was going to be a waitress. Like, was that my life? To have freedom, I had to be a waitress? "And I'd like to find a better waitressing job."

"The world needs waitresses," Grandma Betty said, clearing her throat. "They need people like you to be friendly to the families that come in. Maybe you're the bright spot in their day. We've come to see you at work, and you're very good at what you do. You make people feel good. And the world needs people like that. So if that's what you want to do, then that's honourable and noble."

They accepted my journey, didn't try to interfere, and recognized that they probably wouldn't have any influence over this decision. But it turned out that they could still sway me.

Before quitting school, I started seeing an Indigenous boy from my school named Clayton. I was quite smitten with him—he was well-off, he was good looking. His father was a prominent figure of Kehewin First Nation community, which afforded them positive community status. Clayton's family's land—the Kehewin First Nation land—bordered my family's farm. Plus, his dark, clean cut hair and tall, athletic body was difficult to resist.

When we started seeing each other, I kept it as quiet as possible because I was terrified to think of my dad finding out about Clayton. Lloyd wouldn't have cared, but my father, who I'd heard mutter, "Fucking Indians," under his breath my whole life, would never allow me to date an Indigenous boy. I knew he would pop a top. This didn't stop me from doing it, but it did give me a reason to keep the relationship a secret.

Then one day Dad saw me riding through town in Clayton's truck. He had a thousand questions about what I was doing. When I came clean and told him I was seeing Clayton, Dad's jaw clenched.

"You know, Dolly Girl," he said. "You do a lot of offensive, rebellious things, and we've turned a blind eye. But this is something that I just absolutely can't handle. If you continue on with this relationship with this guy, I won't speak to you again."

I did what he asked. I was disheartened that he could be so racist, but I also knew I had pushed my family's ability to forgive to its extreme. That was the end of me and Clayton, and it was an end for my dad and me in a way too. I'd always have my dad, but I wasn't so sure I still needed him or wanted that in my new life.

§

Without school, I started working as much as I possibly could at the Midtown Motor Inn. One night, a friend from high school, Kelly Biddle, came in and sat in my section. We started talking and catching up and she told me she was waitressing too, at the Fort Kent Hotel. This surprised me because the Fort Kent Hotel had a little dive bar in a hamlet town outside of Bonnyville, but it was famous throughout the area because it was the only venue that offered exotic entertainers. The tired, old building was probably built in the '20s or '30s, and it was the epitome of dive bars. No self-respecting woman in the area would set foot in there. But if you were an oilfield guy or a farm kid over eighteen, you'd be hanging out at Fort Kent. Kelly said she was serving drinks there Wednesday through Saturday—the nights with the live dancers—and bringing in three hundred to six hundred dollars a night in tips.

"I have to work full time to make that kind of money here in a week," I said. The Midtown restaurant was known for casual breakfast and informal family suppers, and I made fifty to eighty dollars in tips on a good eight-hour shift.

"You know, Carmen, we can't even get another girl to help me because nobody will work there," she said. "If you're interested, I can talk to Charlie, my boss. He's this sweet old man who runs the place with his son. I could totally get you in there."

I had been working all morning and barely had fifty bucks in my apron, so her offer sounded pretty tempting. "I don't know if I could do it," I said. "My family would probably go crazy."

"Yeah, but you wouldn't be a stripper, you'd be a waitress, which is the same thing you're doing now."

When she left, I had her number. But I kept looking for other opportunities.

During my search, I came across an ad for a training program that read: *Become a fourth-class Power Engineer and work in the oilfield as a steam operator.* Some of my older guy friends were oilfield operators with their fourth-class power engineering ticket, and they made really good money. I also knew it was a good career with lots of opportunities in that area and possibilities for advancement. And when I researched the criteria, they didn't require a high school diploma. I was a farm girl, so oilfield work didn't intimidate me. I signed up for the training program and started going to classes on Tuesday and Thursday nights from four to ten.

Our part of Canada has vast oilfields, known as the Athabasca oilsands basin, and our oil is plentiful but buried deep underground and stuck in sand. It's not nice and close to the surface like in the famous oilsands of Fort McMurray, where they strip mine the surface of the land to access the sandy oily deposit easily. We can get to our oil by drilling a well, installing a pumpjack or lift system, and steaming the oil below before you lift it up and out of the ground. With in-situ or SAGD methodology, we use superheated steam pumped into the ground to warm and loosen the sticky oil from the sand so it can be pumped above ground in a process called thermal oil harvest. We have thermal oil production and harvest plants all over northeastern Alberta that produce steam in giant boilers and generators, and pump that steam down to the oil deposits through systems of pipes, where it stays in the ground for about a month, improving the oil viscosity, so the pump jack can pull it out of the ground and back to the production facilities. Unlike surface oilsands fields and other methods of extraction and production, SAGD thermal oil harvest operations are clean and tidy and preserve the surface integrity of the ground for local wildlife. Our oilfields look like nature preserves with pipes hidden into the ground. Production like this is known as in-situ oil harvesting, predating SAGD technology, and it's a specialty trade and quite dangerous.

The power engineering program had fourth-class, third-class, second-class, and first-class designations. By the time you got up to be a first-class power engineer, you were a highly decorated person who would manage an entire facility for a company like Imperial Oil or British Petroleum or Canadian Natural Resources. And I thought this would be a great path into a career where I could be in the action. Everyone wanted to be an employee for an oil company because that's where the money was. And they took great care of you. If I got placed with a company for my apprenticeship steam time, then I'd have a good chance of being hired on as an operator when I was done. This was the path I saw myself on.

The program was intensive book work for the first six months. There were fifteen people in my class, and only three of us were girls. But around that time, there was a big push in the energy industry throughout Canada to hire more women and diversify the workforce. I was part of that change, and I did very well in the coursework. We got to learn about large multi-stage centrifugal pumps and gate valves and turbines. At the end, I put my name in the bank to be placed into an unpaid apprenticeship program at Imperial Oil, where I'd have to spend six months doing what was known as Part B of my ABSA certification or "steam time." Imperial Oil Resources, which was called Esso at the time, were leading the industry in occupational health and safety for their workers. They were progressive, and they wanted more women on their team. But getting placed for steam time was a long shot because they were only taking three students.

Lucky for me, I was selected to be one of them. When I got word of my six-month placement at Esso, I was beyond excited. It felt like, finally, something was coming together for me. This was a highly sought-after position. And not only that, but I was placed at their newest, most state-of-the-art plant in the area. The plant was called Mahihkan, and was, like all their other facilities, named to honour the Indigenous people and their names for animals. They had others in the area—Leming and Maskwa. Leming, which was their oldest operating plant and therefore, in the fast-moving energy sector, the least technologically advanced. I was happy to not have been placed there.

On my first day of steam time, at five in the morning, a dark blue Chevy Astro Esso utility van pulled up outside my apartment in town.

"Don Veenstra," the driver introduced himself when I got in. "I'm your D-crew leader."

There were two other people in the van who introduced themselves and chatted with me as we drove. I was part of D-crew, working five days on the day shift, five days off, then five nights on, in twelve-hour shifts. After picking me up, Don drove all over the area, picking up three more people on D-crew in the predawn darkness. Don was a second-class power engineer, and the other crew members were excited for me that it was my first day, and they were really warm and welcoming. Once I got to work, I might not see those people all day because they would be dispatched to different places around the Mahihkan plants and field. Some worked in the water treatment facilities, some worked in the oil production facilities, and some worked in the steam plant. Five in the morning was easy for me after living on the farm, but I wasn't sure I'd be able to work a twelve-hour shift through the night.

The road into the facility was surrounded on both sides by spruce and pine forest, enveloped in the winter diamond glint darkness. When we reached the steam plant, it was lit up and glowing in full glory, gushing what looked like big plumes of white smoke. I had never seen anything like it.

"What's coming out of those huge pipes like that?" I asked, amazed by the sight. "Is that pollution?"

"You know, everyone says that," Don chuckled. "That's just the excess steam—heat coming from the plant. The only reason you can see it is because it's so cold outside. In the summer you can't see it at all." It was minus twenty-seven degrees Celsius that morning.

After all those months of training and learning how steam operating worked in theory, I was excited to see how the science applied to the real world. I couldn't wait to see the big gate valves separating the field to the facility. What did these huge pumps look like in real life compared to our textbooks? The sight of the plant and the idea of being a part of it filled me with awe. At the time, all of Imperial Oil Resources/Esso—Leming, Maskwa, and Mahihkan facilities—were producing collectively about thirty thousand barrels of oil per day. The seriousness and scale of the operation impressed me, and I could easily see why everyone I knew loved their oil industry jobs. These guys were plant workers. It was clean work, not like drilling or working on an oil rig. We were in "operations" or production and harvest, and that was something to be proud of. Some of my guy friends from high school were slugging electrical lines through muddy industrial construction sites as first-year electricians and that looked pretty rough as a day-to-day job or career.

After showing me around, Don introduced me to my site mentor, Al O'Quinn. The work was dangerous, so I was to stay with my mentor at all times. Al was also a second-class power engineer, but he worked as an operator in the water treatment plant and his main job was to teach me. Al was close to retirement, which made him the perfect person to shadow. He had a wealth of knowledge and just as much patience. Often, if I asked Al a simple question about welding, let's say, it would come with four diagrams drawn out on his clipboard and more info than I bargained to learn. I told him about my own welding flash experience and he chuckled loudly. As one of the first few women to work at the plant, I wasn't sure what kind of reception I would get. But I knew to tell the men that I was a farm girl, which meant something to them about the kind of girl I was. It was helpful to say that, and I think Al sized me up pretty quick as a good egg.

Al's job, aside from teaching me, was monitoring a variety of activities in all the different areas of the water treatment and steam plant. After meeting him on my first day, we got right to work. He had his own truck that we drove from location to location, checking on things. Late at night we'd listen to Paul Harvey's *Now You Know the Rest of the Story* segment on the radio. Soon, Al opened up and started teaching me. And I was ever-curious. I peppered him with questions, and he loved it. Soon, we'd talk about everything under the sun, no topic was off-limits and he was quickly becoming the smartest person that I'd ever known. He ended up, I think, really liking me as a person because I was so interested. And after so many years working in the same place, I'm sure my youthful curiosity refreshed him.

Al showed me the whole Mahihkan plant network on that first shift. In his little utility truck, we went out into the field where I saw the giant pump jacks, the biggest in the world. And we toured the steam plant, which was inside a giant warehouse-like building with what seemed a near eighty-foot-high ceiling.

The steam plant was the heart of the dangerous action. Twelve steam generators-boilers, six on each side of the building, each the size of a three-bedroom house, made the steam that was then piped down into the earth to loosen the oil from the sand. Unlike the steam that comes off boiling water, we were making superheated steam by passing it multiple times through giant steam generators. Al and I had to climb to the top center of each one and look through a tiny window into the fire inside. That is what they call the fire-eye, and water is pumped through tubes that wind around the inside of the steam gen drum. After multiple passes through this drum-like structure, the steaming hot water next becomes *superheated*. It was so hot that if one of the pipes were to burst and you were anywhere near it, the steam would cut you in half like a laser knife, Al said. The operator's job was to keep everything contained and functioning properly. He helped me to learn the facility by understanding and tracing the web of smaller pipes that fed and disbursed throughout the facility. I spent a lot of time tracing lines and understanding their internal contents and directional flow.

We had to wear full personal protective equipment, or PPE—coveralls, steel-toed boots, safety glasses that wrapped around, and double ear protection with ear plugs and muffs that attached to our hardhats. Hearing anything when we were suited up was difficult, but I could feel the rotating equipment's vibrating hum through my bones. And the heat that came off as a by-product of the twelve steam generators was almost unbearable inside the steam plant even in winter. Al had to yell anything he wanted to tell me when we were inside the steam plant, but he pointed everything out, and I leaned in to hear his explanations.

I watched as he led me to the backside of each generator, where what we called the taps or the dumps were located. He filled a tray of bottles with the water samples from each of the twelve generators. Then we took those samples to the lab inside the facility. The lab was still unbearably hot, but it was also soundproof, so we could remove our double ear protection and talk. This was where Al showed me the chemistry of the operation. Using several scientific methods and pieces of chem-class equipment, we tested the water samples for anything that might create problems. If the generator feed water contained too much lime or calcium or other minerals, it could build up inside the pipes and potentially cause them to blow when direct fire heat was applied to them. When we looked down into the fire-eye, we had to watch for places on the pipes that were glowing white or red; this meant the pipe had been compromised. If that happened, they'd have to shut the whole generator down and bring in a crew to cut out that damaged section of pipe and repair it. Testing the water every day helped prevent scale build ups ahead of time. If we found something off in our tests, we would adjust the way the water was treated before arriving at the genera-tors. Preventative measures on the water treatment side was imperative to keeping the steam plant running smooth.

The steam we made in the plant helped bring the oil to the surface, and processing that oil coming out of the field was another separate, secondary plant operation. They processed the sandy oil enough that it could be pumped down a major pipeline that ran all the way to Chicago, Al mentioned. Our Canadian heavy crude oil was largely used for road paving and making tar-based products like shingle and other industrial applications. It would need much more refinement to make it to fuel-grade quality.

Although the work was fascinating, it was also grueling. In addition to the twelve-hour shifts, getting there and back on the employee transport added two hours each way. The night shift was particularly difficult. I'd be exhausted, and there was so much to check and keep track of on the job. The worst part was I wasn't getting paid, so I had to work as much as possible on my five off days at the Midtown Motor Inn to pay my bills.

Unfortunately, the manager in charge of scheduling—who'd been so difficult when I was in high school—was still the same. Again, she refused to accommodate my five days on, five days off schedule at Esso, and so I quit. It felt good to get out from under her ruthlessness now, but I had no job.

That was when I ran into Kelly again. When I told her about my steam time and quitting the job that was supporting it, she said, "Well, why don't you come work with me at Fort Kent Bar?"

Although I dismissed it at first because of what my family might think, Kelly painted serving at Fort Kent Bar into a compelling picture. Every Wednesday was known as Wild Wednesday, which was a special show with not one but two girls booked for the night, and it was Fort Kent's busiest night. Kelly said that working two Wild Wednesdays a month would bring in more than enough to cover my expenses. That didn't sound like such a bad idea, and I agreed to check it out.

Fort Kent Bar and Hotel sat on a lonely corner in a hamlet that was little more than an intersection of two roads leading somewhere else. It was a creamy stucco and brick two-story building with few windows and a small sign hanging over the door. If I hadn't guessed it was a dump from the outside, I knew as soon as I walked in. The place smelled like decay and vomit mixed with stale beer.

Kelly introduced me to the owner, a big, jovial man in his late sixties named Charlie, whose family had owned the place since it was built. He was happy to hire me. Charlie didn't care that his legendary bar was in desperate need of a renovation. Everyone loved Charlie. He welcomed all the broken hearts that sidled up to his bar, and he was the one who threw out the guys who'd had too much to drink. And he was thrilled that Kelly had brought in a good-looking young friend to help out.

The bar was the kind of place that might have withered and died if it hadn't been for Charlie bringing the exotic entertainers in. The floor was a combination of dirty old carpet and checkerboard tile. There was a pool room with a juke box off to one side, and the stage in the center. There was even carpet halfway up the walls. Several small round tables dotted the floor on both sides of the stage. The space accommodated about forty people comfortably, but on Wild Wednesdays, it would fill to triple capacity. The stage was floor level with two poles. There was a yellow rope suspended between the support beams that marked off the buffer for the dancers where the patrons couldn't cross. And there were usually two strippers on Wild Wednesdays, and then usually only one would stay for Thursday, Friday, and Saturday.

I didn't have to make drinks or serve food, all I had to do was take drink orders, get the drinks from the bar, and serve them to the guests seated at the tables. Wednesday night, my first night on the floor, Kelly and I agreed to split the room in half. She showed me where to get beers, which I could get on my own; liquor drinks went through Roger, Charlie's son, who was the bartender.

There had to be a four-foot barrier between the patrons and the dancers. Charlie and Roger made this very clear because they could lose their license for adult entertainment if they got caught breaking the rule. Their business depended on nude entertainment—because otherwise no one had any reason to go to Fort Kent Bar and Hotel. The dancers couldn't be trusted to maintain this distance, because getting closer meant a better tip. Those strippers were always pushing the boundaries. Kelly told me to tell Chuck or Roger anytime I saw a dancer break the barrier.

"There's a few rooms upstairs, and that's where the dancers get dressed," Kelly said, showing me the staircase behind a door near the stage.

"What's it like up there?"

"Not very nice," Kelly cringed. "You can check it out sometime if you want, but don't ever go up there when the strippers are here because they're super rude, and they always think that we're going to steal something from them."

§

I had never seen a stripper before. My first night, Kelly and I had about the same number of tables and an equal amount of space close to the stage. The bar opened and progressively got busier as the first show time approached. Then, with standing room only and a crowd well on their way to drunk, the two girls emerged from the door to the upstairs dressed in elaborate costumes with sequins from head to toe. Their spiked heels were six inches high. But with shimmery long pants and sleeves, they weren't even close to naked.

Each one was carrying a little bag over her shoulder and a blanket over her arm, and one of them handed a CD to Roger, who was also the DJ. He'd spent a small fortune on the stereo system; it was probably worth more than the building. He popped the CD in and as soon as the music started, thumping and banging through the speakers, the girls got up on the stage and started dancing.

When that bar filled up, and I was running from the floor to the bar, I knew exactly how Kelly had made so much money in tips. It was standing room only, and money was flying, tips for us and the dancers.

Each show they performed a four-song set, where the end of each song coincided with removal of another article of clothing. First, off came the top, revealing a sparkly bra. Second, off came the pants, revealing a matching bottom. They knew exactly what kind of songs would get the oilfield, blue-collar guys going—Guns n' Roses, AC/DC, ZZ Top—all a little outdated, but still universally appealing to men ages eighteen to sixty.

By the end of song two, they were doing all these wild moves up and down the poles. They did the splits, at which point every guy in the room lost his mind. They kicked their legs high in the air. They were seriously dancing their hearts out, and all the guys were so excited. But the whole time I was thinking, that's not that impressive. I could totally do those same moves. There's no one more flexible than a ballerina, and I laughed in my mind about how easy it was to impress men.

Songs one and two were always exciting, fast-paced rock 'n' roll. Then by songs three and four, the tempo died down and the power ballads came on. The strippers pulled out their blankets and spread them on the floor like they were having a picnic, and this began the sultry, seductive part of the show. They made their way down to the ground in their sparkly bra and panties outfits, where they touched themselves playfully and arched their backs. They got the crowd involved, silently asking which of their last two pieces of clothing they should remove first. Then, off came the piece that got the most cheers. They always seemed to go for the boobs first. The girls with the biggest boobs always got the loudest cheers when she took off her bra. The crowd would go nuts. I learned how visually primal men are and how much they love fantasy.

Between moves on the pole and crawling around on their blanket naked, the girls opened their bags and brought out promotional posters and magnets and keychains featuring them naked. The crowd went crazy over the merchandise, throwing twenties at the stage in exchange for a poster, which they no doubt took home and displayed next to their tool boxes. And each girl took measures to make this merchandise more enticing. One girl licked the key chains and stuck them to her bare butt cheek, making the boys throw loonies and toonies to knock it off and win. The other girl, while lying on her back, rolled her posters into a cone shape and held it between her extended, up-in-the-air legs, allowing the boys to throw their coins into the cone for a chance to win the poster. But oftentimes, some man would stand up, and not want to mess around with the coin game, walk on over to the edge of the barrier, and drop a twenty or fifty down, winning the poster. The hottest girls ended up in bidding wars, and that first Wild Wednesday, I saw a girl make about $1,000 in about five minutes.

Because the crowd was good and the men cheered for an encore, the girls danced naked to one more song. They were kissing by the end of the show, touching each other, in a suggestive burlesque way rather than pornographic, and the crowd was wild. When it ended, naked time was over, and the girls covered themselves in beautiful kimonos and collected all their money off the stage.

Although I didn't know it at the time, Canadian adult entertainment like at Fort Kent Bar was different from other countries', where girls were giving lap dances and taking guys to private VIP rooms. I'm sure opportunities for prostitution came up, because after the show, the girls dressed in their street clothes and mingled in the crowd, signing posters and working on the tips for the next show. And then sometimes, they would duck out of the bar with patrons for a line of cocaine or to smoke a joint or whatever they did. At the end of the night, the strippers often went to other bars to keep partying with guys they'd met at the show. I thought they were skid girls and couldn't figure out what was so great about hanging out with strangers. Even though local guys were pretty tame and safe, I thought it was weird that the strippers hung out with them.

Just as Kelly promised, working Wild Wednesdays was enough money to keep me afloat while I worked on my practicum at Imperial Oil. I tried to keep my new job a secret, but it was such a small town, and before long I started seeing people I knew from one of the schools I'd attended and cousins from one or the other sides of my big family. It took about a week for my mom and dad to find out that I was waitressing at Fort Kent Bar. Kelly's family didn't seem to mind her working there. But mine sure did, and everyone was upset with me, all over again.

After I'd been at Fort Kent Bar for a few months, I started seeing this same table of oil drilling rig guys come in almost every Wild Wednesday. Riggers were their own breed; they were the toughest men, working the dirtiest job, making the biggest money. Unlike the full-time oilfield workers, these crews rolled into town whenever there was new area drilling happening. They'd finish the job and then move on to the next site. These guys made the pipefitters and welders look like wimps. And they weren't the kind of customers who went unnoticed as big loud tippers.

One night, one of the guys at the rigger table insisted he knew me from somewhere.

"Probably here," I said, smiling and serving another round of beers. I was used to guys hitting on me with lines like that about fifty times a night.

"No," he said, furrowing his brow. "From somewhere else."

"I have no idea where you might have seen me," I said. He was tall and handsome with bright eyes, a striking jawline, and flowing hair like Kurt Cobain. He looked like he could be from any small town in Alberta, but he didn't look familiar. "I've only ever seen you here. But I'm guessing you work on a drilling rig?"

"Yeah, you guessed right. I'm a driller, and this is my crew—Sedco 97." He introduced me to everyone and told me his name was Ryan. In the Wild Wednesday commotion, we didn't have much time to talk. But Sedco 97 stuck in my head because I knew we had Sedco drilling rigs working for Imperial Oil at the time.

I didn't have much to do with any of the drilling activity in our giant operation, especially as a steam apprentice. But on the days Al went into the field to check on the drilling rigs, I rode along with him in the truck. The drilling rig operations were even more dangerous than the steam plant.

The drilling rig had a tall derrick, towering and lit up like a Christmas tree at night, and a huge engine cranking away. It was loud and strange mud and fluids were coming out on the rig floor as they drilled deeper and deeper.

When I went back to Esso for my next shift, I asked Al which drilling rig companies were working in our fields. Because I was training to work in the steam plant, I usually stayed in the truck when Al went out to check on the drilling rigs or chat with the consultants.

"Sedco 97 and Sedco 99," he said.

"Well, I want to go out to Sedco 97 tonight when we're working in that field," I said, realizing that the good-looking guy I'd met at the bar the other night had recognized me through my safety goggles, hard hat, and coveralls.

"Why's that?" Al asked, knowing I'd never taken an interest before.

"I met the driller at the Fort Kent Bar the other night, and he seemed like a really nice guy," I smiled. "So, I want to go into the dog house and say hi if he's there."

"Oooooh," Al whistled. He knew I didn't have a boyfriend, so he jumped at the opportunity to play cupid in my burgeoning love interest.

That night, we pulled up to the lease where Sedco 97 was drilling, and Al and I put on all our PPE. Then we climbed the thin metal staircase to the dog house—the nucleus of any drilling rig. Although I could have probably come in anytime I wanted before, being on one of these infamous drilling rigs excited me now that I knew the guys working there. Maybe I could get a tour and finally learn what the heck "power tongs" were.

As soon as I walked inside, the man I'd met at the bar, who was now dressed just like me in coveralls, goggles, and hardhat covered in company stickers, smiled with recognition and said, "I knew I knew you from somewhere."

While Al chatted with the rig consultant, Ryan and I talked. Or he talked and I blushed. The dog house was not unlike any workshop, with tools and equipment and nudie posters from the strip clubs. It was a small bright white space with a simple bench and oily handprints everywhere and was slippery underfoot. I told him about how I was working on my steam time and working Wild Wednesdays when I was off shift from here. And he showed me around, explaining the work they were doing and how the drilling rig functioned.

His rig was on electric rails. Using the latest development in oil drilling technology, the rig would punch (drill) thirty wells on a single pad of land that the geologists had predetermined were ideal sites. The land had been cleared before the rig came in, and while they were there, they were drilling three rows of ten oil wells on the pad. When they finished a well, the rig pivoted and moved along a set of tracks to the position of the next well, making three straight rows of ten wells in a shape like an open box. The wells were shallow and didn't take long to drill, sometimes a well was drilled each day. A drilling rig is meant to be put together at the drilling site and then taken apart in giant sections that are moved on big trucks to new locations, and then put back together again. When Imperial Oil contracted Sedco Drilling, they brought their rig and their own camp infrastructure, including their own trailers and showers and cooks so they could stay on location and work twelve- and fourteen-hour shifts, taking turns around the clock. And once the wells were drilled and everything was safely capped, the rig packed up and moved to the next drilling site, wherever that might be in Western Canada—this is why drilling rig workers are largely nomadic and regarded as oilpatch rovers.

Through the glass window of the dog house, I could see right onto the drilling floor. Under Ryan, the crew included a derrick hand, which was the guy who climbed the two-storey-tall derrick and handled the pipes going in and out of the ground; the motor hands, the guys making sure the drilling rig's mechanical functions were working well; and the mud-hand, who checked the mud coming in and out of the ground; and the lease-hand, who ran errands for the crew. It was fascinating, fast-paced work. With all that heavy equipment moving so fast, I could see how people got their heads chopped off or lost an arm from thick chains slapping around the pipe on the rig floor. All the hydraulic sounds made being on the rig really sensory. And I admired Ryan working in his environment, so when he wrote his phone number down for me, I was thrilled to take it.

Ryan and I started talking on the phone, and soon enough Al started trusting me to take the truck to check on the field activities, so I stopped to visit Ryan then too, occasionally. I loved taking the truck, driving solo across the industrial Canada landscape, thinking about my budding romance with someone who had a badass job, like mine. I learned that Ryan was thirty years old; at my eighteen, this was a sizable age gap. But I didn't care, and he didn't either. I liked that he was a manly man, strong and stable in his life. He made the guys my age look like dumb kids throwing toonies at strippers. They were just so unimpressive to me, whereas Ryan was impressive.

Talking on the phone and visits at work progressed into spending time together outside work as well. While at work on slow shifts, he would write me love poetry and sign off as the "Dog House Poet." He became even more impressive to me. He came to my apartment, and we saw the Lakelands sights. And as winter let up and the temperature started to rise, I showed his crew all the best lake spots to enjoy on their off time to get away from their tiny living-camp shacks. We went camping with groups of friends and spent time outdoors. Then I started taking him around to meet my family on the farm.

Dad and Doris, my grandma and grandpa, and Porky all loved Ryan. He was a blue-collar man's man who didn't hesitate to roll up his sleeves and get to work. And he wanted to impress my family, so he helped on the farm every time I brought him around. He'd grown up on a small acreage near Edmonton. His mom still had a couple acres, where she kept a big garden. My family adored Ryan, and I really adored him too.

When their drilling program at Imperial Oil finished, Ryan started working for other producers on his rig elsewhere in the province. And having a boyfriend was starting to become expensive because we were going out more. I started wanting new clothes to wear, and I wanted to get my own vehicle instead of borrowing Ryan's truck or bumming rides off Kelly. The money I was making at Fort Kent Bar wasn't enough to cover it anymore. Ryan's rig was moving closer to Edmonton soon, which was over two hours away. Before long, the four months I had left in my practicum at Imperial Oil started feeling like an eternity.

That was when I heard about work in *cold flow* oil as a field operator. Instead of working as a fourth-class power engineer in steam plants, the most sophisticated type of oilfield operator you can be, field operators were independent contractors who checked on oil wells across a designated area. These wells were smaller, often one to a pad instead of thirty, and didn't require steam production to extract the oil, which was why it was called cold flow. Oil companies hire these independent field operators to check on eighty to 150 wells each day. You could get a job as a single well battery operator with no education or certification, which made me overqualified for it with my training. The shifts were a week on and a week off, and they were paying huge money—$8,000 a month! That kind of money made leaving my free apprenticeship at Esso to be a field operator sound like a no-brainer. I'd be making more than enough money, and Ryan and I could coordinate our week on, week off schedules.

Without giving it much more thought than that, I explained the situation to Al. "Here's the deal," I said. "Ryan's rig is moving on, and I need to buy a vehicle. I've got too much time left here with no pay, and then there's no guarantee they'll even give me a job when I'm done. I'm thinking about being a cold flow operator. All I'll have to get is wellhead insurance and my own truck, which they'll be paying me enough to afford."

Al listened. Then he looked at me and said, "Carmen, I think taking that job would be the biggest mistake of your life. You're a bright girl and you're really good at this."

"Oh, come on," I said. "What do you mean, Al? How is $8,000 and working two weeks every month the biggest mistake of my life?"

Elan Oilfield, the company hiring private contract operators, was small-time compared to Imperial Oil, which was part of the Exxon Mobil global conglomerate. Elan was what you'd call a "junior producer." And I had one of their most coveted positions—a position that my classmates from training all vied for. From his perspective, I would be giving up a career in the highest end of the oil industry for grunt work with no job security. And Al warned me of what I'd be giving up: "If you leave before completing your steam time, you won't be able to come back."

"Well, why would I want to come back?" I didn't understand why Al wasn't being more supportive of what was obviously the perfect solution to all my problems. "I want more flexibility and to make way more money and get on with my life. I'm eighteen. I can make my own decisions."

Al started laughing (at me). But at eighteen, with my whole life in front of me, and deeply in love with Ryan, I was too impatient to understand why. I couldn't wait another four months; I didn't want to work the night shift anymore, which was kicking my ass. And who cared about job security? Al, who was like a father to me, was giving me fatherly advice. But I didn't want him to be my dad. I already had a dad, and he had been pretty useless anytime that I truly needed him. Al was the one not seeing this as an amazing opportunity.

I gave up my apprenticeship and left Esso and all the wonderful people I'd met there. When I told my family about my decision, they were so proud of me for getting this new lucrative day-time job opportunity. When they asked about finishing my apprenticeship, I lied and told them that there was no reason to finish it because they weren't hiring anyone afterwards.

Even my mom was impressed by the hefty amount of income that I was now making. I'd been giving her the cold shoulder ever since I got my own apartment. But she knew what was going on in my life, and she was proud of me. All I needed was a four-wheel drive truck, wellhead insurance, and to set up a contract company. I went to my Dargis family's lawyer, Alan Fraser, who set me up as CADK Contracting. Mom cosigned for the new truck—a red GMC extended cab 4x4 with a two-inch lift kit that made steering rough but helped with extra clearance on rough lease roads.

I got a job at Elan easily, and they gave me 110 wells to check on my route. I hit my first well at five in the morning and drove all over my region, checking to make sure each well was working properly and producing oil. Many times, after heavy rainfall, I'd pull up to my leases and see the propane bullets tipped right over or gas bubbles seeping from puddles around the wellhead. Elan must have been on a fixed budget during lease construction, as many leases seemed to be somewhat "slapped together," lacking adequate civil earthwork preparation. Each well location had a tank that held 750 to a thousand barrels. Because our oil comes out of the ground with lots of sand and water and other impurities, all of this collects in the tank. The sand sinks to the bottom and the oil floats to the surface. Each day, at each well, I climbed to the top of the tank to check the level. If there was too much sand in the tank, the oil would get too close to the top, potentially causing a spill and damage to the environment. When this happened, I had to get a truck in to remove the oil and another truck to clean out the sand. There were no scientific or elaborate tests or measurements to take. No major risk of severe bodily harm or loss of life if I screwed up. I did manage to hurt myself on one morning run. A burner on the side of the oil tank needed to be lit to keep the oil inside at a nice temperature to aid in viscosity. I turned on the propane gas feed to the burner and carried a long stick with a fuel-soaked rag in my truck for this purpose. I lit the rag and stuffed it deep down to the burner pilot light. Typically, the pilot light would grab the rag and fire up instantly. I waited and waited and then flipped up my safety glasses to peer inside at what could be wrong. Seconds later the propane caught the fuel rag and a ball of fire flashed over my entire unprotected face. It was a flash that dissipated in nanoseconds, but it was enough to singe my eyebrows and my eyelashes down to nubs. My skin wasn't burned at all but my pride was definitely singed too. Other than that bonehead safety-fail moment, this operator job couldn't have been any easier. I felt like I was making money for nothing. Waking up with the birds and hitting the bush to work all day in silence was sublime. I never had to work exhausting night shifts anymore, and I was able to keep the job at Fort Kent Bar on the Wednesdays I was off, just to make even that much more money.

During this time, I was still going back and forth to Edmonton on my days off to visit Ryan. He lived with his mom, Eileen, because there was no reason for him to pay a mortgage with his schedule. She lived in an old trailer on an acreage in Beaumont, which was a small town on the outskirts of Edmonton, and worked as a lawyer. But she was a fascinating, hippie woman who spent a lot of time listening to CBC radio shows and didn't own a television. In getting to know him and his family, I also learned that Ryan had a two-year-old daughter named Zoe.

I understood that he was older and had lived a full life before meeting me, but the fact that he hadn't mentioned her to me for months troubled me. I felt like he'd lied to me, and I became selfish about it. I felt bad for his little daughter, whoever she was, because she had a dad who was out dating someone who didn't even know she existed. And when Ryan asked if I wanted to meet her, I said no, at first.

At that time, my ego was the size of a house. I was making big money, partying hard, earning respect as a hot-shot female operator in the oil patch. I didn't have time or desire to be someone's stepmom. Ryan was really fun to hang around with. And although they seem tough, men like him can be so insecure or immature and will do anything to please. The kind of man attracted to me was always buying dinner, always buying gifts, always giving me gas money, and I took it all like an expectant princess. Men like him liked my ballsiness, my kind of tomboyish-ness in a really pretty package. I think that was what they liked the most: I was unexpected. And I wasn't spending my money to spend time with him, he was spending his money to spend time with me. Otherwise, where was my incentive?

But at the same time, I was always on his side. When Zoe's mother gave him a hard time, I told him not to take her shit. As an ego-tripping teenager, I had no clue what was going on in a parenting situation, but I offered my opinions anyway. I liked the hard-drinking, late-night partying, sleep-all-day lifestyle of oilfield workers. I went to bars with groups of friends, and Ryan was always buying all the drinks. I didn't want to marry him—I was far too young to be thinking about that. But I wasn't interested in finding other men, either. And in my youthfulness, I failed to recognize how quickly things can change.

That was when I lost my job at Elan. What Al had tried to tell me about job security meant that small oil companies went belly up all the time; they were extremely susceptible to market fluctuations. And that's exactly what happened to Elan. The superintendent called all the operators in one day and said, "The price of oil has just dropped so far and our lifting costs are too high. We're shutting down most of the field and wells and letting half of you go."

As the weight of my ridiculous decision to leave Esso crushed me like a boulder, I panicked—I needed the money, I had a truck payment now. I felt awful, and when I looked around the room, filled with people who had families depending on them, people who'd worked for Elan for a decade, I felt even worse. As contractors, we weren't employees, so there were no severance packages or recourse, not even any benefits to cancel.

§

I started picking up extra shifts and working as much as I could at Fort Kent Bar, but even that wasn't close to the big oilfield money I was used to bringing in. And I didn't know what to do. I had no career path, no direction to my life anymore. I was barely making my payments and borrowing gas money off Ryan so I could come visit. But his work started slowing down too as production all over the area sunk into a depression.

Fort Kent Bar was still busy, with plenty of men with money to spend. And I was spending a lot of time there, trying to earn some of it. And the place had grown on me. It was a bit of a home/therapy centre for wayward souls and aging bachelors who liked to drink the day away. Charlie kept a "pay your tab" dry-erase board over the bar counter that had all the sloppy day drinkers' names on it. It was intended to shame these guys into settling up, but Charlie always extended their credit anyway. Getting to know the lonely side of life had a certain charm. A few weeks after getting laid-off from Elan, I was sitting at the bar talking to Roger about why we were only getting one dancer that week.

"Because we're spending all our budget on Hunter Holiday," he said, obviously excited about whoever this entertainer was. "She's so beautiful, she's worth every penny. Just look at her promo package." This was indeed a treat for the patrons as Fort Kent Bar was known for naked girls but not usually gorgeous naked girls. We even had a girl one time that only had one arm.

He passed the folder across the bar, and, sure enough, Hunter Holiday was this gorgeous blonde woman with a tiny waist and huge breasts. Her photographs glowed, and I knew the boys would love her.

When she arrived, and I helped her get signed in and situated, she was just as beautiful as the picture. With her long blonde hair in a high ponytail and her jeans, she didn't look glamorous or over-the-top, but she looked fancy and clean, not like some of the grade-D strippers we were used to seeing. She didn't look like anyone I'd ever seen at the Fort Kent Bar. She was so stunning and I apologized for how gross the bar was.

She smiled and shrugged. "No problem."

"What brought you to Fort Kent Bar?" I had to ask. "This place is a dump."

"Honey," she said, "bars like this are the place to go. I don't love places like this, but any club in these small oilfield, blue-collar towns are where I make the most money. I'll easily pull eight to ten thousand dollars out of this place before I leave."

I didn't doubt it; I'd seen the money flying around the place.

"How long have you worked here?" She eyed me.

"Oh, here and there for about a year. I'm working more now because I recently lost my oilfield job."

"Well, you're really pretty," she said. "Why don't you be a dancer if you need money? You already work here; you already know what it's about."

"Oh, gosh, I could never." I dismissed the idea at first. But then it settled around me like an aha-moment. "You know, funny enough, I am a classically trained ballerina and hip-hop dancer. The only problem is my family would probably disown me. I've given them enough hell over the years."

"Well, you can make a lot of money," Hunter Holiday said, like it was my loss. "If you change your mind, I'm in pretty tight with the agents and I can give you a good word."

She wrote down her personal phone number on the back of one of her cards and gave it to me, and I stuck it in the back pocket of my jeans. That conversation freaked me out a little, and I didn't pick up any more shifts that week while Hunter Holiday was in town. But Kelly went on and on about how awesome she was and how amazing her costumes and routines were and how all the guys went crazy for her and that she probably made $12,000 at Fort Kent Bar.

Kelly didn't know about my conversation with Hunter Holiday. But I kept her business card in my wallet for the next few weeks, while I continued to run low on money. The bright fuchsia card had a full-colour headshot of Hunter Holiday, hair teased to the extreme, and read: "Hire Me! Available for all events that need a bit of fun!" I looked everywhere for other contract operator positions, but couldn't find anything. Then, with my truck payment due and not enough money in my bank account, I pulled out Hunter Holiday's card and gave her a call.

9

FRIENDS IN LOW PLACES

"I was not proud of what I've learned,
but I never doubted that it was worth knowing."
—HUNTER S. THOMPSON

I WAS SITTING IN MY truck outside my apartment, afternoon fading into evening, when I dialed Hunter Holiday's number into my Motorola brick flip phone. And when she picked up, she remembered exactly who I was. I told her I was ready to try at dancing, but I knew very little about the business, aside from what I'd seen at Fort Kent. She explained that entertainers were private contractors, and Alberta had one agency called Independent Artists that booked entertainers in the various clubs across the province. She gave me the number and said she'd put in a good word for me.

After hanging up, I still wasn't sure I could do the job. Getting naked and dancing on a stage in front of strangers didn't bother me so much—strangers don't know you, you don't know them, *but I was terrified that someone I knew might see me*. Still, I needed money, and I didn't want to move back to the farm and be a waitress when all of my other friends from high school were settling into their first year of university. I didn't even graduate. If I could work a few hours away from home, then I could keep it all a secret. I decided there was no harm in checking it out and seeing what was on the other end of that phone call. I called their Edmonton agency office and made an appointment.

Later I left Hunter Holiday a message, thanking her and letting her know that I'd made the appointment with Carl, the booking agent. Then she left me a message, telling me that she was happy to help, call her anytime, and that she'd leave me some costumes with Carl so I'd have something to wear to get started.

The Independent Artists office was located on the second floor of a sign-less, unassuming office building on Argyle Road in Edmonton. Small square windows lined the front and gave the building a '70s retro feel. Inside the office was modern, but chaotic, with stacks of photos and papers on every surface and boxes overflowing with bright fabrics stacked haphazardly along the walls. The receptionist had hair so bleached it looked crispy enough to crumble in a strong breeze. She was a worn-out beauty, with plenty of makeup and ornate decorations on her fingernails and was very obese.

"I'm here to see Carl," I said meekly.

She looked up at me, expressionless, and pressed a button on the office intercom. When a man's voice answered, she said, "There's someone here to see you."

She motioned me toward a hallway to the left of her desk, then went back to her paperwork without cracking a smile or acknowledging me any further. The hallway led to a spacious office. The wall was lined with the small square windows I'd seen on the way in, and fluorescent lights glared overhead.

"Come on in and sit down," Carl said from behind a banged-up wooden desk. His dark hair shimmered in the light, and he grinned like a Disney prince.

I sat in the chair across from him and smiled.

"So let's get to it," Carl said. "You want to be an entertainer and you have been recommended by Hunter Holiday. I see from her note, you're a small-town girl. Nice body. It looks like. Hey, maybe stand up and spin around for me please."

His request was nonchalant, all business, and I did as he asked, hoping my B-cups would look big enough under my tight turtleneck and low-slung jeans. I knew I had a great body—strong, long lean legs, even at five foot four, I had great posture with pronounced clavicle. I liked that even though I was short, I had a great legs-to-torso ratio just like Kate Moss, my favourite petite supermodel. In the mid-90s, salamander bodies were "the look."

"Not bad, young lady," Carl said. "A bit on the skinny side. And I'm hoping that's not a padded bra under there."

It was, but I didn't tell him. His facial expression was serious and unrevealing. I had no idea if he'd give me a chance or not. Maybe sensing my nervousness, he smiled reassuringly and told me to sit back down.

"You can always bump up your breasts and be whoever you wanna be in this business."

I smiled, relieved, when he started telling me how the business worked—everything from the costumes and promotional materials I'd need to the way contracts worked and what the expectations were. I'd need a stage name, he said, for privacy reasons. If I used my real name, then patrons could potentially find me in my off time.

"Have you thought about a stage name?"

"I was thinking Alexa," I said. This was a trendy name at the time, but I didn't know anyone named that.

"That's great," Carl said. "There are no other Alexas in Alberta and the guys will love it. And if you do well, I'll book you on a northern tour for a month, starting in Peace River."

I could tell he was a capitalist, taking into consideration what would make money for his agency and the clubs he contracted with. He had to make sure I'd have a positive impact on the bottom line. But, he said, there was no way he could send me out on a contract until I did an amateur night show. He needed to see what I could do on stage. If that went well, then I'd be in. He gave me the phone numbers for the photographer and costume tailor that most girls used. We couldn't wear regular clothes because everything needed tear-away snaps. And there was no store for stripper clothes, so everything had to be custom made.

That upcoming Friday was amateur night at Showgirls in Edmonton, the most popular city club. But even though it was called amateur night, all the girls had to be prebooked. He signed me up, gave me the bag of costumes and CDs that Hunter Holiday left, and said he'd see me Friday.

When I walked out of the office and back to my truck, I felt so grateful for Hunter Holiday. There was no way I'd have been able to find out about Independent Artists or Carl or anything without her help. She'd even included a pair of platform high heels in her bag. I had everything I needed to get started. When I called to thank her, her phone had been disconnected. I realized then that I never got her real name. And although I assumed I would run into her again, I never did.

§

The timing for my career change couldn't be more perfect. Ryan and I had just started living together in a one-bedroom apartment in Edmonton. I didn't have to go home to Bonnyville and lie to everyone about what I was doing, and no one in Edmonton knew me. I knew a few kids from high school who were in college there, but I didn't reach out to them because I didn't want to explain. I could leave Bonnyville, leave the farm, and start this new life, and I could tell everybody in my family that I was going to school to upgrade high school in Edmonton and nobody would know my secret.

Ryan was still working on the drilling rig, working all around the northern Alberta region. Sometimes he was in Red Earth or Grand Prairie, bouncing around for weeks at a time. So while I prepared for amateur night, he was away working. And I knew that even though I was just trying it out, my life was about to change. Any innocence that I'd preserved within my upbringing would be gone. And I was excited about it. I remember feeling very independent and though I was getting down to the last dollars in my bank account, I felt okay about it because I was about to start making so much money. I was going to be rich. I would never be laid off unexpectedly ever again.

Around this time, my dad was going through personal bankruptcy. Being the kind of guy who runs away from conflict, he left my Grandpa Lloyd to run the farm on his own and went back to driving a truck. This time long-hauling all over Canada and the United States, gone for months.

"Dolly Girl," he told me on the phone, "Doris and I are hitting the road, trying to make as much money as I can. I'll call you as soon as I can."

With my dad on the road, I felt even more empowered and sure I could become an exotic entertainer without anyone finding out. I didn't want to be dependent upon anyone. But at the same time, the only parent who really cared about me was no longer going to be available. He was running away from his own problems.

So far, I had learned that there were only two types of men. My father was weak whenever I needed him; men were weak. Or they were like my grandfather, Pierre—exploitive and cold. And my sense of how to treat men started to change. I loved Ryan as much as I would allow myself. After growing up with such unhealthy familial bonds, I *resisted attaching* too strongly to anyone.

And I started seeing Ryan's weaknesses as well. It always looked to me like his baby mama was pushing him around. If he made more money, he didn't tell her because she'd demand more. He never stood up for himself against her or demanded more time with his daughter, almost like he was under her spell. Although I wasn't jealous of their relationship, I judged him for being weak.

He was gone most of the time anyway. His rig often worked in remote locations, so there were no daily phone calls or frequent visits. The distance between his work camp and civilization was just too far to make it worth it between his long shifts. Cell phone service was spotty. On Sundays, shift change, I'd wait around for 4:00 p.m. to see if he would call. And if he didn't, it meant that he either had to pick up another day of work or he couldn't get away. I was totally on my own if I wanted to be. I didn't have to call back home. I didn't have to call the farm. I gave them enough information to keep them all from worrying.

§

With amateur night a few days away, I focused on getting ready. The bag from Hunter Holiday contained an assortment of sparkly costume pieces. I chose a bright psychedelic kind of yellow and white crop top with a front tie and bell sleeves. There were a cute pair of mini shorts and matching bra and panties that went with it, so I had a full set. She'd also given me a pair of white fake patent leather knee-high boots with towering platform heels. When I put them on, I felt almost six feet tall. I pulled the padding out of some old bras, affixed them inside the costume pieces, and my outfit for amateur night at Showgirls was ready.

For my music, I needed two really, energetic high-tempo songs and then two slower songs. None of Hunter Holiday's CDs really fit for me, so I used my music player to burn my own set. "Intergalatic" by the Beastie Boys was at the top of the charts that year, so I chose that, along with "Love Rollercoaster" by Red Hot Chili Peppers and "Music Sounds Better With You" by Stardust. And then I chose Brittany Spears'"Baby One More Time" and "Doo-Wop (That Thing)" by Lauren Hill to slow things down. These were songs I loved cranking up inside my truck when I was out cruising around the oilpatch. Music let me escape, and the idea of escaping into a new life excited me.

With the outfit and music ready, I practiced some moves and choreographed a routine. I really wanted to nail it on amateur night, but I was at the same time still so nervous about taking off all my clothes and dancing naked in front of people. I'd seen so many girls do it already, and I liked that every show had a structure. At the end of each song, an article of clothing came off, one piece at a time, until you just kind of found yourself naked. And when that moment happened, I envisioned it would be like *ripping off a band aid*. It would be terrible the first time, but if I got through it and didn't die, then it wouldn't be so bad the next time. Mentally, that was how I prepared for it.

On Friday night at about 5:00 p.m., I walked into Showgirls with my bag of costumes and makeup tucked under my arm. The music was low and the bar was empty except for a few day-drinking patrons.

"I'm Carmen," I said to the guy behind the bar. "I'm here for amateur night."

He looked me over and then looked at a clipboard. "I don't have a Carmen on the list."

"Sorry, Alexa."

"Oh yeah," he said. "Gotta use that stage name. You're our only amateur night girl, and you don't go on until 9:00 p.m., but let me show you around."

Showgirls was the biggest, most popular strip club in Edmonton. On a Friday, it would be standing room only by seven. Every night, they had eight girls performing—seven regular girls and a feature entertainer. I knew Carl would be there watching me, seeing for himself if Alexa could do the job. They expected pretty girls who can dance and put on a show. And no matter what, you had to look good naked.

Wood paneling on every surface and swinging saloon-style doors gave the place a Western flair. The bean-shaped stage at the center had black and white checkered flooring and two brass poles. Chairs had been pulled up all around the stage for the close-up pervert row experience, and there were bar-height tables behind with standing room. Then there was seating and tables in a roped-off VIP section that sat up higher than the floor. The DJ booth sat behind the stage, near the dressing room, so we could come out and pass our music to the DJ and get on stage without entering the crowd.

The feature entertainer got her own private dressing room because she did the prime-time exclusive shows and just got special treatment as part of the contract. Everyone else shared a community dressing room. Inside the dressing room, there were no girls, but the faux-marble counter was crowded with cosmetics and ashtrays. Hockey bags overflowed with clothes and shoes and curling irons. The walls were covered in the same paneling as the bar area. Four lighted mirrors and a long, padded bench provided space for the girls to get ready. The schedule was posted on the wall in the dressing room, showing the show times for each girl on each night of the week. When they weren't on stage, they could come and go as they pleased, which was why no one was there yet.

"Any questions?" the bouncer asked.

"Okay, well, if there's nobody sitting in the bar as a patron and it's somebody's turn to go on, what do you do?"

"We still put them on. We don't care if they're dancing for one person or just us at the bar. They go on. That's how they get paid." He explained that the dancers' contracts worked out to about eighty dollars per show, or maybe fifty or sixty dollars if you were new or not so great. They were expected to dance for at least four three- to four-minute songs, four times a night for six days. That was how the dancer fulfilled her contract. Tips belonged to the dancer—they didn't have to share with the bartenders or DJ, though it was customary to give them something, especially if you have a good night.

I had four hours before my amateur show, so I asked the bouncer if I could get some food.

"Sure, we have a full kitchen."

"I'll have a burger, fries, and a Coke," I said.

"Okay. But you know you can drink for free while you're here. Our girls get free drinks."

"Then make it a rum and Coke."

I found a spot at the end of the marble counter where I put my bag. I didn't have much, just the one costume. I sat in the dressing room, taking it all in. I didn't touch any of the girls' things, even though I was dying to see what they had. A bar stuffed with hanging costumes lined one of the walls. Each hanger held a four-piece costume, with the matching top, bottom, bra, and panties. And each costume was more ornate than the last. Touching the sheer fabrics, the sequins, the satin, I was astonished. They were all hand-crafted and original. I may have been a farm girl, but I was still a girl who liked pretty, frilly things. Their costumes were reminiscent of theatrical productions that I'd been a part of with ballet, just a bit sluttier. Their footwear was just as amazing, from sky-high black patents, spike heel boots to the most broken-in heels I'd ever seen. It reminded me of dance, where we worked so hard to break in a pair of new pointe slippers and then kept them forever because they were so comfortable. I felt like I was backstage at a theater. It may have been a little sleazier and a little sketchier, but it felt the same and featured rum!

I ate my burger, read my book, *The Rum Diary*, and waited. Then, about thirty minutes before the first show, all these girls flood into the room. I was still tucked in the corner, picking at fries, with my face in a book.

"Hey," one of them said. "You must be the amateur girl tonight."

"Oh my God," another one squeaked. "We don't get a lot of amateur girls. It's so exciting."

They had 1,001 questions. Who are you? What's your name? They were all so beautiful—far more beautiful than the girls I'd seen at Fort Kent. And I wondered if they were this pretty, what could the feature look like? But they were all very nice, very excited for me and the tips I'd make. They were exuberant, gregarious, kind of drunk, and loud, all shuffling through the dressing room. The music on the other side of the walls started amping up and the bar was coming alive.

But as nice as they were, they were also devious. We got into a conversation about the entertainer lifestyle and I asked, "What do you do when you're on your period and you have a gig? Like, what do you do?"

"Oh, well, you just decorate your tampon strings," one of the girls said. "You put sequins on it."

The room got quiet.

"Really?" It sounded so ridiculous, and I didn't want to mess anything up, but that sounded pretty gross. "That's what you do?"

Then one of the other girls burst into laughter. "Don't tell her that. That's not what we do."

"You wear a tampon, obviously," another girl said. "And you cut off the string or burn it off with a lighter before you put it in. That's what most girls do."

They were just messing with me, and I stopped being horrified. One of the girls started lining up shots of tequila in a row for me. One asked if I wanted to do a couple of lines of blow, another produced a joint of marijuana. And I hadn't thought about numbing myself to prepare for a show at all and quickly decided against it. If whatever poison I picked actually worked, then I'd become dependent on having to do it for every show. So I politely declined and lit a Player's Light cigarette instead.

When the show started, I peeked through the door and watched some of the other girls on stage. Some were decent dancers, others were lazier. These girls were making three, four, or five hundred in tips in a four-song set, and walking by the DJ booth, back to the change room, they flipped him a fifty-dollar bill. Mondays through Wednesdays weren't as big for money, the girls said, but Thursdays through Saturdays made up for it. We all sat there chatting and rotating, getting ready at the mirrors, according to who was up next.

The DJ kept talking up and promoting the fact that they had an amateur dancer that night. The patrons loved amateurs because they were the girl-next-door type, ultra-newbie, where they could witness innocence lost and I could not understand why that *was so desirable?* So, the club was happy to have me. They'd been promoting it on their city-wide radio ads all week. They didn't use my name, thank goodness. But I was kind of thrilled that they were making such a big deal. And it was even better that I was only eighteen. One of the girls was twenty-seven, which was old; in this business you couldn't be young enough.

One of the girls, who was beautiful but had cellulite on her bottom, gave the DJ a hard time about using red lights during her show.

"What's the deal with the red lights?" I asked one of the other girls.

"Red lights make cellulite stand out," she said. "If you have cellulite, red light makes you look like an orange peel."

That they even knew this made them seem so professional in my mind.

All the girls were booked through Carl at Independent Artists. When I mentioned that if I did well that night, he said he'd send me on a northern tour, they all had something to say about Carl. They didn't seem to like him that much, which surprised me. As a booking agent, they saw him as a necessary evil who did as little as possible for 15 percent of our contract value. And you damn near had to be sexually involved with Carl to get the best contracts.

"He didn't come on to me," I said. I thought he'd been nice enough.

"That's because you're new, and you don't have fake breasts," one of the girls said. "Carl likes one type of girl, and if you're that type, he'll keep you booked solid." I had been wearing a padded bra since I was fourteen, and it seemed like I could replace large breasts with dancing skills and still make money. I hoped my small breasts wouldn't hinder my success. At 8:00 p.m., the first riffs of Guns N' Roses' "Welcome To The Jungle" pounded outside the dressing room.

"What's happening? Why is everybody losing their mind right now?" I jumped up from my seat to look out the door.

"Oh, Sally's going on. She's our *feature creature*. She's doing her animal show." The girls were nonchalant about it, but not unkind. They'd seen the act before.

"Her animal show?"

"Yeah, the guys love it. She does it every night and it's a real crowd-pleaser."

The DJ announced the feature entertainer, Sally Stardust, and the crowd roared. By this time, the club was stacked to the roof. Everybody was just starting to get that nice glow on. Canadian boys drink like fish, and our beer is strong. I watched through the door as four bouncers carried what looked like a wild animal in a cage toward the stage. She wore a loin cloth bikini, had paws on her hands and feet, and a mask covering everything above her nose. Her blonde hair tumbled and spiraled in a stunning mane, and she'd painted stripes on her arms and legs to look like a tiger. The lights were low and the music loud. As the cage got closer to the stage, the crowd got crazier and crazier.

As the song tore off and the tempo kicked in, she started acting like a beast inside the cage, scratching at the bottom, pulling at the bars, snarling at the men. I fell into complete sensory overload. Every seat in pervert row was full and guys were packed in to the walls. The lights flashed, she kicked at the cage until one bar gave way, then another. When she crawled out and stood up, snarling seductively the whole time, she was simply breathtaking. And her dance was the sexiest, most intoxicating dance I'd ever seen. She worked the pole, she dropped into the splits, she tipped into back walkovers. Her dance was professional-level choreography. The whole time I watched her, entranced, spotting pas de bourrées and plies that I instantly recognized from ballet study. She did all sorts of amazing things that I'd never seen anyone do before, and she did it with such swagger. She used all her abilities as a dancer to fuel her confident, cocksure routine.

As she took off her loin-cloth and got down to her bikini set, she kept her mask on. She was a leggy blond, taller than me with a little bigger breasts that were still on the small side, doing all sorts of amazing things I've never seen in my life before. When she was naked, but still masked, she got out her posters and merchandise, and the money started flying. Hundreds, fifties, all flying at her. It got to the point where the crowd didn't care if she was naked or not, they just wanted to see her face. And in the last few seconds of her final song, after everyone had their posters and the keychains had been knocked off her nipples and the show drew to a close, she finally ripped off her mask. Her blonde hair tumbled down around her beautiful face, and the crowd went wild.

I was completely astounded by Sally's show. She probably easily pulled out $1,500 in tips in ten minutes, which justified becoming this kind of entertainer. She invested in her costumes. She invested in her dancing skills. She invested in props like the cage (which any of my welding friends could easily construct). The crowd loved it. And that's why the clubs paid more to have her. None of the other girls, who for the most part lazily sashayed across the stage, impressed me the way she did. Sally was a dancer. Sally was a true *entertainer*. And I wanted to know her. I wanted to be like her.

I knew I could be, too. I had a lot to learn, but I wanted to try. She made me see the possibilities.

After she'd put on her robe and collected all her money and gave a little love to the crowd, she came down off the stage, past the DJ booth and community dressing room where I was standing at the door. She walked right past me, not giving me the time of day or even noticing I was there. She had to be exhausted. She went into her private dressing room and closed the door, while a bouncer parked himself in a seat to make sure no one from the crowd decided to go find Sally. I waited a few minutes, and then went to her door.

"I'm the amateur," I said to the bouncer. He knocked and told Sally I was there to see her.

"Sure, it's okay," a soft voice called from inside the dressing room.

The bouncer opened the door for me and I stepped inside. Sally was sitting in front of her mirror, glistening from her high energy show and smelling like a piece of peach fruit even from across the room.

"I loved your show," I gushed.

She sized me up, head to toe, with her gaze, and said, "You look like a good kid; I can tell. Why are you here? This business is gonna ruin you if you don't watch out."

I looked over at her huge dressing room counter and saw at least a dozen empty mini wine bottles scattered around. Sally wasn't much older than me.

"I need the money."

"Don't we all?" She laughed. A cigarette hung from her full lip. "Well, you'll make lots of money just *make sure* to tell everyone that you're brand-new for as long as you can. Boys love that. That's their favourite thing. You can't ever be 'new enough' for boys, they're honestly the hardest and easiest to please all at the same time."

She winked at me, and then a bouncer came to tell me that I was up in twenty minutes.

I looked at Sally and smiled. "I have to go."

"Hey kid," she said as I was leaving, "just remember that you can end this at any time you like. Be smart, save your money, and keep your nose clean."

The bouncer pushed me out of the dressing room and closed the door behind me.

Minutes later, as "Intergalactic" started playing, the DJ called out to the roaring crowd, "And now, to take it all off for us, like never before—coming to Showgirls. First time ever. Give it up for Alexa."

Out I went on the stage, where I climbed the pole with my thighs, and danced all the moves I'd been practicing in my apartment. To the crowd, they were having the best night ever, with Sally's wild animal performance and an amateur in one night. Everyone looked so red faced and bleary eyed drunk, but I thought they were gonna lose their minds.

During my show, as I swung upside down on the pole, I noticed Sally come out of her dressing room. She came up to the edge of the stage and placed a hundred-dollar bill down for me. She raised her mini bottle of white wine and winked a toast to me.

After my performance, Carl was waiting for me by the DJ booth when I came off stage. He was smiling and nodding when he said, "Girl, you nailed it. We can definitely work with you."

I was excited and nervous, but I didn't have much time to think about it. Carl booked me for a northern tour starting with a stop in Grimshaw the following week. With Sally's hundred dollars, I made $650 in tips in about fourteen minutes. All I could think about was how rich I was going to be.

Carl set me up with the photographer all the girls used for an emergency shoot that weekend. Orland, the photographer, staged and took all my photos, providing things to wear and a hair and makeup artist who made me look as beautiful as possible for the camera. He kept pushing for spread open leg shots, but I refused. If my face was going to be in the picture, then I had to keep it classy somewhat. Bare breasts was as far as I would go. And the next day, my emergency promo of glossy posters were ready. When I unfurled them, I felt like a supermodel; really, I looked about fifteen. Armed with merch, Hunter Holiday's old costumes, and the six hundred and fifty I'd made on amateur night, I was ready to go up north.

Seeing only dollar signs, I couldn't wait to dance my way across Western Canada. It seemed like the perfect opportunity—I would be far away from home, making a ton of money to pay my bills. Ryan was busy with work. And I was seeing places I'd never seen; meeting people and having adventures sounded fabulous. There seemed to be no downside. If I should have felt immoral, dancing naked in front of strangers for money, it didn't matter to me. I only cared about what was happening in the moment and my bank account.

§

Carl didn't tell me much about my three-day stop in Grimshaw, but he said it was important to prove myself in some smaller markets before I could get more lucrative jobs in Edmonton, Calgary, and Red Deer. Grimshaw was a hamlet, with a hotel, like Fort Kent Bar, and not much else. When I went inside to check in, the worn-out place had a bar, pool tables, and a small stage. A man in his sixties with a body like a barrel, a horseshoe hairline, and a lopsided face was the only one there.

"I'm Alexa," I said brightly, even though the venue made me want to cringe. Fort Kent Bar was like the Taj Mahal compared to this place.

"Ah, the princess of the week has arrived." He, the owner, didn't smile or express any warmth, like he was annoyed with me, and perhaps strippers in general, before I even arrived. He explained my showtimes, that I'd be staying upstairs, and how everything worked. There were no other staff at the bar—no bartenders, no DJ, no servers to help. Just him, serving drinks and pressing play on the CD player at showtime.

He led me up a dark, dusty stairwell to my room, and I thought about Kelly taking the girls upstairs at Fort Kent. After her warnings, I hardly ever went upstairs. But here I was, not only going upstairs in a place just as bad, but I was going to be staying.

"This is your room," the owner slurred, swinging the door open and motioning me inside. Then, perhaps preempting my complaints, he shuffled back downstairs and left me alone. The small room had a broken down melamine wood dresser missing most of the knobs and a bed shoved in the corner. I dropped my bags down on the floor and, wishing I had a set of tongs, pulled back the covers on the bed. Long strands of every colour hair you could imagine, from black to brown to blonde, covered the sheets. Period blood stains dotted the center. Week after week, girl after girl had slept here, and not once had those sheets been changed. I shuttered and vowed never to touch the bed again. I imagined girls complaining about having to sleep in this room, stomping down the stairs and having a fit about how disgusting it was. To me, it felt like the basic necessities of my contract weren't being met. That was when I knew why he'd referred to me as the princess of the week. But I was new, and I wouldn't whine or gripe. I'd just tough it out.

At three in the morning, after my last show, I spread out the blanket I kept in my truck on the floor of my room. The blanket was ugly, but plush, and I made a pillow out of a few sweaters. The room hadn't been swept ever, probably, and from the floor I could see piles of dust in the corners and around the perimeter. I tried to imagine beautiful, talented entertainers in this place, and knew this was the kind of gig a girl got as punishment. There in the darkness, the hard floor beneath my tired body, I thought about Carl. He needed to satisfy the client, and I was too new to know any better. But he hadn't warned me or given me any indication that Grimshaw would be gross. He left it for me to discover on my own, like he wasn't just testing to see if I could perform, but also if I could put up with the gross living conditions that sometimes went with the job. I would never come back to this place, no matter what, I decided.

I slept until noon, and with four hours to kill before my first show, I took my book downstairs and sat at the bar until I had to get ready. Thankfully, the three days passed quickly, and I was back on the road.

I drove up to Peace River and found the next club, where three other girls who were going to be working with me that week were already gathered. The club owner was putting us up in a house he owned for that purpose; this was pretty common, the other girls explained. It was often cheaper that way for the club owners, who were responsible for accommodating us as part of the contract, than getting hotel rooms. And night after night, I did the same set over and over, tweaking it and experimenting with other music as I went along.

I noticed lots of the other dancers accepted offers from guys in the crowd to hang out in other clubs at the end of the night. They often went to the local late-night bar, getting free drinks and staying out late. Even though I wanted the other dancers to like me, I always declined these offers. I wasn't that interested in hanging out with any random local guys, most of whom were our same age. I didn't want to be friends; I just wanted to take their money. And I definitely didn't want to make any mistakes that would put my new career in jeopardy. I'd already heard rumours of girls getting blacklisted from clubs or picked on by the other dancers for being disliked. So, after every show, I loaded up on snacks at the vending machine and went back to the house and watched Letterman or read my book.

But part of it was that I didn't really respect or identify with these girls. They seemed like weak, lost souls, looking for companionship. I didn't need that. My goals were mercenary. When the money was made, I wanted to go to bed so I could be fresh to do it all over again the next day. Sure, I'd have a drink or two while I was signing posters and mingling in the crowd, making the guys feel less lonely and more important than they really were. But after I left the club, that was my time. Making friends made no sense because I'd be in a different club with different people in a week. And as I got to know them and watched them perform, I came to see myself as better than them. They weren't even that pretty. One had dyed her hair so much that it broke off and she had to wear wigs. None of them could dance.

And I soon noticed that most entertainers were always high on prescription drugs or whatever they could get. It was like they couldn't get right with themselves for what they were doing. It didn't sit right with them. I wondered why it didn't bother me more. But at the farm or when I was slicing meat in the butcher shop, there was no modesty. It was just biology. It was just physiology. It was the body, whether animal or human. The butcher shop stripped away anything I felt about shame and physiology. When you tear away the hide off of an animal, or rip flesh from bone, you're essentially or figuratively violating it. You're just getting to the meat, you're getting to what you need. So taking my clothes off and getting to the money felt oddly similar. For me, it was easy to see dancing naked for what it was. The only type of shame I harboured was if somebody recognized me. Being ten hours away from my hometown, I wasn't worried about that at all. I felt proud that I could rock it, make that money, be nice, and go home for the night.

Saturday night, the club owner paid me for my shows, less the 15 percent for Carl, and, with my contractual obligation fulfilled, sent me on my way. And I was on my own to get to the next gig by Sunday night. Some of the girls carpooled with friends from club to club, but since I didn't know anyone I wanted to ride with yet, it was just me in my truck from Peace River to Fort St. John in British Columbia.

Even as far away as Bonnyville, I'd heard about Fort St. John's hard reputation. Guys would talk about picking up cocaine habits when they passed through. It was a take-no-prisoners oil and gas town that wasn't for the faint of heart. I'd always been intrigued by the wild side of life, so I couldn't wait to see it for myself.

I'd seen Edmonton and Red Deer Rebels patches on motorcycle jackets in bars before. And I definitely noticed some Hells Angels patches on a few backs in the Showgirls VIP section at my amateur night. But before I walked into the club in Fort St. John, I don't think I'd ever seen a real biker bar. The place was called Northpole. It sat on the outskirts of the town's main drag and looked like a bar built in the '70s that had been retrofitted to be a strip club. The inside was all black, dark and dank and boozy smelling. There were a few other girls already there, waiting to check in. And when the manager or owner or whoever he was came out to receive us, it was hard not to swoon over his Jax Teller-like swagger.

"Alexa?" The Edmonton Rebels logo was emblazoned the back of his black leather vest, and his eyes sparkled. "I heard you did amateur night at Showgirls."

"Oh, yeah?" I said, blushing under his spell. I had never seen such a good-looking tough guy.

"I wanted to be there. I'm often in Edmonton for business, and they said you really killed it."

He smelled amazing. *He looked like sex.* And he was being really nice.

"I'm John," he said, passing me the contract. I signed as he explained to me and the two other girls how everything would work. While the other girls checked in and signed their contracts, I sized them up. Both of them, Annie Monroe and Joey Amoure, looked like they'd been in the business a little too long. Pushing thirty, they were very pretty, but neither one looked like she could dance. One had nice breasts, the other didn't. I was like the feature entertainer compared to them, even though I was new and not getting paid that much. These girls were no competition at all, I suspected.

But they both seemed pretty cozy with John the biker. He hugged them and greeted them like they were all old friends. I remember thinking, Wow, how do they know each other so well? How long have these girls been dancing around a stripper pole? They were so friendly that I wondered if my initial assessment had underestimated them.

After checking in and getting a tour of the club, a driver took us to the corporate house where we were staying for the week. The other two girls were obviously close friends.

"I'm Alexa," I introduced myself in the car.

"Alexa, huh? I'm Shay and this is Jolene. Those are our real names and you can call us by our real names."

"Okay, I'm Alexa," I said, smiling. I didn't mean to be unfriendly, but I wasn't ready to be too friendly either.

My standoffishness didn't faze them; they didn't even seem to care. They just kept chatting with each other.

At the house, a bungalow engulfed in overgrown bushes, we settled into our rooms and had the rest of the night to relax. We didn't start working until Monday at 4:00 p.m. The house had couches upholstered in a woodsy brown plush fabric, plain panelled walls, and a television, which was where I found Shay and Jolene after I unpacked. I sat on the couch opposite them.

"What do you want to watch?" Jolene asked me.

"Anything's fine," I said. I watched the television and stole glances at them. They both seemed so confident and at home with each other. "How long have you been friends?"

"Since forever," Shay beamed at Jolene.

"We've been friends since we were both fifteen," Jolene beamed back at her.

"Fifteen?" I was shocked. "That's a pretty long time."

"Yeah," Shay said. "It was so much better in this biz back then too."

"What do you mean?" I was dying to know more about the business I was getting into, and they seemed to be friendly with all the right people.

"Girl," she said. "We used to get picked up in limos. The club owners would buy us fur coats at the end of the year."

Shay explained that there weren't nearly as many girls back then competing for the same contracts. And the money was about two times as good. As she talked, Shay pulled the biggest bag of weed I had ever seen from a box that had been sitting on the table. There had to be two ounces in it. Then she pulled out an electric coffee grinder. After finding a place to plug it in, she pulled a bud from the bag, pulverized it in the grinder, and rolled it into a thick joint.

The whole time she was talking and rolling her joint, I was shocked that a person could consume so much marijuana they needed a motorized bud buster. I didn't want to be the babe in the woods on the first day at work, so I turned away as soon as I realized I was staring.

"Do you smoke weed?"

"No," I said, "I tried it a few times. I'm not very good at it. All it does is make me sleepy and hungry, and pretty uninteresting."

"Oh my God." Shay laughed. "I don't know what I'd do without it."

"So what about you?" Jolene asked. "Where are you from?"

I told them about Bonnyville and the farm and everything I'd left behind. I think they pitied me because no one knew what I was up to, and that I was out here alone. I told them all my friends were in university, but I liked wild times and adventures and making money. And I found myself drawn to them. They were confident and funny, unlike the forgettable girls I'd met in Peace River.

"Where are you going after this week?" Shay asked.

"I'm going to Grande Prairie next."

"We're gonna be in Grande Prairie next week too," Shay said, perking up like she was excited to have me along.

"You're gonna love the club and the club owner," Jolene said. "And you're gonna make a ton of money."

Shay and Jolene only worked in Edmonton and on the northern circuit, travelling for four weeks and then taking six months off between tours. It never occurred to me that we could pick and choose where and when we were working. I asked them a million questions. What are the good tours? What about southern Alberta? And they told me about who owned what, what the crowds were like, how a cowboy town was different from an oil-patch town, where the best drugs were to be had, everything.

"You guys must know everyone," I said. "John sure was welcoming to you."

"Oh yeah," Shay said. "And John's brother runs Grand Prairie. You'll love it; there's a lot of club guys there."

"What do you mean, 'club guys'? Is that motorcycle gangs?" I was so naïve, but Shay and Jolene covered the basics—motorcycle gangs had their hands in most of the clubs around Canada, often as fronts for illegal activities, cash businesses are perfect for 'cleaning money' I gleaned. When I asked about specifics, like who runs Independent Artists, Shay gave me a side eye, like she wasn't sure she could trust me with that information yet. And I didn't press her. When she hesitated, I just asked a different question, piecing together how the business worked.

The crowd at the club in Fort St. John was a little older than the last crowd, blue-collar guys closer to Shay and Jolene's age than mine. It was thin Monday and Tuesday, but by Wednesday night, the place started filling up with guys eager to show us a good time after the shows. Shay and Jolene, like the girls in the last town, were open to spending time with patrons after leaving the clubs. They were all about the free drinks. And Shay and Jolene were so tough. They were dainty little things, but Shay carried herself like she wasn't afraid to slit someone's throat. Shay was twenty-nine. Her dirty-blonde hair fell down past her shoulders, and she was thin with the smallest breasts I'd ever seen. She was flat-chested, but I knew from watching her show that she had the biggest nipples I'd ever seen. When the cold air in the club hit them, they stood off her chest, like they were made for hanging keychains off of or your winter coat. She was intimidating and beautiful all at the same time. I felt safe when I was around her.

At the end of a busy night, when we were finishing up in the dressing room, Shay said, "Hey, we're going to this club after this. You should come with us."

"I don't know," I hesitated, even though I wanted to go. But a girl could easily go missing or find herself in an uncomfortable situation so far from home. "Is that safe?"

"Oh, you're so adorable." Shay laughed and pinched my cheek. By this point they were treating me like a little sister. "Nothing's gonna fucking happen to us. Nothing's gonna fucking happen to you when you're with me and Jolene because John is gonna make sure of that."

"Oh, is John coming with us?" I knew I'd feel safe in the company of a big, bad, muscly biker.

"No, he doesn't have to," she said. "He knows everybody in this town. If somebody fucking does anything to us, he'll hear about it. They'll be taken care of."

Of course I went. I was thrilled and intoxicated by the world Shay and Jolene could show me. And I was flattered that they'd taken me under their wing. I needed it to get ahead in this new crazy world I found myself in. I imagined myself never going back to the farm. I was so intoxicated by the rough side of life of these motorcycle gangs, these strip clubs, this money, and how different it was from what I'd assumed. I felt like I knew the farm well. I knew what sleepy little towns were like. I knew what being a good girl was all about, and all of that was incredibly boring, certainly not for me.

That night, I went out with Shay and Jolene. When we went into a civilian club, hair teased and dressed in skimpy tops and heels only a stripper would wear, we stood out. The hometown girls knew exactly who we were and where we'd come from, and they stayed away. All the hometown boys, however, couldn't wait to be around us. Shay could walk into a bar, have a few words with the DJ, and minutes later, he'd be playing her songs and she'd be running the dance floor. Even with her clothes on, she was a performer, and she had so much swagger. She didn't care who was watching her, and I was amazed.

Jolene was a little more maternal and reserved. Also at twenty-nine, she had three kids and a husband at home who worked as a boilermaker in the boilermakers union. Jolene had long, gorgeous, dark brown hair that touched the top of her bum and tiny little waist. Her hair was about four inches longer than mine. Her body was amazing for someone who'd had that many babies. When I asked her how her husband dealt with her being a dancer, she said, "Honey, you know what it's like in the oilfield. He's trying to become a manager, and in the meantime, we have kids to feed. And he's totally fine with me as long as I'm with Shay."

I tried cocaine for the first time, running into the bathroom and snorting it off Shay's special ring. We had a great time that night, and many nights after, partying hard and sleeping it off the next day. I felt no lingering effects. Cocaine seemed so great, it kept me awake while we were out and was easy to sleep off. Shay and Jolene had taken the bus, so at the end of our week in Fort St. John, they rode up to Grand Prairie with me. And just as they said, the club was amazing. It was huge and busy, crowded with oilfield workers, construction workers, welders, riggers, and pipefitters. The city, which was bigger than Peace River and Fort St. John but not as big as Edmonton, was a fun place to spend the week with more exciting clubs to go to after work and more sexy bikers to meet. We pulled a lot of money out of there too.

I'd never been around bikers before. I knew farmers and blue-collar workers. One night after work, when one of them—a guy named Jim— started coming on to me, Shay warned me never to date a biker.

"Why not?"

"Their loyalty goes like this: the brotherhood, the bike, the dog, and then their woman, in that order," Shay said. "Even though Jim's just a prospect, you never want to owe the Hells Angels anything."

"What's a prospect?"

"It just means he's not a full-fledged member of the brotherhood."

"What does he have to do to become a full-fledged member?"

"You know, I don't really know how that works," Shay said, shutting down this line of questioning. "I'm not sure what to tell you, kid."

I knew that she knew and that was a lie. But I was too new to be let in on all the secrets. And I took her advice, telling them all about my boyfriend, especially when they got too interested. Being friends seemed to garnish the most respect anyway. I found that we were all kind of misfits, strippers and bikers alike. They treated us with respect, even protectively, all of us misfits together.

I also gained a deeper understanding of the lifestyle and the feelings or sentiments behind it. Shay liked to smoke weed all throughout the day because no matter how experienced she was in this world, there was still something that she was running away from. There was still something that didn't sit quite right with her about being an exotic entertainer, or maybe it was something else? And I started to suspect that all of her bravado was a bit false, even though she never let on. Every time she rolled another joint, it was to outrun some uncontrollable anxiety that seemed to be chasing her right on her heels.

But at the same time, I felt like the strippers and the bikers were like me. They were take-no-prisoners people too. After my upbringing, I identified with these people. I knew what it felt like to be misjudged by society and rejected by the normies. I wasn't the dirty butcher shop girl; I wasn't a little boy with a unibrow. I wasn't a trouble-maker looking for more trouble. I was a talented, beautiful, independent woman, and finally I was in a place where I could see it and so could everyone else. And I felt so much safety in the embrace of Shay and Jolene. I felt like with them, I could do anything. We could do anything.

10

INTO THE CLUBHOUSE

"You can't get it right if you can't relate. Trade the cash for the beef for the body for the hate. And my time is a piece of wax fallin' on a termite that's chokin' on the splinters."
—BECK

AFTER MY NORTHERN TOUR, I had $18,000 in my pocket. When I walked into the Independent Artists office back in Edmonton, the receptionist, crispy-hair-Debbie, greeted me with a warm half smile and called me hun, as if I'd passed the test and been initiated. I thought she was weird. But I guessed that she liked me now.

"The club owners were all very pleased," Carl said when I sat down in his office.

"Well, you know, a little warning about what Grimshaw was like would have been appreciated, Carl."

He looked at me coolly from across his desk and said, "If you want something good, you have to work for it."

He wasn't there to entertain my complaints, he had an agency to run. Now that I had some money, he explained, I needed to invest in real costumes and a full photoshoot.

"You have a week off. You should take care of all that now," he said. "Then I can book you for work here in Edmonton."

Working in Edmonton excited me. There were lots of clubs, and I had my new friends Shay and Jolene in town. They weren't working because they liked to take time off between tours. But I wanted to work, work, work. I wanted to turn my $18,000 into $40,000, and then $80,000, and then $160,000. Ryan was away working in Red Earth, so far north the highway ended. He couldn't even call me unless he borrowed a truck and drove somewhere with cell service, and he'd be there for a while. I didn't have anything else to do but work and make money.

Carl gave me contact information for a photographer and costume maker who worked in the industry and had quick turnaround times. I'd heard from some other girls that Shaundra, the costume maker, was the sequin go-to gal who could fix me up with costumes, tall boots, and acrylic platform heels. My hand-me-downs from Hunter Holiday were okay for places like Grimshaw, where guys were rolling in from the oilfields and weren't picky. But if I wanted to work in the fancier city clubs, the standards were a little higher. And costumes had to be custom made because tearaway, sequined bras and panties weren't the kind of thing you could get off a rack.

"Be prepared," Carl said. "She's not cheap, but she's fast and does great work."

§

After observing what the other girls were wearing on tour, I'd already sketched out a few ideas. Sexy nurse and naughty school teacher were, of course, classics, so I sketched ideas for those. I wanted mine to be better than all the other girls' versions. And I tried to think of music to use with them, like Rough Trade's "High School Confidential" and Van Halen's "Hot For Teacher." For the nurse, there was Motley Crue's "Doctor Feelgood" and Bon Jovi's "Bad Medicine." Those songs, even ten or more years old, were popular with the blue-collar crowd. But I wanted something a little bit different, so I came up with a sexy race car driver, gangster, and businessman and sketched that too. I played around with a few other, un-themed designs, all with matching sparkly tearaway bras and thongs. The whole process brought back memories from ballet, where a mom measured us and made recital costumes based on sketches for upcoming productions.

Shaundra's place was outside St. Albert, on the outskirts of Edmonton, at the end of a long driveway in the woods with only a keep out sign to mark the turn. Two barking pit bulls guarded the run down house. As soon as I pulled up, a woman with long, salt and pepper hippie hair came out and called them off, assuring me they were friendly. When we stepped inside, the dim light made it feel like dusk despite broad daylight outside. Houseplant cuttings crowded every windowsill.

"Welcome to Shaundra's costume and tailoring," she sang and rhymed like she'd done it a thousand times before. "My fabrics are second to none, and my stitches never run."

After quick introductions, she sat me down and looked at my drawings.

"Nurse and teacher costumes are absolute career staples," she said. "I've made hundreds, but rest assured: no two Shaundra costumes are alike."

She loved the race car driver costume and said it was a first for her. Shaundra exuded warmth, and her quirkiness delighted me. She was like a glam slam Romanov Gypsy. When I stripped down to my bra and panties so she could measure my body, I felt comfortable enough to be vulnerable.

"I wish my breasts were bigger," I said. "I'm thinking about getting a boob job."

"Oh, honey," she said, "that's so typical. Are you sure? Carl tells me that you're a trained dancer and that you've got some moves. That should get you by. Give the boys a refreshing take on what they see."

I felt bolstered by her perspective, but also like she was maybe a bit out of touch with what real boys liked. I could tell from my northern tour that big, delicious, squishy fake breasts got the bigger tips. I was busting my ass in artistic dance form, while the girls with the fake ones could just walk across the stage. I kept that to myself, not wanting to hurt her feelings.

"Still," Shaundra said, wrapping her measuring tape around me, "if bigger breasts is what you need, let's create the illusion. How about we sew in a little skin-coloured faux fur into the lining of your sequined bras. That should give a nice bump to what you already have."

This sounded like an amazing idea, until I was naked. "What happens when I take it off and the illusion is broken?"

"If they happen to be disappointed, tell them your nipples are just *too sensitive*, and that any other fabric is simply way too abrasive on your perky, pretty boobies." She wrote down a measurement and looked at me. "Trust me, boys fall in love with an illusion, and it's how you spin it that saves it. And they probably won't even notice." Boys were a little easy to impress, I'd noticed too.

I thought that was quite brilliant. Maybe boys really weren't that smart and could be teased with the idea that your nipples are just too sensitive for any other fabric. And Shaundra—not only a master costume maker, but also a master marketer—was confident that that would eliminate the problem.

At the end of our session, we had eight costumes planned. I bought three pairs of thigh-high boots in black, red, and white, and two pairs of acrylic platforms. My tab came to $7,000, half the money I made up north. But I walked out of Shaundra's feeling empowered and excited. Everything would be ready for pickup in six days, just in time for my Edmonton shows.

The same way we couldn't buy costumes in a store, girls in the business couldn't just go to Staples Business Center for promotional material. My experience with Shaundra was so wonderful that I assumed working with the new photographer, Randy, to create new posters, key chains, stickers, and magnets would be just as amazing.

Darkness cloaked the downtown Edmonton studio when I arrived for my evening appointment. Randy greeted me and introduced himself, assuring me that he was Carl's guy and doing me a great favour, the way he had done for all of Carl's other girls. Boxes for portrait seating, faux Roman columns, backgrounds of draped fabric, and other props cluttered the studio. And he had a hair and makeup artist on hand to get me ready.

The makeup gal motioned me into a chair. She had a timid way about her, almost as if she was afraid or intimidated by Randy. I sat down and she went to work, teasing my hair and applying makeup. False eyelashes were a must, she said, and she wanted to make me look a little older. But she didn't engage with me or my ideas about how I wanted to look. While I watched Randy setting up props and checking lighting situations on his light meter, I told her where I liked my hair parted and that I wanted to play up my full lips and high cheek bones. She nodded and kept working. My chair faced away from the mirror, so I didn't really know what she was doing until she said she was done.

I got up, looked in the mirror, and gasped. She'd teased my hair into a mess and caked my face with heavy makeup and pink frosted lipstick. I looked like I was ready to appear in a Whitesnake music video.

"Thank you," I said, aghast, "but this is ridiculous." I took over her tools, taming my hair and softening the makeup the way I wanted it, with a smoky eye and way less blush.

"What are you doing?" She was angry at me, and I didn't care. I glared at her, threatening her to stop me, lest I cut her. Finally, she shook her head and disappeared into the studio shadows. After a few tissues and revisions, I looked passable. But the session didn't improve from there.

Randy had already chosen a black chainmail bra and panty set. I wasn't naked, but it was very peek-a-boo. After getting dressed, he motioned for me to come onto a draped sheet of gray background fabric and sit in a chair. When I tried to tell him what poses I had been thinking about, he dismissed my ideas and started positioning my body the way he thought the boys would like best. By this time, I'd seen lots of examples of promo from the other girls. Some played with suggestion in a classy way, with a little nudity and more focus on the face, while other girls went full porn. That seemed to be the direction Randy envisioned for me. In each pose, he pushed for more vulgarity. I was always confident and secure in my body and nudity, but I had never felt violated like this before. When he put his hands on my legs and spread them apart, I stopped him.

"This is too much," I hissed. "I am not some Gumby doll that you can move around and take full monty photos of."

He shook his head, and irritation flicked across his face. I knew my place as the new girl, and I didn't want to overstep any boundaries. But at the same time, I wasn't going to let him push me in an uncomfortable direction.

Shot after shot, I resisted and he grew more impatient. By the time we were done, after the makeup and tension with Randy, I was so worried the pictures would be horrendous. And when he told me the total was $3,000, I balked. I had no problem handing Shaundra seven grand, but three thousand for a terrible experience made me seethe. I paid it, and stormed out of the studio, feeling like I'd been ripped off and fearing what the photographic results would be.

Three days later, when crispy-hair-Debbie called from Independent Artists to tell me Randy had dropped off my promo material, I raced over to pick them up. When I unfurled that first poster, expecting the worst, I sighed with relief. The pose was me standing in nothing but the chainmail bra and knee-high black patent boots. I crossed my legs at the ankles, bumped my bum out to the side, and twisted my upper body toward the camera. A tiny bit of nipple showed through the chainmail, and my hand rested suggestively over my lower lady parts. My head was cocked over to the side so my long brown hair cascaded down past my shoulders. The photo was actually cute. A note from Randy in the box explained that only *one* image turned out well enough to use, so he used that same one for everything. Variety would have been better, but it was okay considering what I had to go through to get that one decent picture.

Carl walked out of his office then and said, "Oh, you got your promo. Let me see it."

When I showed him, he shrugged.

"That's pretty tame," he said. "Maybe a little too cutesy and not enough dirty."

He went back to his office and I looked at Debbie, who seemed numb to the whole conversation. She basically couldn't wait for me to pick up all my boxes of promotional items and get out of the office. Which I did.

A few days later, Shaundra called to tell me my costumes were ready and waiting for me at the agency. After picking them up, I spent the whole afternoon trying them on in front of the floor-to-ceiling mirror in my bedroom. They fit like a glove, and Shaundra's work was remarkable. I felt so glamorous. They were stunning!

If I'd told my girlfriends from home that I spent $7,000 on costumes, their eyes would have bugged out of their heads. Most people working regular jobs wouldn't make that much in months. I had that kind of money no problem, and now I had the tools to make a lot more. But I couldn't call any of those girlfriends to tell them about it. What would I say? I wasn't upgrading or working a regular job. When my family members called to see how I was doing, I kept it brief and lied about work. I told them I was waiting tables at a breakfast place. Still, even though I couldn't be honest about it, my new life intoxicated me. I wasn't Carmen anymore. I was Alexa. Alexa had new costumes, Alexa had new promo material, Alexa had a very lucrative job, and Alexa was where I liked my life to be. The more dissociation I could add between Carmen and Alexa, the better.

§

When I called Shay to tell her about my costumes and promo, she invited me to come hang out at her house. Shay and Jolene had regular, normal-girl lives in Edmonton. I thought those two girls were really undercover badasses. They seemed to know everybody in my new world, including all the scary people, and they were very well received. Of course I wanted to hang out and get to know them better.

Shay lived with her big rottweiler, Tyra, outside Edmonton. The small house sat on several acres of rural land that looked like any other rural yard I'd seen near Bonnyville. When I arrived, she showed me around. There were motorcycles parked on the edges of the property and, remembering how much fun I'd had riding dirt bikes around the farm, I asked her if she rode.

"No, those are my friends'. Lots of people park their project bikes out here because I have space."

Shay kept a tidy home. It was clean and remarkably uncluttered, and it smelled wonderful in there. I'm not sure what I expected, visiting my first stripper friend in her home environment. But I was surprised. She lived the life of a normal single girl, with her awesome dog and little house in the country.

"Where are you working next week?" she asked as we settled into her couch. "I heard you're working in Edmonton."

"I'm going between two places, St. Pete's and the Yellowhead." It was a split booking where the clubs were close together in the city, and I was expected to perform in both each night.

"St. Pete's is new," she said. "And it's really, really nice inside. The clientele is good too—a lunch crowd. You'll make most of your money at lunch and then after nine."

The Yellowhead was named after the section of the Trans-Canada Highway that goes right through the city of Edmonton.

"It's a trucker type of club," Shay said. "You'll get lots of truck drivers passing through."

When she said this, I thought of my dad. Although he wasn't the type of man who hung out in strip clubs, he was a trucker. The thought of seeing him there sent a shot of panic through me. Although highly unlikely, I hadn't thought this through very well; of course I could run into people I knew, even with the big city buffer around me. For the first time, it dawned on me what a stupid kid I was. I tried not to think about it, instead absorbing everything Shay could tell me about the different clubs, the clientele, and what to expect working there. I soaked it all in.

Shay lived alone, but her phone rang off the hook. Every twenty minutes another friend called her to make plans. On the center of her coffee table sat an ornate, pearl-inlayed box that was probably two feet long and a foot tall. After we'd chatted for a while, she opened it, revealing what must have been the master supply of her marijuana. The box was full of green buds. She pulled a few out, plugged in her coffee grinder, and buzzed them. Then she rolled a joint like a complete and total pro on a Snoop Dog tour with one hand and offered it to me. I passed, so she smoked it herself. We talked for hours that afternoon, and about every forty-five minutes, she reached back into her box, loaded up the bud buster, rolled a joint, and smoked it. In a way, she reminded me of Grandpa Lloyd, sipping off his cup all day long. And her tolerance was obviously much higher than mine. Each time she offered it to me, I passed. I didn't particularly love the way it made me feel. I preferred uppers over downers, I learned. I preferred feeling sharp and in control, the way I'd felt when we did cocaine in Grand Prairie.

For the first time in a long time, I just wanted to make a new friend. I told her about riding dirt bikes and growing up on the farm, searching my past for some common ground with this woman I thought was a complete badass. I told her about how I thought I was making such big money in the oilfields, working two weeks a month for $8,000, and we both laughed because we both knew that was nothing. Then I explained how I lost my job and started dancing because I needed the money.

"How did you even get into it?" she asked. "It's not like you can look up a number in the Yellow Pages."

"So," I said, "I was working at this place near Bonnyville called Fort Kent Bar, and one week our entertainer was this awesome girl called Hunter Holiday. I told her about my situation, and she gave me the number for Independent Artists."

"You mean Tanya?"

"I don't know. Is that her name?"

"Yeah, that's Tanya. She's so great, isn't she?"

"I can't believe you know her," I said. "She gave me all those costumes you saw me wearing."

"Oh, yeah, she's a good bitch," Shay said through a cloud of pot smoke. "I haven't seen Tanya for a while, but if you run into her, make sure you tell her that Shay says hi."

"Yeah, you betcha," I said, thinking, wow, what a sorority. If you were in with the right people, this business wasn't so bad.

Late in the afternoon, as our conversation waned comfortably, I took the joint when Shay offered it to me. Twenty minutes after sharing it, I started yawning and feeling tired.

"I'm freaking hungry," I said.

Shay laughed and said, "Oh, you're so adorable. I'll start the lasagna."

The plan was to take dinner over to Jolene's, where I could meet her family. While Shay worked in the kitchen, I curled up on the couch and basked in the glorious afternoon sun, feeling like I had a new friend, like I was in a safe place. There was a giant rottweiler standing guard outside. It all felt so new and different from anything else I'd felt in my life. And I slipped into a deep afternoon nap.

Over an hour later, I woke up to the smell of lasagna baking in the oven. Shay had covered me in a blanket and tucked me in. She was smiling when she saw me stirring on the couch.

"I'm so happy you woke up," Shay said from the kitchen. "I didn't want to disturb you so you could take a nice rest."

She seemed so excited to have me there, excited to be entertaining someone. She didn't know me all that well, and I didn't know her well either. But I could tell she enjoyed taking care of people. And I appreciated her so much. She felt like the big sister I never had. Being Maurice's big sister, I was the one that was always taking care of him, making sure he had enough to eat, making sure he was okay, making sure he had clean clothes, making sure he had someone to talk to. I never had anyone taking care of me like that before.

I was so hungry, we ate before we left. She talked about Jolene and her family. She had three kids and a husband, Darren, who worked as a boilermaker.

"What about you?" I asked. "Have you ever been married?"

Shay put her fork down and her eyes filled with tears. Then she told me about how she got married when she was twenty-five to the love of her life, a guy she met when he was a prospect hanging around the Edmonton Rebels. Their relationship was passionate and loving, and Shay got pregnant with twins, thrilling them both with the promise of future joy. But at five months along, she lost the twins in a late term miscarriage. It was horrible, she said, recalling the D&C procedure and how broken she and her husband both were over it. One of the babies was a boy and the other was a girl. And it savaged her body, leaving her unable to have children and with C-section scar but no fruit. She and her husband eventually got divorced over the endless depression that followed her. Ah, the heavy weed usage—I got it now.

I sat there, watching her weep and try to pull herself together, and didn't know what to say. Those experiences were far more adult than anything I'd ever been through. I could see all the pain behind her eyes. And Shay was a tough person. She could go from loving and taking care of me one minute, to ready to cut somebody in the club if they tried to take advantage of us. She had all these tough friends, like the Edmonton Rebels and the Hells Angels, and she was the one in the crowd that you didn't want to mess with. Seeing her losing control, tears in her eyes, telling me that all she ever wanted to be was a mother, I understood why she smoked so much weed. She reached for it first thing in the morning, and she reached for it last thing at night to dull the pain of her loss—not only of her children, but also her dreams.

§

When we arrived at Jolene's, she greeted me with open arms.

"Oh, my goodness, Carmy," Jolene said. "Come on in. I'm so happy that you're here. I don't get many visitors from 'our life,' if you know what I mean." She winked at me and I let her call me "Carmy."

The curvy, sultry Jolene I'd seen dancing on the stage on our northern tour lived a completely different life at home. Three red-headed children filled their mobile home with energy and noise. Kids' artwork hung on the fridge, along with pictures of happy babies and grandparents and cousins. Jolene looked like a regular mom, and she had three little freckled faces with eyes filled with wonder and love for her and their life. Regardless of what stereotypes or preconceptions people had about exotic entertainers, we were more than what met the eye.

"Is that our lasagna?" asked Jolene, gesturing at the pan Shay was carrying. "Darren is due home any minute now."

"Carmen fell asleep on the couch, and she was super hungry when she woke up," Shay joked. "So, you know, I had to give her some of the lasagna. That's why there's a giant big piece missing."

"Oh, you were smoking with Shay today?" Jolene smiled at me.

"Yes," I said, sheepish. Jolene just laughed and thanked us for bringing dinner.

When Darren came home, he looked like a completely normal young husband. We all sat around the table like a big family. He and Jolene had been high school sweethearts. Their oldest daughter was ten; they'd had her when they were twenty. And they had a hard time making ends meet until Shay, who Jolene was always close with and who always associated with the wilder side of life, got her into dancing.

"You're okay with that, Darren?"

"Oh, she loves me. I'm the only one for her, and she's the only one for me," he said. "Ain't that right, Mama?"

He leaned across the dinner table and kissed Jolene. "You always come back to me."

"Yes, I do," said Jolene. The kids knew their mom had a job that took her away for a few weeks at a time, a few times a year. But they didn't know what she was doing. Jolene and Darren shielded them from that. The money helped them pay for vehicles, trips, and, they were hoping, a down payment on a bigger place. Jolene paid for Darren's training and supported them during his apprenticeship. They accepted each other, lifted each other up, and were obviously a strong union as husband and wife. Sitting there with them, I fell into the deep, warm, loving embrace of their family, and appreciated how they let me in. No judgements, no questions, just pure unfettered acceptance.

Later, Shay told me to grab my promo pictures out of the truck for Jolene to see.

"Oh, my gosh, Carmy," Jolene said as she unfurled the poster. "This picture is awesome. Look at you. You didn't have to *blast the cookie*." That was industry talk for vagina. Jolene and Shay agreed that some girls were too vulgar and distasteful, which made me feel better after Carl's snide cutesy comment.

When I told Jolene I was working at St. Pete's and the Yellowhead next, she said, "Carl told me I'm too old to even work at St. Pete's. He won't even book me there because you have to be young for the white-collar business crowd, and I don't cut it anymore. But I've worked the Yellowhead a few times. It's pretty divey, but you'll pull out a lot of money out of there."

§

The next week, I checked into the Yellowhead, feeling excited to use my new promo and costumes. The place was a huge mega complex that'd had its best days in the '70s, with eight floors of hotel rooms above the exotic entertainment club, a restaurant, and a gaming lounge with video lottery machines. The guy who checked me in showed me around and warned me about leaving my stuff lying around.

"We've had a few thefts recently, so be careful," he said, leaving me in the locker room-style dressing area. I'd just spent a fortune on amazing costumes, so of course I made sure I didn't leave a single thing out. I had my apartment in Edmonton, so it wasn't like I'd packed for a week away. I kept everything in my smaller hockey bag.

For the first performance, I wore my new sexy nurse costume and danced to "Bad Medicine." Shay and Jolene had showed me a few new moves on the pole, so I rocked it. Then at the end, when I pulled out my poster, the roaring crowd of truckers went crazy. Money flew from their hands onto the stage. I tossed out key chains and magnets, and teased them with the one big poster I brought for the show. At the end, I'd meet the guy who won it, which was always part of the allure for bringing out the cash for the poster. Lots of guys whipped out fifty-dollar bills and hundred-dollar bills. I closed my eyes and waved my hand over the crowd to make my decision. When my finger landed on a guy in the front, he dropped a hundred dollars on the stage and the poster was his. I couldn't cross the buffer to hand it to him, so I rolled it into a tight tube and popped it over. He caught it with one hand and all his buddies cheered and slapped him on the back.

Then the show was done. I pulled on my Kokanee beer bathing suit, which was high cut at the bottom and low cut at the top. Then I started picking up my money. Shay taught me a great trick using a strong magnet on a telescoping stick that fit in her bag to quickly grab all the coins off the floor. It made collecting the money easy and fast so I could get the heck off the stage.

After changing into my street clothes and putting on a fresh coat of lipstick, I headed out to sign the poster and meet the guy who won it. He was sweaty and drunk and named Jesse. I wrote, "To Jesse, breast wishes. Love, Alexa," and kissed it, leaving a red print. Then I packed up my costumes and hurried across town for my next show at St. Pete's.

Billy Joel's "Piano Man" was playing when I walked in the club. The patrons were dressed in suits, freshly knocked off from work at the office. It was a whole different kind of club than I'd ever seen. The bar and stage area gleamed with modern silver and glass finishes. All stripper poles are brass because they are grippier than any other metal and let you get a firm grip with your hands or thighs to do all of those amazing acrobatics, but these poles sparkled in the lights. I did my race car driver show, with the checkered flag spandex outfit Shaundra and I had designed. The long pants had hosiery clips that held on the legs, and during the show I unclipped them to reveal the skimpy shorts underneath. The crowd went wild over the clever convertible nature of my outfit. I danced, handed out promo, picked up my money, and hustled to change, meet the crowd, and get back to the Yellowhead for another round.

That week in Edmonton, with four or five shows a day between Yellowhead and St. Pete's, every day for six days, I made approximately

$26,000 in tips, plus my rate per show. And I had the time of my life—showing off my new costumes and promo, and then going home each night to my own bed. Like Scrooge McDuck, I drifted off to sleep dreaming of my ever-growing money-bin.

If I had run into any of my old friends during that time, they may have looked down on the direction my life was going. But I couldn't understand why everyone didn't want to do this. I had an amazing job, and everybody else was a chump. All of my friends were going to university to study hard to maybe in four years graduate with a useless liberal arts degree and make $30,000 at an entry-level job, if they could find one. I was having fun, wild times and making so much money; I didn't need to waste my time upgrading chemistry, thanks.

§

That Friday morning, Shay called and asked if I wanted to go to a party at the clubhouse Saturday night after my last show.

"What's the clubhouse?"

"It's just the clubhouse. They're my friends, and it's invite-only. Some of them saw you on amateur night. Do you want to go? I promise you'll have an amazing time."

I knew from her vague answers that she was talking about the Hells Angels, and of course I wanted to go to the clubhouse party. Just being asked, my stomach fluttered and my heart raced; I felt like I was being accepted and brought into the fold of a new world. This would be unlike any other party experience in Edmonton. I was sure of that.

After my last show on Saturday, I went back to my apartment to get ready for the party. Not having any idea what to wear, I dressed in a sweater and tight jeans. Then I went to pick up Shay at her acreage. The whole ride back into Edmonton, she kept telling me about what an amazing time we were going to have. She smoked a joint, and then she pulled out her cocaine ring, took a sniff, and offered it to me. With one hand on the wheel, and one hand holding her hand steady under my nose, I took a pull off it too. By the time we arrived at the clubhouse—a house somewhere deep on the south side of Edmonton—I felt like I was on top of the world.

I barely knew my way around the city, so I followed Shay's instructions without paying much attention to where we were going. We stopped in front of a nondescript house in a residential neighbourhood. Shay led me around back, where she knocked on a side door. The faint sounds of music suggested a party inside. After a few seconds, a huge man opened the door. He practically filled the doorway, and as soon as he saw Shay, he bent down, picked her up around her waist, and held her, legs dangling in the air, in a giant hug.

"Shay, great to see you. How are you?"

"Bear!" She embraced him back. "I haven't seen you for so long. I've missed you. How are you?"

"Good, good," he said. "The boys are downstairs, you know where to go. Help yourself to a drink."

Shay stepped past him, and then Bear glared like I wasn't welcome.

"Come on, Bear," Shay said. "You know I told the boys that I was bringing a guest tonight. She's totally cool, she's with me. She's new at the agency. Some of the boys saw her at amateur night and said it was okay to bring her."

Bear looked me over from head to toe. I'm sure I looked bewildered and terrified, and I didn't know why she didn't just tell him my name. Then, finally, he gave me a nod that implied I could go inside.

We cut through the kitchen, where a few people had gathered, and headed for the basement. A wood-burned sign at the top of the stairs read: "Loose lips, sink ships." We walked down the stairs to another door, where the noise of the party increased. In the moments before Shay opened the door, I didn't know what to think. Newspapers associated the Hells Angels with club bombings and other crimes around Canadian cities, so a part of me was afraid of what I'd find inside. My head and chest pounded with excitement and fear as we walked through the door.

"Shay!" Several people yelled when we entered the basement. She greeted everyone while I hung back and watched. The crowd of bikers looked exactly like Hunter S. Thompson's descriptions. There were big, fat bikers, beards like ZZ Top's, scraggly guys, guys with bandanas, and muscular, hot guys, most wearing motorcycle boots and sleeveless vests emblazoned with patches. Some guys, dressed in collared shirts and khakis, looked a little clean cut to fit in this crowd. I learned later that these were the lawyers. Based on what I'd seen on the news, they definitely needed those.

A brother poured drinks and handed out beers from behind the bar, where an actual decorative motorcycle gas tank overflowed with twenty- and fifty-dollar bills. It looked like a lot of money, but it didn't seem like enough to pay for the house and all the booze and all the lawyers.

"What do you want to drink?" Shay asked.

"I don't know."

"Well, let's get you a Boilermaker," Shay laughed, ready to hit it. "Like Darren."

We laughed, because Jolene's husband Darren worked as a boilermaker. And it really was a drink too. The bartender put two shots of whiskey next to two pints of beer in front of us. Following Shay's lead, I dropped the shot into the beer and chugged the whole thing. Then Shay gratuitously waved her hand and ordered a round of those for everyone in the clubhouse.

Everyone loved her fire-starter party-girl nature. That night she blossomed the same way she did at the clubs up north. Over and over again, guys came up to her, saying things like, "Aw, Shay, you know I want you," and "When you gonna be my girl?" She'd just toss her dirty blonde hair, laugh, and brush them off like they should have known better in the first place.

I stayed next to the bar, but Shay got pulled in a million different directions by people who wanted to talk to her. I watched her and the crowd and chatted with the bartender. The atmosphere was laidback—no cocaine or bags of mushrooms or other hard drugs being passed around or consumed. In the corner, one of the brothers sat strumming a Neil Young song on the guitar. He looked like an old hippie, with a bandana around his head like Axl Rose, and the kindest eyes I'd ever seen. We started talking about Led Zeppelin and The Doors and life, and by the end of the night he was calling me sister.

By around four in the morning, everyone left was either passed out or about to. The only girls left besides us were dressed like hookers in skirts that Shay and I might wear on stage but nowhere else. These women tolerated Shay but wouldn't talk to me. And they were hanging off the guys like laundry on the line.

When we got ready to leave, the guys started greasing on Shay, saying, "Why don't you come home with me tonight?" She swatted their hands away and said, "Not tonight; I have to take my little girl home."

I had barely moved from my spot by the bar all night, and I when I stood up, I felt dizzy. I was pretty drunk—too drunk to drive home. Shay collected me, and we walked up the same short flight of stairs, out the door into the early morning light, back to my vehicle. Shay was pretty drunk too, but she insisted on driving us back to her place.

"I don't want you to risk getting a DUI," she said. "I know the way, and if anyone's getting a DUI, it's going to be me."

Back at her place, she totally took care of me, getting me undressed and into some of her jammies, tucking me into her guest room.

I woke up the next morning to Jolene's three kids jumping on my bed, yelling, "Wake up, Carmy," and a giant spread of breakfast that Shay and Jolene had prepared. We ate, and Shay pulled out the crayons and colouring books she kept for when Jolene brought the kids over. I noticed her giant box of weed was missing from the table, tucked away where no little kids could find it. And when Shay needed to smoke, she snuck out for a walk around the yard and came back with everything fine. Shay and Jolene were like a happy family, and I was the special guest.

§

I had the week off after my split booking in Edmonton and before my southern Alberta tour to Red Deer and Calgary. Shay and Jolene were still riding off cash from our northern tour, but I tried to persuade them to come with me. "We'll have so much fun," I implored, desperate to keep our fun rolling. "See if Carl will book you for the tour too."

"Maybe," Shay said.

The more time we spent together that week, the more questions about the Hells Angels I slipped into conversation. That was when she told me they owned Independent Artists, our agency.

"They're the ones that make all the money off us working out on the road," Shay said. "Carl doesn't get the whole cut from our contract; Carl's just their bitch. That's why I can call Carl and say, 'Hey, Jolene and I are joining Alexa in Red Deer next week.'"

I was in awe of all this. With her associations with the brotherhood, and Carl being their bitch, Shay could make Carl her bitch. To me, what could be more powerful than having connections and power over Carl? I could not believe my good fortune of falling in with Shay.

"You seem to be pretty popular with these guys," I said. "Have you ever been in a romantic relationship with any of the brothers after your ex?"

"No way," she said. After splitting with her ex-husband, there was no way she could take up with another club member ever again in her life.

"Well, why is that? They seem to be such good people, and they seem to really protect you and take care of you."

"Yeah, that's why," she said. "Carmen, you are never allowed to date any of them. You can fuck one of them if you want. Or all of them, I don't care. But never be one of their women. They value everything in life according to this hierarchy, remember: first the club, second the brothers, third the bike, and fourth the dog. Girlfriend isn't even on the list. Unless you want to be on the bottom of that totem pole, don't ever go down that road. If you never date them, they'll treat you like gold. Oh, and lots of times in the different clubhouses all over the place, like in Red Deer and Calgary, they'll show you all sorts of stuff that 'fell off the truck.' Beautiful coats, cool stereo stuff, and they'll try to give it to you. But as soon as you take it, then you owe them. Don't fall for those traps. Never put yourself in that kind of vulnerable position."

This made total sense to me. I had watched her be the gorgeous star of the show all night, drinking for free and brushing off the advances, gaining respect. She wasn't fetching them drinks or hanging on their arms like the other skeezy girls we saw. And if I followed her lead, I would have the best they had to offer. I wanted to be a tough girl like Shay.

11

SOUTHPAW TOUR

*"You have your way. I have my way. As for the right way,
the correct way, and the only way—it does not exist."*
—Friedrich Nietzsche

UNLIKE OTHER WINDOWLESS, DARK CLUBS, natural light poured in through the windows of Nisku Airways. Not far from Edmonton, Nisku—the first stop on my southern Alberta tour—was an oil and industry hub. Exotic entertainment was so popular at this venue, they had two stages with two girls dancing even at lunch. The bar could seat over two hundred business travellers and tradesmen, and they filled the place at lunchtime, making that time of day as lucrative as the night shows. And the stage lit up from underneath, bathing the dancers in a warm, flattering glow. After seeing places like Grimshaw, Airways was like stepping into the sunshine.

The better lighting may have made my costume illusion more obvious, because during my first show, when I flung my fur-lined bikini top off, baring my smaller-than-they-looked breasts, a heckler in pervert row said, "Hey, that's false advertising!"

"Well, you know, my nipples are just that sensitive," I coyly smiled at him, even though I didn't feel like smiling. "I need the fur inside because the fabric is simply too abrasive."

He and everyone else in the front row looked thoughtful for a second, then seemed even more turned on. Shaundra was right; it worked like a charm. The guys were dumb enough to fall for a simple illusion. I kept dancing, but felt empowered by this sage woman trick for manipulating men. Men were like playthings—shallow, and when presented with sexual innuendo, easy to manipulate. And I felt so relieved that my ruse had worked.

Getting closer to the weekend, the evening shows brought the Hells Angels crowd to Airways. Big guys in leather and patches commandeered a section of tables. Some I recognized from the Edmonton Clubhouse party, and they invited me to sit with them. Bravado hung like fog over this crowd, nervous and anxious to be liked, I brought out my corniest, most cringe-worthy jokes. I asked one of the bearded, burly bikers what do you call the white stuff that gathers in the bottom of women's panties?

"I don't know," he said.

"Clitty litter."

His wide head flew back in laughter, and then he made me repeat the joke for everyone. They loved it. And they seemed to like me. I was saucy and great at hiding any anxious feelings about mingling in such a rough crowd. And, with Shay's warnings burning in my brain, I was careful not to send any signals that might be misinterpreted. A flirtatious touch on the shoulder was okay when signing posters for the guys in pervert row, but here I kept my hands to myself.

I told them about growing up on the farm, which immediately earned me the nickname Farm Girl, and I talked about my brother, who was still back in high school in Bonnyville. Maurice had earned himself a brawler's reputation, getting in fights and winning every time.

Maurice, bouncing from my mom's and the farm, was struggling in his own way with our childhood and our upbringing. He became quite a scrapper. And for this tough-guy reputation, everyone at school loved him. Maurice was the only person from my old life who knew what I was doing. I told him about my job, about the clubhouse party and the Hells Angels—I trusted him with everything. And I secretly wired money to his bank account so he could buy whatever he wanted. Because I could, and likely because of lingering guilt, I wanted him to have everything his teenaged brain could imagine. When he proudly told me about the fights he got in and won, I worried. I saw it as a manifestation of him struggling to process our upbringing. He was acting out.

But on the high school grounds in Bonnyville, bravado and being tough and fighting was how you established yourself on the food chain. I kept an eye on him, and I used his great stories to feed my new Hells Angels friends at Airways. In a club with a reputation for brawling, they recognized a kindred spirit in my brother. I regaled them with stories of how my currently undefeated six-foot-tall brother owned the BCHS smokers' alley with his left hook, even cracked a kid's eye socket.

The Hells Angels surprised me too. One brother told me how excited he was about an upcoming toy run, where they collected and donated toys to children's hospitals. I had heard about them running drugs, shaking down Johns, and racketeering. Even though I never saw any of this firsthand, the stories circulated like folklore. This was the first time I heard about them doing anything charitable. They supported the community in their own way, whether it was sincere or a carefully crafted ruse to keep friendly with the law. No matter. These Hells Angels brothers definitely lived up to the name and enjoyed every bit of barroom intimidation that came from them simply waltzing over to their makeshift VIP zone. Wearing their vests, they could part the crowd better than Moses parted water.

At the end of my week of work at the Nisku Airways, the brothers gave me two white T-shirts that read, "Support the Big Red Machine," in small red writing on the top-left corner. One was a ladies' extra small for me and one was a men's large for my brother. I'd talked about him so much that week that they wanted Maurice to have a T-shirt too. They assured me that anybody who knows what "Support the Big Red Machine" means knows what that means; it was a subtle way to support the club. I thought that was pretty amazing, kind, and generous of them.

I liked getting to know the brothers throughout the week, but noticed my workmates were unfriendly and skittish. Most girls with me at Airways popped Ativan and benzos like it was candy and were not afraid to line up cocaine rips on the dressing room counter before a show. Uppers, downers, they all had their favourite poison. None were sober, most twitched when they spoke, and they never looked me directly in the eye. None of these girls were ever invited to sit at the brothers' tables.

With only two days off before the next tour stop in Red Deer, and worried that I hadn't made any new girlfriends, I called Shay and begged her to call Carl and get booked for Red Deer or Calgary or both with me. "You said you loved working at the French Maid in Calgary," I said. "We'll have an amazing time if you come."

"I don't know, Carms," she said, "I'm pretty comfy at home this week. And I'm getting too old for week-after-week gigs, you know? Carl will flip his lid if I demand a last-minute booking. And I got some bad blood with girls down in Calgary, you know."

"Oh, you're too old at the ripe age of twenty-nine," I teased. "Come on, please."

"Okay. I'll call Carl, see what he says."

Within five minutes, she called me back to tell me that I'd better get my liver ready because she was coming. My alcohol tolerance had increased considerably since we became friends. I was so grown up now, I could drink two boilermakers within minutes and keep them down too.

I picked her up the next day at noon, and we drove up to Red Deer, halfway between Edmonton and Calgary, the two major cities in Alberta. We arrived early, so Shay could take her signature two-hour bath. Shay hated being rushed. She was a sleepy, hooded-eyed, pretty little sloth.

Our venue for the week was the Gentlemen's Club, and they had recently installed a glass shower stall on the stage next to the brass poles. When we were checking in, Shay and I looked at each other like, "Okay? What are we supposed to do with this?"

The club rat guy checking us in said, "You don't have to use it if you don't want to. Just go with what feels natural."

"Okay," I said, freaking out. But Shay was unfazed. I could see the wheels in her mind spinning. She was beautiful, but she was twenty-nine and lived a hard lifestyle in a competitive business that favoured youth. She had to get creative.

Shay knew eight out of the ten girls on our week-long shift at the Gentlemen's Club. They hugged her so hard she winced. One girl, Charity, instantly gushed her man problems to Shay, as if picking up their last conversation. Shay introduced me to everyone, and they accepted me as one of Shay's closest friends. I knew that if she was with me, that acceptance and making friends with the other entertainers would be effortless. Watching Shay was the easiest way to learn this world, to get in there and dominate it, make money, have friends, have these crazy adventures. I was still so new and wanted to integrate into this world. It felt so natural, like I'd finally found my people in a misfit tribe.

At the same time, I tried a little too hard. Ten seconds after meeting Charity, trying to be cool, I started blabbing about how I knew some of the brothers from Edmonton. I even name-dropped a few guys I'd met. Later, Shay laid it out straight to me.

"Stop being so cocky, Carmen. And tuck that shit in with the brothers. You never, ever name-drop. Got it?"

"Yeah," I said. "I got it."

While we were in Red Deer, I bought Shay and myself rollerblades and taught her how to skate in the park on the paved bike paths. She was awkward and uncoordinated but willing to try as long as we took smoke breaks on all the benches. I was loving the big sister thing, and even if rollerblading wasn't Shay's favourite, she played along.

At ten on Thursday night, the club was packed with rowdy, drunk college kids, standing room only. The bouncers were working overtime. I stood on the edge of the crowd to watch Shay's show. She always danced to '80s rock, music so old it made the DJ's roll their eyes. And tonight was no different. When Air Supply's "Making Love Out of Nothing at All," came on for her fifth song, I groaned. It was a great song, a beautiful song, but so old. It was one of Shay's favourites. But instead of unrolling her blanket and getting down on the floor, Shay got in the shower!

She turned on the water and adjusted the temperature, testing it by playfully splashing water on her cookie and flicking it off her fingers into pervert row. She had so much swagger. Once the temperature was to her liking, she stepped in the glass shower. The side with the shower head was tall, the other two sides only came up as high as her knees, so everyone could see. She smoothed the water over her face suggestively and rubbed her neck like she was all alone and no one was watching, and the crowd went wild. As the song tempo ramped up, she picked up a small bottle of blue liquid. She squeezed it into her hands, rubbed it on her body, and as she lathered and lathered, the bubbly foam grew until bubbles were spilling over the edge of the shower. The foam kept growing, higher and higher, until she had no choice but to exit the shower, soaking wet. So many bubbles.

When the chorus erupted, slippery and glistening, foam stuck to her everywhere, she got down on the stage floor to finish the show. Sloshing and thrashing, money rained down onto her. Coins hit her chest, bills landed in her foam-filled hair as she arched her back and spun on the wet, slick stage. At the end of the song, the crowd roared and demanded more. She blew kisses graciously, put her robe on, and exited the stage. She didn't even pick up her money; she left the sudsy mess and cash for the staff to clean. That was Shay, the queen. Back in the change room, the girls gushed and gushed over her show. I was gobsmacked. I hugged her and started up a "Shay, Shay, Shay" chant that took over the dressing room.

§

Calgary was like the Dallas of Canada; our oilfield industry sector was younger, but the industry ruled the area. The city gleamed with shiny skyscrapers, filled with global oil producer headquarters and white-collar money. And on clear days, we could see the white-capped Canadian Rockies off in the distance. French Maid, the name of the club where we were working, was downtown in the middle of it all. It looked like a tuxedo inside: classy, black, and white. Lunch was especially popular for the white-collar business crowd. Then at night, the place filled up with people from all over the area. Monday through Saturday, there wasn't a slow night of the week. This was a place to wear your most elegant costumes. And the girls were glamorous, mostly Calgary circuit girls, who had fake breasts and didn't have to work very hard.

A few of the girls were from Ontario, three provinces east. Based on what they said, the exotic entertainment business was completely different there. They'd never seen the four-foot barrier, and they complained nonstop about the Alberta Liquor Control Board who made the rules. They also didn't have much in the way of dancing skills or performance talent. Even their costumes were kind of ratty and unkempt. But they also complained about making so much more money back at home.

One girl who worked there was named Ariel Andrews. She was a ditzy, classic blonde with a perfect body and not much to say. The guys in this crowd loved the upscale arm-candy type of girl. They weren't taking posters to hang over the tool box because they worked in offices. But they were often looking for a date to an upcoming event.

Ariel was a couple years older than me, and she'd just had her breasts done the year before. She fit the cookie-cutter Marylin Monroe mold that the business-types loved. Shay was more like a biker-chick. I was more brazen, like Shay, which is why she liked me so much. These other girls weren't like us. But Ariel desperately wanted to be friends with Shay. Shay was gracious and patient and matronly, and she entertained Ariel as best as she could. But as soon as Ariel left the room, Shay would tap on her temple and whisper that Ariel had some issues in the head—she was "crazy."

I noticed many of the girls popping pills—heavyweight pharmaceuticals like OxyContin and Percocet. No one was ever sober, not even Shay, who smoked marijuana and drank. It didn't take much for me to become wasted because I was so inexperienced. But Shay seemed to like keeping me young and innocent. She wanted to protect me, and she didn't want me to be like her. And, of course, I was always very rebellious and pushing those boundaries with her. When we went out, I'd goad her for attention at the bar and say, "Hey, Shay, I'm onto my fourth tequila shot."

"Yeah, I can tell," she'd say snarkily. "You're losing control. You think you're in control and you're not. You're just a kid." A few times she even intervened and grabbed a shot that someone had bought for me before I could take it.

Ariel made Shay crazy all week. Then Thursday at four, when Shay and I were arriving at the club to get ready for our shows that night, we heard shrieking coming from the dressing room. It sounded like someone was being murdered inside, and girls came running out, bumping into us as we were trying to get in, saying, "Don't go in there. She's fucking crazy. She's totally fucking lost her mind. Just stay away from there."

"What the hell is going on?" I asked Shay.

"I don't know, but I'm definitely checking it out."

We opened the door and Ariel was screaming, rocking back and forth in a corner wearing a soft pink silk robe, looking at the center of the room and pointing at this disgusting *bloody tampon mess* in the center of the carpet. Mascara-stained tears streamed down her face. And with one hand balled in a fist, she was knocking on her head over and over again.

Without hesitation, Shay flew right over to her, picked her up off the floor, shook her shoulders hard, and said, "You need to fucking calm down. What the fuck is wrong with you?"

"I'm gonna die. I'm gonna die," Ariel cried. "I left this tampon in my body for *six days*. I'm gonna die. I just realized it. I pulled it out."

I hung back by the door, watching this girl having a bout of major psychosis. And granted, I was terrified too. I'd never thought of what would happen if you forgot about a tampon in your body and left it there for six days. But she was so nuts, she could have simply lost track of reality or time. Who knew how long it had actually been in there. Either way, there was a bloody mess in the center of our dressing room.

When Ariel shrieked again, Shay slapped her with an open palm right across the face. "Get your shit together and calm down."

Ariel crumpled to the ground into the fetal position, whimpering and breathing heavy like she was having a panic attack. Shay slid with her all the way down to the ground and brought her into her arms. For several soft-sobbing minutes, Shay rocked her back and forth and comforted her until she was calm.

I'd never seen anyone lose it like that before. Feeling useless, I stood watching, then grabbed an armful of paper towels. Making a thick wad in my hand, I picked up the tampon and threw it in the trash. Then I grabbed more towels, wet them at the sink, and dabbed it on the floor to clean up the mess. We all had to use that change room, and we had a busy night ahead of us. It looked like the blood stain was going to stay no matter how much I scrubbed or dabbed it.

Shay asked Ariel where her medication was, and Ariel, still breathing fast and heavy, pointed at her station at the dressing room table. Shay motioned for me to grab her bag. When I passed it to her, Shay helped Ariel take her Ativan with sips from a vodka spritzer to wash it down. In about fifteen minutes, she was Ariel again.

The rest of that week, the other girls treated Ariel as if she had the plague. She was a social pariah now. Ariel didn't bother anybody; she kept it together and did her performances. She sat in the opposite end of the club the rest of the time and didn't spend too much time in the dressing room. But we were hard on her. She was ostracized by the rest of the girls for her moment of weakness. There was no forgiveness for her breakdown, and it cast a shadow on the rest of our time there. And once it got out that she was a loose cannon, there was no way she'd ever get booked there again. The agents were quick to put you on blacklists or to book you at gigs in places like Grimshaw.

§

While in Calgary, I called my friend Kelly from back home. She knew about my career, but she lived a normie life. Her mom helped her get an administration position at a natural gas company headquartered downtown. She dressed up every day and rode the elevator up to her office job in an ivory tower building. And Kelly was so excited I was in town, she called in sick to work on Friday and picked me up so she could show me around town.

Calgary is a beautiful, picturesque city with parks and natural landscapes. And everything was brand-new. New high rises, new pavements, new city infrastructure, all hip and modern. I saw her apartment—a classic, urban bachelorette pad—and met her new boyfriend, Shane. He had fiery red hair, freckles, and a wake 'n' bake weed habit like Shay's. He was going to SAIT, the Southern Alberta Institute of Technology in Calgary, where tradesmen got their trade tickets. He was a second-year electrical apprentice. It felt good to be with Kelly, who knew about my new career because she'd worked with me at Fort Kent Bar. It was like having a touch of home in my new life. I liked that I didn't have to explain this job A–Z, like I did with Maurice's thousand and one questions.

I told her all about the French Maid, and teased her about quitting her boring job and making nothing but money with her huge natural breasts and perfect size-two body. Kelly was a beautiful girl with strikingly large hazel eyes, like a tiger. And I didn't want our day to end. I wanted to spend more time with her. She made me remember the good parts of back home, and she was so welcoming and nonjudgmental. So, I persuaded her to come see me that night at the club.

The nighttime crowd at the French Maid was still white-collar, lots of lawyers and oilmen, and they liked modern Top Ten music. My show had a hip-hop vibe with lots of Eminem, who was so popular then, and some Naughty by Nature, as much as the DJ's allowed me to push my hip-hop tracks. And Kelly loved it. She was amazed to see me doing advanced moves on the pole and using all of my flexibility; I'd come a long way from playing on the pole at Fort Kent, goofing off with her. At the end, I gave her a poster, signed, "Breast wishes, Love Alexa." We had a great time, and I confided in her that I'd been researching a plastic surgeon in Calgary. Seeing so many naked women with breast enhancements, some clearly had better results than others. I learned that what you had before the operation would be the same afterwards, only bigger. So if you had lopsided or tuberous breasts, augmentation would amplify that, unless you had a great doctor. I always asked the girls who had the best boobies, who did their breasts, and the answer was usually Dr. Waslen in Calgary. I had resisted believing that breast size mattered that much, but there was always just a tiny bit more money to be made with bigger ones. Often times, with clever costumes and better dance and promo items, you could make more money. It was hard to recreate that approach every time compared to simply just having larger breasts. Kelly insisted I stay with her for the consultation, instead of in a hotel room. She was thrilled. It was settled.

§

Back in Edmonton, Shay was worn out from two weeks on the road. She wanted to retreat to her acreage and take a break before we all went to the infamous Slack Alice club in Penticton, British Columbia, for the Peach Festival. But I felt completely energized. I was young. I wanted to hit it. I wanted more adventures. I wanted more money. I wanted to keep going.

During those weeks off, Ryan was coming home from several back-to-back drilling rig hitches, and we were both really excited to reconnect in our little apartment. Neither one of us had been spending much time there. I cleaned our place from top to bottom, went grocery shopping, and stocked up the fridge, wanting it to be perfect for when he arrived.

Our relationship had been distant, limited to occasional phone calls for months. As soon as he pulled up, we crashed into each other's arms. I had so much to tell him, I gushed all about the new friends I had made, jobs I went on, people I had met, including the Hells Angels. I told him about all the money and how I was thinking about getting my breasts enlarged. But as I talked and talked, he went quiet.

Guessing his unease was about Shay and the brothers, I assured him that they were actually solid fellows who would never hurt me. In fact, I felt quite safe with them. He insisted that everything was fine, but our weekend of reconnection was off to a bumpy start.

The more time we spent together, the source of his hesitation became clear. It bothered him that I was so happy, that I was blossoming, and he felt left behind. And he seemed to resent the way I insisted on paying for everything. I just wanted to spoil him, and I thought he would be thrilled that I was making it rain. I thought any man who worked hard as a breadwinner would like a break. But it emasculated him. It was like he cared for me less as I became more confident and more powerful and wealthier than him.

He became irritated and annoyed at nearly everything I said. When we were talking about a headline in the Edmonton paper that week, and I said police corruption was actually pretty prevalent, he got mad like I was siding with criminals. It was like he thought I was becoming indoctrinated into a new belief system while he was away working the rigs, and he was probably right. I was. I had access and acceptance in a different kind of wealth and power system, and I liked it.

The visit ended as awkwardly as it began. Neither one of us was willing to concede our views, and a quiet line in the sand was drawn. But we interacted like we were both scared to talk about it, knowing that even if we unpacked that disagreement, our personal thoughts wouldn't change. After seeing how my Pépère Pierre could so easily guilt and manipulate my mother, I had a low threshold of tolerance for a man using care as a disguise for *control*. With nothing resolved, he left for work before I had to head to the infamous BC Peach Festival.

§

A few weeks later, Canada's most stunning landscape opened up for Shay, Jolene, and me as we drove ten hours from Edmonton to Penticton. I'd never been past the Rockies, where the wheat fields and prairies of Alberta turned into fruit orchards and rolling hills. The whole drive, they regaled me with their stories of what the Slack Alice club was like when they first went in 1988. It sounded absolutely wild, like a late-80s dream: big hair, neon spandex, and hair metal music everywhere. All of Shay and Jolene's favourite things.

Sunday night we rolled into town and went to the club to check in. Outside, a row of forty show bikes were lined up, all chrome and flashy paint and leather. It was definitely our kind of club. Shay and Jolene hugged every big bearded biker in the place, one after another, like old friends. But this no longer surprised me. They were famous everywhere in this underground world. Like Penny Lane, *Almost Famous* groupies.

Slack Alice put their girls up in a luxury waterfront hotel that featured parasailing over the Okanagan Lake. We had a great time that week, taking daytime rides on the brothers' show bikes, wearing bikinis and cutoffs, sunning ourselves on the beach, and eating the juiciest peaches. I even got Shay up in the blue-bird sky on the parasailing adventure tour. The whole time, the warm wind whipped our faces high up over the water. She humoured me, but she clung to the rigging ropes, terrified and wishing it were over. I loved making her be younger.

While we were there, we met BC girls who worked under an agency in Vancouver called Best Entertainment. They told us all about doing club openings overseas and making so much money they were considering retiring. I listened. I asked questions. I took it all in. And I got the number for an agent, Kevin, from Best Entertainment. Back in our shared rooms that night, I gushed and gushed about how wonderful that would be if we could all go to Europe and see the world and take our adventures overseas. Both Shay and Jolene dismissed the other girls' talk as most likely bullshit. But I didn't think it was bullshit at all. These girls were rolling in designer goods, many laid as gifts at their feet while on stage, abroad.

The first thing I did when we rolled back into Edmonton was call the agent, Kevin, from Best Entertainment.

"I want to work overseas," I said, straight to the point. "How does it work? And what do I have to do?"

I told him about the girl who'd referred me to him and said that, if he needed a reference, he could call Slack Alice's in Penticton. Kevin, who sounded excited and enthusiastic over the phone, told me where to mail a promo package and said he'd let me know.

That week, I express mailed him my headshots, body shots, and promo merchandise package. A few days later, he called me back and said that I was very beautiful. I got a glowing review from the club owner at Slack Alice's in Penticton; I was a great dancer, had top-of-the-line costumes, and was definitely welcome back.

"But," Kevin said, "your small breasts are a problem. We can definitely get you jobs, but they're not going to be the best jobs." He said he had a couple opportunities coming up in South America—one in Panama and one in Santa Cruz, Bolivia.

"I'll take whatever you've got," I said. "And I'm getting my breasts done soon."

"Great," Kevin said. "I'll fax you the contract."

I gave him Shay's number because she was the only person I knew who was adult enough and had a fax machine. And I told Shay that I needed to borrow her machine to receive a contract. I'd come over later that night, and we could sit down and look at it together. In my imagination, Shay would see my contract and want to get in on the same deal. Everything seemed like it was falling into place until I got to Shay's.

"What the hell, Carmen?" She was furious with me. "Why would you even want to do this?"

"Oh, come on," I said. "You and Jolene have been working the Alberta circuit for ten years. Don't you want to see what else is out there? Aren't you curious what these Ontario and BC girls are talking about?"

"No, I don't," Shay said. "I thought you were joking when you brought this up."

Jolene, with three kids and a husband, maybe couldn't get away like that. But I didn't understand why Shay didn't want to try.

"I can't go anywhere, Carmen. I just can't." She used the dog as an excuse, but her reclusive ambivert nature was starting to show. She may have been a popular party girl, but she was also a bit of a hermit, locking herself away in her little house on her little piece of property, surrounded by broken-down vehicles and bush. Then it dawned on me that maybe she couldn't get a passport. She ran around with an outlaw crowd. I didn't know if she had any prior convictions or if she'd ever been to jail—she didn't offer that information and I didn't ask. But it was possible.

"All right. Well, I guess it's just gonna be me," I said. "Will you at least look over the contract with me?"

And she did. It was a new club opening, which was good because new clubs meant more money from big crowds of people checking it out. The contract looked like a great deal. So I signed it and sent it back to Kevin, who said he'd let me know travel details as they were finalized in the next couple weeks.

I didn't realize that the handful of exotic entertainment agents in Western Canada all knew each other. Kevin must have tipped off Carl that I'd signed with him, because Carl called me, and he wasn't happy.

"I don't get it. You're making great money, and I know you're hungry," he said. "I had this Saskatchewan-Manitoba tour planned out for you, only to find out you've signed with another agency."

"Carl, I can work for you too," I said, firmly believing this was possible.

"Don't even think about it," he spat. "Unless you cancel your contract with Best Entertainment, you're done working in Alberta."

This was not ideal—I really thought I could balance working jobs for both agencies. Who were they to decide for me anyways? But I wanted adventure, so there was no way I was cancelling this contract. Going abroad was the future, even if it meant working in Alberta was the past. I thought about calling in a favour from the Hells Angels and asking them to shake Carl down for treating me that way. But Shay was upset with me too. I knew some of the brothers, but she was my real connection to them. And she'd warned me about going into debt with them. So I decided to take my licks from Carl and let him calm down. And worst case, I could always move to Vancouver to get more regular work from Best Entertainment.

I wasn't desperate for money, but I did want to keep working while I waited around for my trip to Bolivia. One opportunity did present itself, but it was the kind of opportunity an exotic entertainer takes when she's out of options.

Pinky's Showroom in Edmonton was arguably the most famous, the longest-running strip club in all of Alberta. It started in the '70s, and every club in town came after it. Pinky's was legendary. Paul, the owner of Pinky's, also owned the famous Kingsway Hotel next door, which was a Klondike-style place, legendary in its own right. And he'd had a falling out with Carl years ago, so Shay told me he had his own agent.

"Paul's a crusty old man, but he's fair," Shay said when I called her to tell her that Carl blacklisted me. "If you wanna get booked at Pinky's, which is basically where all the girls who get blacklisted from their agents go, you have to talk to Cheryl, their agent."

Of course, Shay knew Cheryl. She hadn't worked there in years because nothing made Carl madder than having one of his girls on the stage at Pinky's. But I had nothing to lose.

"Let's go there tonight and see what's up," Shay said cheerfully.

The bar was hopping, and I knew right away there was money to be made. The club had light-up plexiglass flooring, two brass poles, and maybe too much brass on everything else. Pictures of all the showgirls who'd performed there over the years lined the walls. If you started at one end, you could spend half an afternoon looking at all the vintage pictures of glam slam women with teased hair, waterfall bangs, blue eyeshadow, and pink frosted lips. I loved those days-gone-by pictures; it was like staring at ghosts of strippers past. But the closer I examined them, the more used up the girls in the photos looked. I could see why they ended up at Pinky's. And judging what I saw on the stage, I would definitely be the best-looking, most talented, hottest little performer they'd had in a while. I would do my getting-famous money show for this crowd of sad saps, that would make them feel important, I reckoned. The "money show" I'd designed consisted of just my sparkly green underpieces with fake Benjamins that I rubber-cement-glued onto my skin to create a mini-dress. During the money themed song set, I removed the fake bills, a handful at a time and threw them at the crowd, to their delight. After no bills remained stuck to my skin, I was left in my green sequin bikini.

We asked for Cheryl at the bar, and after a few minutes she came down to meet me. I told her I was experienced and looking for work, then I showed her the promo package I'd brought. She was instantly pleased.

"You betcha," she winked at me in a most lesbian way. "Can you start next week?"

Yes, I could. She explained that once I did a week here, I couldn't come back for two months. I was leaving for Bolivia soon, so this sounded great to me. And just like that, I was back to work.

I pulled out all my classic rock routines for Pinky's, and it was awesome. I got to know the club owner, Paul, and made good money. It was an easy gig. Mid-week, there was a knock on my hotel dressing room door and I answered it. There stood a teenaged Indigenous girl who asked me if I wanted anything from the Kingsway Mall next door. I didn't know what she meant. She explained that if I wanted anything from the shopping mall, from any store, she would steal it for me and I would buy it from her at a half-price discounted rate. She was a "booster." She looked desperate and I wanted new 501 button up Levi's, size 26-inch waist and 34-inch length. Sure enough, twenty-five minutes later, I got my new jeans—delivered to my door and I paid her full price for the convenient service. Boosters were awesome. You helped them, they took all the risk, you got what you wanted.

That Friday night, when I arrived to get ready for my show, Shay met me at the bar. She wanted to hang out and take a walk down her own Pinky's memory lane. When you're at Pinky's, they give you a hotel room, even if you live in town, because they don't have a dressing room. They put all the girls up in one part of the hotel and gave us each a key to an unmarked door that led from the hall by our rooms to the stage. This way it was safer for us to move around when the place filled with patrons. Shay followed me upstairs to my room, which I used strictly as my dressing room, never partying hard enough after work to need the place to crash. I didn't even put my costumes on the bed until I'd covered it with my own blanket. Once Shay saw that the place was still a dump, she went downstairs to the club while I got ready.

I performed and saw Shay in the crowd, drink in hand. Then when I put my Labatt Blue bathing suit on and robed up and was out in the bar signing promo and merchandise, she found me.

"I've got drinks for us," she said. "Let's hang out for a while; I want to see who you're working with."

Without the communal dressing room, I hadn't gotten to know any of the other girls very well. But when the next girl, Sandy B. Mine, came on, Shay recognized her right away. Her eyes bugged out of her head when Sandy walked on the stage.

"Oh, do you know Sandy?" I said. Sandy B. Mine was tall, with long tanned legs and long blonde hair. She was kind of a lazy entertainer, relying on her looks rather than her moves. And the crowd was lukewarm to her. I'd met her in the hallway and talked to her one night after my show. "Boy, do I ever," Shay said. "That fucking bitch."

"What? You guys have a history?"

"Yeah. Let's just leave it at that."

"I actually saw her earlier today," I said, keeping the conversation going without really knowing what I was doing. "She had her little daughter up in her change room."

"Wait, what?" Shay said, visibly affronted by this information. "She's got her daughter, HERE?!"

"Yeah, she's the cutest little thing, with pretty blonde curls," I said. "I just talked to her in the hallway. She's quite a little sweetheart."

"You know how fucking disgusting it is to have a kid in your room when you're working for the week?" Shay took a long sip through the straw of her drink. "That just disgusts me so much, you can't even imagine."

Being nineteen and not motherly at all, I couldn't understand why Shay was so upset. Obviously a club wasn't an environment for children, but the way the hotel was set up, it wasn't like she had her kid in a strip club at the bar. I never even considered who might be watching her kid while she was downstairs performing.

After Sandy's performance, she came out into the crowd and mingled for a while. Then she sat down at a table of men and started drinking. An hour later, she was still sitting there with a drink in her hand.

"Maybe her daughter isn't really here. Maybe she was just here for the day," I said when Shay brought it up again.

But Shay couldn't let it go. She wanted me to describe the little girl again. "She was a little blonde girl, about four?"

"Yeah. But how do you even know her kid?"

"Oh, I know her," Shay said. "Don't worry about that."

I changed the subject, and we both left the club a while later, not saying anything else about Sandy or her daughter. And I didn't give much more thought to Shay's reaction. I resolved that it wasn't right to have a kid anywhere near this environment, indeed.

The next day, Shay called me and said she was coming to visit me again. "I'll be there early, before four, so we can hang out before your show."

I assumed she was bored and looking for something to do, so I agreed to meet her at the bar. When she came in, there were a few patrons hanging around, but it was too early for the evening crowd. The first show didn't start until five, so we sat and had a drink.

We were talking and having fun like always, when Sandy B. Mine came in and saw Shay. Before I knew what was happening, Sandy came straight over to Shay and grabbed her by the neck.

"You fucking did this, didn't you?" Sandy yelled, hysterical. Her long fake nails like claws on Shay's throat, isolating her trachea tube. "They came and took my daughter away from me today. You did this."

But Shay wasn't having it. She stood up, ripped Sandy's hand away with one arm, and grabbed Sandy around the neck with her other. Then she pulled Sandy, who was several inches taller than Shay, down and started kneeing her in the face, over and over again. The bouncer and the bartender rushed over and pulled the girls off each other. It was too late though, Sandy was injured badly and quickly.

Sandy's nose and face were a bloody mess, and she was still screaming at Shay, "I know you did this. I know it was you."

The bar manager fired Sandy immediately because we weren't allowed to fight like that and everyone witnessed her as the aggressor. Then Shay and I were ushered straight up in the owner's office and interrogated about what happened.

"Why did this happen?" Paul boomed from across his desk. "Why is one of my girls getting fired for fighting? And what the hell are you doing in my club, Shay?"

Shay just straightened her halo and said, "I came in to see my friend, Carmen. I don't even know this 'Sandy.' I have no idea what she's talking about. She must be crazy."

After satisfying the owner, he sent us on our way. But before going up to get ready, I said to Shay, "Obviously you know her. What's going on?"

"Oh, I know her. She's my ex-husband's baby mama, and that little girl deserves a better mother than that piece of shit. *That little girl should be mine.*"

Apparently, after our talk the night before about Sandy's little girl, Shay called social services and had the little girl taken away from her mom. She unloaded on this poor woman because she had something Shay lost in her late-term miscarriage. Because Shay lost her babies, Sandy and her daughter symbolized what she couldn't achieve with the same man.

"I don't think she should have a daughter," Shay said. Thankfully, at the club owner's suggestion, Shay left after that.

For the rest of the night, I didn't know what to think. Shay never spoke about her ex-husband much or what their relationship was like. And I agreed with Shay, in a way, that a kid shouldn't be left alone like that. But at the same time, that cute little girl was taken away from a mom who obviously loved her. I sympathized with that little girl. It brought me right back to waking up in a new house after my mom had stolen us away from my dad in the middle of the night. I had seen girls engaged in all sorts of questionable behaviour, from cocaine in the club bathroom to breaking the four-foot barrier trying to make more money. I wasn't a snitch. And we didn't know the whole story about Sandy and her daughter at the club. Seeing Shay, seemingly without care, getting involved like that, feeling like she was in the right, was alarming. Maybe Sandy was a bad mother, but where was that little girl now?

These kinds of problems were way over my teenaged head. But the more I thought about it, the angrier I was at Shay. She flat out used me. And the look in her eyes, when she was smashing Sandy's face on her knee, was like she was on fire with pent up glee for pain. I knew she could be violent, but I'd never seen it firsthand. It was like she harboured some old vendetta and finally the stars aligned and she got her revenge on this woman she despised. Everywhere Shay and I went, Shay knew everybody. Shay knew everything about what happened in these clubs ten years ago. But who was she, really? Was she using me? Did she really care about me? Did she really want to protect me every time she drank my tequila shots that I didn't want to take?

Sitting with Hells Angels, being in these clubs, having these types of adventures, making this type of money felt surreal to me. It was a fun job. It wasn't hard like farm work or dangerous like being a power engineer. But I had been naïve. Seeing Shay, seeing the girls breaking down with mental illness, seeing how they needed to be completely numb to do what I was doing sober, and seeing that some of them had children waiting in the club wings was starting to really intimidate me. For several days after that, I holed up in my apartment and stayed away from everyone.

§

I knelt on the carpeted floor, scanning the South American travel guide shelf at Chapters bookstore on Whyte Avenue in Edmonton. They had Brazil, Venezuela, and Columbia, but nothing on Bolivia. All I found was a few pages in a regional guide. So Bolivia was apparently not a popular destination. Eager to travel and see the world and get a little distance from Shay, I was just waiting around for my tickets and itinerary to come through from Best Entertainment. I decided to take the regional guide, and picked up a few Grisham novels I hadn't read yet. On the way to the register, I noticed a new novel called *Memoirs of a Geisha* by Arthur Golden on the new books display. The jacket read, "We enter a world where appearances are paramount, where a girl's virginity is auctioned to the highest bidder, where women are trained to beguile the most powerful men, and where love is scorned as illusion." It sounded like something I could relate to, so I bought that one too.

I threw myself into preparing for the trip, carefully planned the shows that I would do and packed a full suitcase of my props, wigs, and costumes, loading up all of my best posters, keychains, and magnets. As a Virgo, I liked to plan. But I also felt a sting of dumb naïveté.

Not working for those weeks took me back to losing my oil well operator job and learning how fast your life can change financially. I vowed to never be so blind again, and I hoarded as much of my money in a savings account as possible. And I grew increasingly repulsed by girls who raked in the cash, squandered their earnings on nonsense like couture clothes, and yet still drove around in beat-up cars. They acted as if youth and beauty were permanent, and this annoyed me to no end.

If there was one person I didn't mind spoiling at all, it was Maurice. I forever worried about him, his coming-of-age journey, and his cocky willingness to scrap anyone who ticked him off. His fights were usually coming to the defense of someone who was being picked on. I admired that about him; he wasn't usually a provocateur, but rather a defendant, or so his stories went . . .

For his eighteenth birthday, Maurice came to visit me in Edmonton. I presented him with his "Support the Big Red Machine" T-shirt the Hells Angels brothers had given me weeks earlier, and I told him about its subtle innuendo—anyone who knew what it meant would know to back off. Indeed, weeks later, he reported that a few customers from his work at BMW Monarch oilfield supply shop asked where the hell he got *that shirt*. He was an outside sales agent who made sure oil companies had all the valves, pumps, fittings, and oil well lifting systems that they needed for capital and maintenance projects, perfect for his gregarious and jokey nature. Maurice had dropped out of high school too, and was coasting on his high-level charm and charisma.

He asked me to call him Moe instead of Maurice, probably his way of turning away from our French-Catholic upbringing like I had. I always thought we were similar, both too arrogant for our own good, overly confident, people who might cut you if you got too close. Farm kids and butcher shop kids, peas in a pod. But more people liked him. I think because where we came from, a girl couldn't be pretty, smart, and nice and still be liked. You could be two out of the three and that was okay, but never all three. It was usually too much for most to process. Most men don't like pretty girls who are tough and intimidating, as I was learning with Ryan's growing resentment over how much money I could make as a dancer, unapologetically and without shame.

To celebrate Moe's birthday and legal ability to booze in Alberta, I took him and his college pals to Whyte Avenue and filled them with all the booze they could handle, round after round, bar after bar. The first time Moe saw street performers playing with their guitar case open for tips, he and his redneck pals jeered and sneered at these low-lifes trying to grift passers-by for money. They wanted to pop "these bums." I had thought the same thing about street performers when I first moved to the city. After living there for over a year, and fearing one of the brawly boys might punch a street performer, I highlighted how wrong they were. These people were at least offering music instead of a begging cup, and I encouraged them to think about what the songs added to the atmosphere on this legendary

Alberta avenue. They agreed and quickly switched gears and demanded that I now give the man some money. They put in song requests like "Jesse's Girl" by Rick Springfield and "Your Love" by The Outfield and "Enter Sandman" by Metallica. Singing along, having a grand time, the boys made new friends with every street performer. And the good times continued well into the night.

Back at my place, after his friends funneled more straight vodka down his throat, Moe passed out. I placed him in my bathtub in case he wretched, and shook his shoulders every few hours to make sure he wasn't completely poisoned. His groans assured me that he was gonna be okay. And the next day, I sent him back to Bonnyville with an epic hangover.

§

Every day I checked the mail for my flight tickets to Bolivia. When they arrived, I had a full itinerary of instructions and plans to follow. I would fly from Edmonton to Vancouver, and have a three-hour layover to meet the other girls and our agent, and we would proceed together from there. I wanted to get away from Shay and had avoided her calls for a week. Now, I didn't have to think about any of her mess brewing or about anything serious at all. I was outta here. Perfect.

12

AFTER BOLIVIA

*"Dear optimist, pessimist, and realist—while you were
busy arguing about the glass of wine, I drank it!
Sincerely, the opportunist."*
—LORI GREINER

BACK FROM BOLIVIA, I CRASHED through the door of my Edmonton
apartment, home from the most insane and dangerous gig. I had been in
the same clothes for days and the stench of disgust was palpable. I was
disgusted with myself. How could I have been so stupid and naïve?

That first shower back home after Bolivia did more than wash my body
from airport grime. I sat and cried on the shower floor with my knees
tucked tight and hoped the extremely hot water would cleanse my marrow.
I hated crying. I hated the feeling of lumps growing in my throat because
I didn't want to succumb to the act of crying. I couldn't stop it this time. I
felt incredible gratitude for my Canadian passport privileges and for Tom
and the Bolivian-American Consular Agency. Without them, I would no
doubt still be stuck in some sort of drug-cartel-family nightmare. I tried to
imagine what would have happened to me if I'd stayed and hadn't escaped

Elena's compound when I did. Terror and horror crept up again, inside of me. Did Jacey stay? Did the Consular Agency rescue her? I was terrified for her too. How was her story going to end, when mine felt like I had escaped by a paper-thin margin?

Anybody who hadn't known I'd been an exotic entertainer for the past year certainly knew now. Rumours from the past year about what I was up to turned into bonafide, fact-checked tidbits of small-town salacious gossip. I was sure of it. The tears of relief, grief, and disgust for self mixed with the shower water and I watched them swirl down the drain. I was defeated and found out. But this wasn't the hardest part. That was still to come. I next needed to make it right with Grandpa Lloyd and Grandma Betty.

I drove all the way from Edmonton to Bonnyville alone and in complete silence, obsessing over the reactions I may encounter from my family. I didn't know what to expect and tried to imagine what I should say, practicing little scripts of justification. If they were angry, I'd say this; if they were quiet and sad, I'd say that.

Hill and Valley Ranch looked the same, but smaller when I pulled in. Had everything from my past literally shrunk? Everything in my hometown seemed to be getting smaller—I was developing a more macro view of the world and how I fit in it. I had been avoiding the place since I started dancing. And now that my secret was out—my worst fear realized—this was the last place I wanted to show my face. But I had to come home. My grandparents had pulled money from Grandma's teacher pension to get me home from South America, and I wanted to pay them back right away. I sat at their kitchen table with an envelope of cash and told them how grateful I was, how sorry, and that I wanted to do something for them.

"I'm putting an extra $2,000 in here for you."

"Oh, no, no," Grandma said, getting up from her seat at the table to clear a glass leftover from lunch. "You don't have to do that, Dolly Girl."

"I want you to have this money. I want you to do whatever you want with it, buy something that you might need for the farm." They always needed something, some sort of tool or piece of equipment or medicine for the cattle.

She had a hard time taking my money, but I stuck it in the envelope and left it on the table. Before she could protest any further, I put on my old rubber boots and went out to find Dad. He'd been away driving a truck for almost two years, running from his financial problems, trying to repair his bankruptcy. But he was back at the farm now, working and rebuilding his credit. And when he found out what I'd been doing and that I had to be rescued from Bolivia, he was upset. The whole ordeal had been unsettling for everyone. I walked the path over to his house, the house I'd lived in as a kid, and sat down with him.

"I paid Grandma back today, Dad. That's why I'm here."

"I don't know what to say, Carmen," he said, settling into the chair across from me. "It seems like you're putting yourself at great risk."

"Dad, I've been doing this for eighteen months now, and haven't felt like I was in any danger until I went to South America. And I'm fine." I wanted to protect my dad from worrying about me—I didn't tell him about hanging out with the Hells Angels. I wanted him to know the situation was okay by keeping a positive attitude about everything.

"You know your mother is going to find out now; everyone knows. And she's going to lose her mind."

"I have zero intentions of seeing her," I said. "I haven't seen her in almost two years, and I'm not going to start seeing her now."

"I just don't understand how you could do something like this and feel okay about it."

"You know what, Dad. I'm wealthy. I have a cash positive balance because of what I'm doing." Still a cocky nineteen-year-old, I defended myself. "You're broke. You just went through bankruptcy. I figured out my life, you should figure out your life. And I don't think you should be judging me when you need to figure out your own financial situation."

He looked at me hard and then hung his head, his argument deflated. My side of the story wasn't inaccurate. And I think he realized that I was an adult who could make my own decisions, whether or not he liked my decisions or was shamed by them.

I didn't spend much time in Bonnyville. That night, I shuttered myself in my old room at Dad's house and stared at the ceiling in complete country silence until I fell asleep. Then the next morning, before everyone woke, I was back on the road to Edmonton.

By the time I got back to my empty apartment in Edmonton, I felt like so much had changed. Ryan was gone, as usual, and things weren't exactly going well between us anyway. For over a year, I'd been living very much in the moment. If you live in the future, it seems that your life passes by so quickly. And if you live in the past, you're usually depressed. And if you live in the now, one year can feel like a lifetime has gone by.

With my international dreams behind me, and the Alberta and British Columbia scenes fully explored, I started thinking about heading east toward provinces like Saskatchewan or Ontario, cities like Saskatoon, Toronto, and Niagara Falls. Maybe even Montreal because I spoke French. A girl I met in Penticton mentioned that she'd be heading east soon to see if the clubs were as good as we'd heard. Her name was Annika and we'd had a fun-filled time at the Peach Festival. Maybe she'd like a shotgun rider? The idea started to grow—I still couldn't work in Alberta because of my falling out with Carl, and it would be good to get a little extra distance from my family and their shame. I was still avoiding Shay, who thought I was still working in South America on my contract job. When I called Annika, she said she was leaving in a few days and would be thrilled to have a road partner.

Just like that, my plans were settled. But I felt I couldn't leave without calling Ryan first. I couldn't get a hold of him, of course, but I did have his boss's number. The rig push was like the big boss, and he had a direct satellite line that crew family members could call in case they needed to reach someone in an emergency. I left a message for Ryan: I'll be back in a few months, and don't be surprised if you call and find me out east. The call was perfunctory. After all our conflict over my job and meeting Tom in Santa Cruz, Ryan was the last guy on my mind.

§

The prairie passed outside the windows of Annika's Chevy Cavalier on our drive east. We stopped in Saskatoon for a week of work at a club owned by the same people as Showgirls in Edmonton. We partied with the Saskatoon Hells Angels near every night, made a decent week's worth of scratch, and were next back in her car on Sunday, skipping over Manitoba and heading for Toronto.

Annika chattered the whole drive. She grew up in Poland and came to Canada after finding her fiancé dead from suicide at seventeen years old. In quiet moments I rested my head on the window and watched the prairie lands, fence posts, and late summer bumper crops fly by. I closed my eyes, imagining Hill and Valley Ranch lands and what my dad and my grandparents and Porky would be doing at that exact moment. My heart ached. Harvest was always my favourite time of year. The low-slung sun glazes over wheat fields beautifully, rivalling Tuscany.

Then my thoughts drifted over to every steamy, freeze-frame memory I had of my time with Tom, every smart thing he said, every giddy chat that made my head and long hair fly back in wild laughter. How he was the kind of guy that I wanted to find again, and only that kind of guy would do for me.

It took us a day and a half of straight driving to reach Toronto, in the center of Canada. We took turns at the wheel, only stopping for gas. And, boy, did folks in Toronto think they were the center of Canada, all right. This was a completely different world and political scene altogether. Toronto is the New York City of Canada. And it did not disappoint! This is where I ran into the dreaded, vile, liberal left-wing policies and politics that my farm family had warned me about. We'd been taught in grade school that Canada was diverse and multicultural, but we didn't see much of that back home in Alberta. Here, we saw every colour of skin tone. I liked the sharp contrast from anything I'd seen growing up out west. Toronto was a beautiful city with lots of parks and pretty freeway drives and *big ideas* to explore.

Whiskey A Go-Go was our club destination. We didn't know the club owner or the agent; we planned on just showing up at the club, finding someone important, and asking, "How do we work here?" The Toronto girls we'd worked with before weren't talented or busting their butts dancing up on stage. And they didn't have much for costumes. But they talked about how the money here was so much bigger. Annika was a busty blonde, and I was a dark maven. We had this, we thought.

For $1,000 a month, we got a hotel suite with a kitchenette at the Howard Johnson in Markham. We didn't realize just how far the hotel was from the club or how big Toronto really was compared to Calgary and Edmonton. That first night, we slept until three in the afternoon the next day. Assuming correctly, we had to get licenses from Toronto Vice to work as exotic entertainers in the city. At the police department, we filled out paperwork, gave our fingerprints and social insurance numbers, and left with photo IDs. These moments reminded me just how seedy my career was. I *hated* getting licensed.

When Annika and I walked into Whiskey A Go-Go, it was 911 night, which was a monthly special with discounts for police officers, firemen, EMTs, and other first responders. Eminem's "My Name Is" blasted through the speakers so loud it took my breath away. I loved the modern, fresh, big-city vibe right away. Dressed in our skanky best, we wove through the crowd of clean-cut young men with perfect teeth. Not a biker to be found anywhere.

The manager, Dave, shoveled us into his loft office because it was too loud to talk on the floor.

"Let's make it fast, ladies," he said. "Why should I hire you to work at Whiskey's?"

Annika twirled for him, showing off her hot Polish body, while I promised I could dance better than he'd ever seen. We rolled out our promo posters, which he gave a quick glance. "Yeah, sure, I guess they'll do." He steepled his hands on the top of his cluttered desk. "But it's different here than out west. Can you party with our customers?"

"What does that mean?" I said, looking at Annika. I was used to mingling with the crowd and signing posters, but I wasn't leaving the club with any patrons and wasn't about to start that, either.

"We offer a champagne room where, after you're done on the main stage, you dance and entertain tableside." He stood and pointed out the giant window that looked down on the club floor. Beyond the stage was a walled-off area with small stages and poles set up right next to tables. Girls, dressed in skimpy gowns, rhinestones, and long gloves, draped all over the men. We didn't have any of those types of costumes.

"Sure," we said, eager to do whatever it took to salvage a near two-day car drive across the country.

"Great," he said. "You can start tomorrow."

He photocopied our licenses and suggested we hang out to get a feel for the place. Annika and I went out to the bar and watched all the feature performances. Sure enough, they were lazy. Costumes weren't anything elaborate, more like silky, slinky, low-cut, high-slit gowns. And big-breasted girl after big-breasted girl sauntered lazily around the stage. But still, money rained down on the main stage dancers. Annika, who did elaborate acrobatic routines, and I knew our performances would be much better. We high-fived each other and we were so excited. We'd make fools of these girls tomorrow night and every night after that. The crowd would go wild for us. We were sure of it.

Everyone in the club was drunk and full of testosterone. These police officers and firemen were all the kind of guys we would call meatheads back home. So many of them reminded me of Tom. I liked good looking, muscly, competitive men; I already knew that was fast becoming my type.

Before we left the club, we toured the champagne VIP areas and saw the mini tableside stages. The girls sashayed their hips and shoulders. When a song finished and another started, the girls peeled off a layer of clothing, until they were either naked or the patron invited them to sit down. There was no touching allowed, but these girls were too close to the patrons for my comfort. Someone could easily reach out and make contact with these girls. Me, maybe, tomorrow night. The thought of this made my stomach turn and my teeth clench.

No money was being exchanged, so I wondered how it all worked. I was definitely not in Kansas anymore. And I wasn't sure how I felt about it. We'd heard horror stories of American VIP rooms, but this seemed pretty tame. Annika caught one of the dancers coming out of the restroom, and she explained that they got paid by a credit card tab when they worked the champagne room. The patrons picked which girls they wanted to dance by their table. That was where the prettiest girls made all the money. Every song the girls danced to, the waitress charged the table fifty dollars. That got added to the cost of the overall tab, which included the cost of sitting in the VIP area and a bottle of champagne that ranged from $350 to $5,000. So, if you were lucky enough to get picked to be in the tableside area, then you were probably making anywhere from three thousand to eight thousand dollars a night, depending on how busy you were and how much your tables tipped.

Annika and I didn't have slinky gowns made of silk and satin, we had sequins and themed costumes. But the next night we went for it, thinking we could give them a taste of something different. I chose my sparkly catsuit that zipped from between my breasts down to the inside of my knee, so I could peel it off and reveal my prettiest sparkly bra and panties, which would be good for hanging out in the champagne room. I picked modern music too—no more country or '80s hair band rock at Whisky A Go-Go. DJs at prominent clubs got access to new songs before they were available to buy on CD, so Annika and I called our DJ friends from Edmonton to make playlists for us. The DJs at Whiskeys actually preferred to play their own music, but we wanted to be in control of our own shows. I wanted my show to be badass. I wanted to be modern. I played Rage Against the Machine and Korn, finally getting to dance to something from my own era. It couldn't have been any fresher.

Since Annika and I were new, fresh meat, the DJ talked us up all night. When I went on at nine, the club was jam-packed. The DJ pumped up the music and introduced me, saying I'd come all the way from out west. I felt a little like I was back at amateur night, only this time my moves had advanced. And this time I was truly nervous because I did not have big breasts and all sixty of the other girls working there did. I knew I had to make a good impression on stage if I wanted to be invited into the VIP area where the real money could be made. I performed an elaborate pole routine, pulling out all my tricks—spins, splits, walkovers, you name it. Money piled up on the stage. None of the other girls had promo merchandise, but I brought mine out. I unrolled a poster and the crowd went wild because they weren't used to that.

When I was done, I put on my Coors Light bathing suit and picked up all the cash—hundred-dollar bills and fifty-dollar bills. The DJ came on and said, "Hey, wasn't that a great show. If you got a poster from Alexa, she'll sign it for you. Come find her at the main bar."

Then I went back to the change room and put my same stage costume on. I wanted to make sure people in the crowd recognized me, especially the champagne room crowd. Then I went back out to the bar. Two seconds after I got to the bar, the bouncer tapped me on the shoulder and said, "You're requested in the VIP area."

Keeping an eye out for Annika, who was up next on the main stage, I headed to the VIP area. The bouncer led me to the table that had requested my company. I sat down and introduced myself and started putting together how the champagne room worked. The table was a group of high-level Nestlé salesmen who were entertaining clients. At first, I really didn't even know what to say. If this were a Hells Angels scene, I would have felt more comfortable. Thankfully, the salesmen started talking.

"We really enjoyed your show, Alexa," one of the men said. "You can really dance. Were you professionally trained?"

That opened me up a little—I told them about all my years in dance. They loved that. But they didn't ask me to dance.

Annika showed up in the champagne room after her stage performance. I winked at her from across the room. She was a gorgeous, leggy Polish girl, blonde with big breasts, laughing and throwing her head back like Marilyn Monroe. I watched Annika, who danced song after song, from across the room and started to worry about how much money I was making. It looked like she was raking it in. Because I wasn't dancing, I had no idea how much money I'd make, if any.

I stayed at that table all night talking to two of the businessmen who really liked just talking to me. They didn't ask me to dance any further. They just wanted to talk to me about my life out west on the farm and the work I'd done in the oil industry. They seemed to think it was cute that this stripper girl had smart things to say. And it seemed like my tiny breasts weren't really that big of an issue at all, as long as I had swagger. That's what really mattered. At the same time, I knew that large breasts completely disarmed men. You could be a complete and total airhead, but if you had breasts, they would like you anyway. And they would tip you. I was worried because most men didn't tip for clever conversation.

Later, back in our room, Annika was thrilled. She made over $3,000. I was satisfied too—making $2,000 for sitting around and talking by the grace of those salesmen tipping me. We both laughed at the crazy world we were living in and how different it was from back home. There were no more agents, no more Carl's or Eddie's and we gleed at cutting out the useless middle-man structure of back home agent-scabs. We could work directly with clubs and club owners in the east of Canada.

"I like it here," Annika said. "I'm never going back west. This is for me." She really felt like she found a home in Toronto. Even after a couple days, she talked about enrolling in the University of Toronto. She was twenty-four and already conscious of the fact that her looks wouldn't last forever. She loved the multicultural feel of the city and could see herself putting down roots in Ontario. Although going back to school and putting down roots weren't totally out of the question for me sometime in the future, I wasn't that sure yet. The maverick lifestyle still pulled at me. And I wasn't even sure Whiskey's was going to work for me. I made my money dancing, performing on stage. Sitting at a table, talking to men, hoping they'd tip seemed less reliable and unappealing to me.

When I told Annika that I was worried about the champagne room, she said, "Honestly, Carmen, all of that would change if you had breasts."

When you had breasts, you didn't have to dance that hard. You didn't have to talk to anybody. It was just easier to make money. To do this job. That's when I decided it was time to call the doctor. I'd been collecting names, researching, and letting the idea roll around for long enough. The next day, I phoned Dr. Waslen in Calgary and made an appointment for a consultation.

§

When Ryan got my message from his boss, he called me on my cell phone, furious. "How could you cross all those provinces without even talking to me about it?"

All I could do was chuckle. He was gone all the time, out of reach; what did he expect? Did he think I'd be a good little wifey girlfriend and wait for him at home? I had the right to roam free. Thanks.

Granted, maybe I was a little more maverick than any other girlfriend he'd ever had. He'd never been with a dancer, and I wasn't a stripper when we met and started dating. He made it very clear that what I was doing was too much for him. But at this point, I didn't even really care. I had had an amazing time with Tom, who saw me for who I was and was fine with it. I knew it was possible to find a confident man. I was living life. I wouldn't be single for long, if I wanted. Dating, in general, was never on my mind.

"If that's the way you want it, that's the way you want it. No problem," I said. I told him that I'd been in Calgary for a few days, staying with Kelly and seeing the plastic surgeon. "If you have time off, you can drive down and we can say good-bye in person."

"I'll have to think about it," he said, ending the call. But I didn't care if he said yes or no. I was more excited to meet with Kelly, have a great visit with her, and see Dr. Waslen to get the implant process started.

And then, as soon as Ryan was out of my life, as if by some cosmic event, *Tom called.* I had been living like I would never hear from Tom again. He had become a beautiful fantasy that played in my mind and had no chance of materializing. And that fantasy played on a continuous loop, especially on 911 night at Whiskey's. Tom wasn't exactly a cop. He was part of major investigative units that attempted to thwart multimillion-dollar drug deals from entering the United States. That was pretty badass in my opinion. Cops didn't exactly have the best reputation in some of my circles. But I really liked Tom; I liked that type of guy. So, when he called me, I was thrilled.

On that first conversation—and several after that—we talked for hours about life in the months since we'd met in South America. When I told him I'd been thinking about him a lot, he said he'd been thinking about me too. In his intoxicating slight Southern drawl, he admitted to having looked Alberta up on the map so he could see where I lived. And my favourite thing I liked about him was that he already knew I was an exotic entertainer. He was fine with it. He saw it for himself in Santa Cruz, Bolivia. He thought it was wild and fun.

"So why didn't you call if you'd been thinking about me?" he asked.

"I was too embarrassed," I giggled. "You're such an accomplished adult, your business card even looks serious and 'official' and I felt like a dumb kid. I wouldn't know what to say."

He didn't think I was a dumb kid, and we started talking almost every day. He thought I was intriguing and refreshing. I told him about Toronto and my upcoming trip to Calgary and how I was thinking about getting my breasts done. At this point, I still felt like the only reason I was doing it was to make more money.

"What do you think?" I tested him. "Should I get breast implants? I don't really feel like personally that I want to. I like my body the way it is."

"I like your body the way it is too," he said. "You're absolutely stunning and beautiful. Not every man likes big breasts. Men tend to be either T or A guys. I'm more of an A guy and you've got a really great A. I think you're wonderful just the way you are."

I appreciated that about him. He didn't seem to be like all the dumb meathead boys and men that just went gaga over a fake pair of breasts. Still, I thought of exotic entertainment as my "so far" career. And I needed to win at my career. I needed to make the kind of money Annika was making. If that was one surgery away, I decided to go for it.

§

The next week, I hopped on my flight from Toronto Pearson Airport—the largest airport in Canada—and flew to Calgary. The only place I'd ever flown to was Santa Cruz, so this experience gleamed in comparison to riding on the twin engine cargo plane from Panama to Bolivia. The airport was so big it was hard to navigate. I thought I was in the right terminal, then almost missed my plane when I found out I wasn't anywhere near where I was supposed to be. At nineteen, everything seemed so new and hard to figure out on your own. But I made it back to Calgary and took a cab from the small Calgary Airport to Kelly's apartment.

She was still doing her nine-to-five at the natural gas company, still with the same boyfriend, Shane. And she loved my stories about all my adventures since I'd seen her last. She listened with her mouth hanging open.

"You're so lucky to be having these experiences," she said.

Although I was having fun, I also felt like I was risking my family, even though the cat was out of the bag. Everyone knew what I did; at least now I was doing it far away in Ontario. Kelly's family seemed to be much cooler than mine. They never had a problem with her working at Fort Kent Bar, when my family couldn't even handle the fact that I was waitressing there.

"Kelly, you have beautiful natural breasts," I said. "If you want to try it, you don't have to spend a dime. I'll give you some costumes and we can do this together."

She laughed at the thought. She couldn't possibly, she said. She and Shane were getting more serious, and it seemed, to me, like he was a little controlling. When he came home from work, he was grumpy and hard to get to know. And probably because guys like him don't like girls like me. I was a confident, take-no-prisoners Virgo, and Kelly was an ethereal, floating-on-air Libra. She thought he was amazing and let him run the show. But Shane didn't blow my hair back. And I think maybe he could kind of sense that. He got very nervous when I was around Kelly, like I was a bad influence. And maybe I was. For normie women, there was risk of producing over-confidence if you spent a half-day in my presence. But I would never wish sleeping on a disgusting floor in Grimshaw on any of my friends.

The next day, Kelly joined me for my appointment with Dr. Waslen, the plastic surgeon in Calgary who was known to do the best boob jobs in Western Canada. He was also the most expensive. In 1999, he charged $15,000, easily two times the usual amount, because he was the only doctor using a method that minimized scaring. Instead of cutting under the breast and leaving the long traditional scars, he made a discreet opening along the edge of the nipple and used that to cut the pectoral muscle and create the pocket underneath to slip the saline implant in. Then he filled the implant up through a small hose, closed the valve off, and sealed it. For most women, scaring wasn't a big deal because it would be hidden by a bikini. But my job was to be naked in public, and I didn't want any visible scars.

"I want extra-large breasts," I told the doctor, sitting in a crinkly paper gown in his exam room. "Not just a little bump up; I want a significant increase without looking like a porn star."

He looked at my body and fitted me with a few different sizes. Then he suggested going with a 590 cc saline implant.

"Isn't that a little too big on my tiny body?"

"Not necessarily. You have broad shoulders," he said. "If I put 375 or 425 cc implants in you, which is standard, they're going to look smaller on you."

"I do want them to be bigger than normal."

"Well," Dr. Waslen said, "your body can handle it." That was good enough for me. Most girls complained of Dr. Waslen's poor bedside manner. Indeed, he was gruff but proficient and serious. I liked that about him. I was about to have my first ever surgery and I didn't need my doctor to be *pals* with me. I needed him to make me look good and not kill me on his table. He was perfect, I surmised.

I paid the deposit and booked the next available appointment, which was six weeks away. Kelly agreed to help me home from the surgery and to let me recover at her place for a few days. Then I flew back to Toronto to wait.

Back at work, without big breasts to rely on, I got creative. I went back to my 4-H Beef Club public speaking days and dropped all shyness. I needed to be a performer all night long, whether on stage or with tableside chit chats. Annika and I had already outfitted ourselves in the Whiskey A Go-Go style, with slinky silky gowns. I accessorized with sequins, which was part of my signature style. Underneath my gown, I wore sparkly bikinis. I cut my hair in a shoulder-length bob to show off my shoulders. And I got my lips done. Annika and I both went to a surgeon in Toronto for Artecoll injections. In the late '90s, the trend was still lining your lips with a dark liner and filling them in with a clear gloss. After the fill, our lips looked amazing. Men just sat and stared at my mouth, watching me talk.

§

Not long after we started talking on the phone, Tom asked me to come visit him in Florida. The flight from Toronto to Fort Lauderdale, where he lived, was only two hours, and he enticed me with the promise of palm trees and beaches and hot Miami nights. So I bought the ticket with plans for a Thursday to Tuesday stay. I didn't want to commit to a full week because who knew what would happen when I got there.

When my plane landed, I de-boarded and Tom was waiting for me on the jet bridge right outside the plane door! He spoke to the attendant and pilot, flashed his US Customs badge, took my bag and my hand, and led me into the airport. I've never seen that type of VIP curbside service in my life. And I think he was trying to impress me with his job perks.

"Did you fill out your customs card on the plane?"

"Yeah, I did. It's right here." I gave him my paperwork, and he ushered me through the customs clearance. He flashed his badge around and got me through without waiting in line. But he didn't let me skip it altogether—he seemed careful not to abuse any powers and made sure all the rules were followed. This fascinated me because it was so different. A Hells Angel—a different kind of authoritative man—sees a rule and largely disregards it completely. But Tom, who had all this authority, all this capacity, was a stickler for the rules.

"Wow," I said when we were through. "That's pretty amazing, Tom. You didn't have to do that."

"I know that you've never landed in the United States before," he said, carrying my luggage. "Welcome to the USA."

I had butterflies in my stomach, absolutely smitten with him. I felt the same way I did when we were walking the streets of Santa Cruz, him taking care of me. A gentleman who wasn't afraid of me or my lifestyle, who didn't think I was going to hell in a handbasket like my family and Ryan. Tom was different from everyone else. He saw me for who I was and he liked it. To me, nothing could feel more amazing.

Florida was like a tropical paradise with heavy heat, sunshine, and palm trees swaying in the ocean breeze. The upscale Miami and Fort Lauderdale area felt so American. We found Tom's new Camaro parked in the airport lot and sped to his house.

"I'm going to introduce you to my friends tonight," he said as he drove. "We're going to dinner at this kind of casual oceanside kind of place."

"Okay," I said, thrilled that he wasn't afraid to introduce me to his friends.

Tom lived in a small house with a low clay tile roof and lush tropical landscaping in a giant subdivision in Broward County. Inside, he showed me around the basic kitchen and sparsely bachelor-decorated living area, making sure to mention the guest bedroom. There was no way I was sleeping in the guest bedroom. I'd already had an amazing sexual experience with him in Santa Cruz, I couldn't imagine sleeping anywhere but with him.

Las Olas Beach, where Tom and his friends loved to hang out, was the closest beach to his house in Broward County. On our way to dinner, I couldn't tell where one city ended and another began. Fort Lauderdale blended into Miami and it felt like the city landscape never ended. At the restaurant, I met his best friend, Knoll, and several other work friends. They all got such a kick out of Tom's young Canadian girl, and they all spoke with a drawl that I couldn't get enough of.

Over and over, we kept asking each other to repeat what we'd just said just so we could hear it again. They almost died when I said, "I can't wait to see what's going on and get out and about." To them, "about" sounded like "a boo-t." And I too was giving it back to them with their slow drawls. The best part was that they seemed to already know a lot about me, adding some legitimacy to everything Tom had told me. It could have been bullshit; I didn't exactly trust men, and I didn't know him all that well. But they said he couldn't seem to stop talking about me, which was really nice of them to say, and it was nice to hear.

This was around the time when the United States and Cuba were fighting over the refugee boy Elian Gonzalez. He and his mother had been coming to America by boat to find her sister, who was already living in Florida. But the mother didn't survive the trip. The sister in the US and the father, who was back in Cuba, were fighting over where the boy should stay. Until I came to Florida, I'd never heard about this controversy, and I was excited to learn about such a dramatic cultural event as it unfolded. We even had to take a different route to avoid the protesters, who had been blocking roads in the fight to keep the little boy in the United States. I had no idea there was such a large Cuban population in southern Florida. I was a twenty-year-old from Canada—I didn't know anything about anything. But Tom never made me feel stupid for asking a million questions. A lot of men liked that; it makes them feel needed. I learned this lesson from many, many tableside chats with men from all walks of life. He didn't find it annoying. He found it attractive, wildly attractive. And he told me he loved my never-ending curiosity.

When I asked Tom about his work, he couldn't tell me much. But I did notice that often, when his cell phone rang, he had to slip away to take the call. He did tell me that he managed lots of informants, who he'd built relationships with and was acquiring information to help with investigations. He had a master's degree in criminology and was rising up the ranks in administration with the United States Customs Agency quite nicely. We laughed at the very large differences in the types of "agencies" that we both respectively worked with. And he told me that he enjoyed being on the *tactical team*. He carried a concealed gun and his badge almost all the time, and he even had an M16 under his bed. When he asked if I wanted to see it, I said no thanks.

Later that weekend we drove a few hours north to Ocala, where he was born and raised and his parents, Martha and Lamont, still lived in his childhood town. The name Lamont sounded so southern I thought of sweet tea and pecan pie and debutantes dressed in ball gowns. What kind of girl doesn't fall in love with that sort of imagery? And Tom spoke highly of his family, which I liked. I always loved the idea of family, even though I never had quite that normal family life myself. The drive up through central Florida revealed a whole different landscape from the bumping Miami night life. Here, horse farms, gator tours, and small towns spread out in all directions. We stopped at a roadside eatery called the Cracker Barrel, which was apparently a Southern American experience that would legitimize my whole trip to the deep south USA.

"You have to try the grits," Tom said. "They're amazing."

"What are grits?"

"You'll see."

The restaurant had a store filled with trinkets and antiques to look at while we waited for a table, and Tom explained that Cracker Barrels are all over the States. Everybody loves Cracker Barrel for authentic Southern food, he said.

At the table, after ordering our grits, I started telling him about what we eat in Canada, like perogies, kutya, meat pies, sugar pies, sucre a la crème, and all the French and Ukrainian cultural dishes that I knew by heart. Then I asked him, "What other foods are weird down here?"

"Well, grits is definitely a big one," he said. They also ate *okra* and *collard greens* and all the dishes I could get on the Cracker Barrel menu.

When the grits came, they looked like porridge or cream of wheat, which made me want to put brown sugar and milk on top of it.

"You could do that," he said. "Some people put jam in it to make it sweet. But most people eat it with butter or hot sauce."

"I think I'll go for the jam instead," I said, preferring sweet things.

I cracked open the jam and started rubbing it over my grits, when a little old lady who happened to be walking by the table stopped and said, "Only Yankees put jam in their grits."

Then she turned away, mortified, and kept walking. I didn't know what to think.

"What just happened? What is she talking aboot? I thought all Americans were Yankees."

Tom laughed and explained the Mason-Dixon Line and the Civil War. I had learned a little American history in social studies classes, but really nothing to the extent that Tom explained. And even though the country had united, some cultural divisions still existed, alive and well. This opened up a conversation about his values and what motivated him to get into law enforcement. And everything sounded so altruistic and had a stand-up quality, feverishly against anything to do with racism. He said more than anything, he valued honesty.

"I never tell a lie," he said. "I was born and raised to never tell a lie no matter how hard the truth is to say. The truth is your salvation."

Of course, this sounded great, but it also made me feel a little like I was lying by omission. I'd been drinking the whole time I was in Florida in every bar and restaurant we went to, but I was still considered underage in the States. Tom hadn't asked my age, and I hadn't told. And I didn't dare tell him I had friends in the Hells Angels. But even if I wasn't being my whole self, I liked the person I was when I was with Tom. I liked that I could tell him about how disappointed my family was in me, without him judging me. I liked that I could be a regular person. A regular girlfriend.

Martha and Lamont were lovely, welcoming people, just like Tom. We sat around and played card games and Trivial Pursuit. Question after question, I had no idea. I had no answers. I felt like a moron compared to these three older people who'd gone to university. The only question I could answer was what colour do potatoes turn when they're rotten and become poisonous?

"Oh, I know this one," I said. "Green."

They all laughed because they didn't know that. Although I was intimidated, I also felt like they at least found me funny and charming. Tom had warned me that his parents would be fine to let us sleep in the same room at their house, but we ended up staying in the family cabin on wooded property a short drive from their house. After all, Tom was thirty years old.

When I suggested taking a walk through the woods to explore that night, Tom said that would be a bad idea unless I had a pair of snake boots.

"What do you mean?"

"There are venomous snakes all over the place here. So, just to go for a walk in the woods at night is not the best idea. You should have the proper gear on."

I was surprised again. Up in Canada, we had other terrors in our woods. Wolverines, bears, moose—but nothing venomous. Florida was so wild.

The next morning, we made our way back from Ocala, down to Fort Lauderdale, back to Tom's place. On my last night there, Tom joined me outside while I smoked. He didn't smoke cigarettes and went for a ten-mile run every morning. But he did like cigars and lit one up.

"Oooh, is that Cuban?" I asked, knowing those are regarded as the best.

"No," he said. "I would never smoke a Cuban cigar in the United States."

"Why not?"

Tom explained the whole Cuban embargo to me, about how anything Cuban was illegal and Americans couldn't travel there. I laughed at this because Canadians travelled to Cuba all the time. It was a popular winter destination, just like Mexico.

"Not for Americans," he said, ripe smoke from his Arturo Fuente swirling around him. "I've been to Cuba for work, but only for work. I can't go there as an American citizen and then enjoy the beaches like you guys can from Canada."

As he told me all this, I thought: Who is this guy? He was always on the moral high ground, always ethical. He was a walking definition of integrity. Even when nobody was looking, he was doing the right thing. And I started remembering every time I'd smoked weed, every time I did cocaine, every lie I'd ever told. My entire career had been pretty sordid, on the rough side of life. Ryan was my somewhat boyfriend when I'd slept with Tom the first time in South America. I wasn't the same kind of person as Tom, but I felt inspired by him. He made me want to be a better person.

Then I asked him, flat out, "Are you sure you're okay with me being an exotic entertainer? Because most men I've met aren't okay with it at all. It intimidates them."

"No, it's fine." He puffed on his cigar and looked at me. "You're honest about it, it's what you do. I don't have a family. I'm not a single dad or anything like that. I want to have a good time with life too. I just really like spending time with you and I hope you like spending time with me."

To myself I thought, Oh my God, boy, do I ever.

§

By the time I got back to Canada, Annika was already tired of the hustle and bustle in Toronto and talking about going down to Niagara Falls.

"Toronto's too big," she said. "Niagara's only a two-hour drive, and there are some nice small towns along the way. And girls are making way more money at the Twilight in Niagara Falls than they are at Whiskey A Go-Go."

We were always on to the next "best place" it seemed, and I loved it. With nothing to lose, I agreed to check it out. We left on a Friday afternoon and drove down the Queen Elizabeth Way, the major highway down to the southern border and the town of Niagara Falls. On the way we passed orchards and places like Hamilton, Canada's Steel City, and St. Catharines, little towns I'd heard of but never seen. The summer air felt warm, and it was an absolutely beautiful part of Canada, a different climate from up north. When we arrived, we got a hotel room in Niagara Falls and went to the Twilight Club that night.

The Twilight on Friday night felt like pandemonium, crowded, drunk, and blaring music. A naked girl was walking on her hands around the parameter of the low stage, driving the patrons wild. Then she popped back up on her legs and performed one of the most amazing acrobatic pole routines I'd ever seen. Her name was Tessa, and money poured down on her. Then patrons started lying down on the stage with ten-dollar bills on their faces. Tessa came up and gave them a little close-up booby show, then picked up the bills off their faces with her breasts, the original "motor boat" I'm sure. I had never seen anything like it. There were bouncers all over the place to make sure the patrons kept their hands tucked behind their backs and to themselves.

That's when I noticed that not only was it raining down tips, it was raining down *American greenbacks*. Even though we were in Canada, the Americans came across the border to go to the club where the drinking age was nineteen instead of twenty-one and to enjoy the full-monty shows. At the time, the Canadian currency was about sixty-six cents on the American dollar. Just with the different currency, these girls were making more money than we could make in any other place.

Around the main stage, the club had several smaller platforms where girls were dancing. The club was wild and fresh. And we wanted to work there. We found the club manager, who explained that our Toronto licenses wouldn't work because Niagara Falls had its own licensing system.

"But you guys look great," he said. "I'll call up Whiskey A Go-Go and make sure you're as good as you say you are. And if you get your licenses and everything checks out, you can start tomorrow night."

Annika and I went back to our hotel, and first thing in the morning, we went to get our licenses and called our manager, Dave, at Whiskey's to see if he'd call and put in a good word for us at the Twilight. And that night we started working and making a ton of US money in Niagara Falls.

"I'm tired of hotel rooms," Annika said after we'd been there a few nights. "Let's get an apartment."

"That sounds like a great big commitment," I hesitated. I needed a permanent address to give Dr. Waslen, but I didn't want to sign a lease. "Can I just live with you? I'll help pay bills, but I want to be able to roll with the wind and go wherever I want, whenever I want."

This was fine with her, so she found a place. I gave her some money, and then flew to Calgary for my surgery.

§

Everything I knew about having implant surgery, I learned in the dressing rooms. Make sure you keep your bandages tight for the first month because that will help with the swelling. They'll look outrageously huge at first, but that's just swelling. You won't be able to sleep on your stomach. They'll look great in about a month.

Even after talking to every girl I met with breast implants about their experiences, my anxiety level before the surgery swelled. I had never had surgery or been put under anesthesia. I'd never even broken a bone. The doctor explained all the risks of anesthesia, that one in a million people die because they're allergic to it.

"Are you allergic to anesthetic?" the doctor asked.

"I don't know. I've never had it before." It terrified me that I didn't know and could possibly die from an allergic reaction. Kelly held my hand the whole, entire time; being the best, most supportive friend I could ever have. In those last moments before they took me in, I joked about how lucky she was to have great breasts naturally without going through all of this. And when it was time for the procedure, she said she'd be there when I was done.

Surgery seemed like I'd closed my eyes for a moment, then opened them to find it was all over. But it felt like a train had parked on my chest, and I itched all over because, it turned out, I did have a mild allergic reaction to the anesthetic. My chest was wrapped so tight that I couldn't see much, but I did seem to have more down there. They'd given me 577 ccs of saline in each breast, which brought me up to a full double D, but I couldn't tell in my bandages. When I was fully awake and cleared to go, Kelly eased me into the car and drove me back to her apartment.

Every bump in the road sent a shock of pain through me. I had to keep my elbows tucked in at my sides because extending my arms any further felt excruciatingly painful, which the doctor said was common because they'd cut, stretched, and sewn back together my pectoral muscles. And they'd given me Benadryl for my allergic reaction, but my skin still itched so bad I tore my skin scratching with my fingernails. After getting me settled in her apartment, Kelly went to the store for a stiff bristle hairbrush that I used to scratch the itch without ripping apart my skin. I could scratch and scratch away.

The next morning, Shane and Kelly left early in the morning for work. Around nine I got up and made my way to the kitchen, my elbows still tucked in like I had T-rex arms. Moving them felt like my muscles were ripping, and the squishy implants felt so strange. I could actually feel them inside. Kelly had left the cereal and milk at a reachable level for me, but even the carton of milk was too heavy to lift and pour. It was awful.

Later that night, Kelly helped me take a bath and change some of the bandages. Slowly, she unwound the covering and revealed my breasts for the first time, bruised and battered. When I saw them, I broke down and cried.

"Kelly," I sobbed. "What have I done to my body?"

My breasts were a black and blue swollen mess. My nipples were bandaged and bruised. And I felt sad for what I had done to myself. My emotions were running higher than normal because of my pain medicine, and I cried and cried while Kelly tried to comfort me.

"You know, Carmen, this is just the swelling," she said. "They said it would be like this for a while. But every day you're going to feel a little better. You wanted this, don't forget about that. And go back to the reason why you did this in the first place."

She was right, but I felt more depressed than I ever had in my life. I even felt some religious regret in my delirium. My body was my temple, and look what I'd done to it. But every day I felt a little better. My arms still ached when it was time to fly back to Ontario, so Annika met me at the Toronto Pearson airport and carried my bags for me. Then, back at our apartment, she got me set up with a mountain of pillows in the clawfoot tub of our new bathroom. I couldn't lie down flat because it was too painful, but the tub kept me propped up at the perfect angle. I slept in that tub for a week. And before long I could tell that I was going to make it. Of course, I was going to be okay.

13

CROSSING BORDERS

*"I had always hoped that this land might become a safe
and agreeable asylum to the virtuous and persecuted part
of mankind, to whatever nation they might belong."*
—George Washington

BACK IN NIAGARA FALLS, WITH six weeks of recovery before I could return to work, life slowed down. I played tourist and got to know Niagara Falls, which I never really had time for before because I always wanted to work. I went to the Madame Tussauds Wax Museum, packed picnics, and explored different vantage points for viewing the falls. The rumbling vibration and hum of the water felt soothing and healing. I even treated myself to lunch at the revolving restaurant, where every hour it made a complete rotation, putting the whole city and falls on view from the tables. I'd sit with my book and journal and just watch it all pass by the window. I liked being alone.

While I didn't like being out of the game and not making money, this was the first break I'd taken since starting down the exotic entertainment path. At our apartment, I had a blow-up air mattress with sheets and comforters and two pillows and my clothes, living out of a suitcase in my room. I didn't care about getting a bed or furniture or any of that. I just wanted to sleep and get back to the club. Even in Alberta, I'd never really taken time off. So now that I was forced to do it, I embraced it.

Annika started working less during this time too. She checked out a college in St. Catharines and talked about going back to school and working with children in some capacity. And while I was proud of her, I really couldn't relate. I thought about going back to school and upgrading, but it just didn't feel like the right time. All I wanted to do was make money.

Although I couldn't work, I did haunt the club, talking to my DJ friends and girlfriends and hanging out in the dressing rooms. Not only did the Twilight draw tourists from America, but the Buffalo Bills often came across the border to hang out there. Athletes love exotic entertainers. They love that they can party and have a wild time in the clubs with them. Strippers were like a secret society, so they weren't out selling pictures. And taking pictures in clubs was a big no-no anyway. So athletes would come in with their entourages and spend thousands.

Two Middle Eastern brothers owned the Twilight, and they were all business. Every night, they stood at the corner of the club and watched the floor and made sure that everything was okay in the VIP sections, and no patrons were getting too crazy or trying to touch the girls in inappropriate ways. And they had a lot of bouncers on staff. So, it was a very safe place to work, we found. But like many clubs, an undercurrent of shadiness ran right through the place.

One day, three Eastern European, blonde, *very young* girls appeared in the change room. They looked about seventeen on a good day—too young to be working in a club in Niagara Falls, where you had to be at least nineteen. None of them spoke much English. The dressing room at Twilight was large enough for all forty of the regular girls to have her own station. It was like choosing a spot on the school bus, once you sat down, that was your spot. One of the Eastern European girls—a leggy, gorgeous girl named Renata—got the spot next to my station. And she was friendly, eager to learn English, and looking for friends. Although she didn't know much more than a few English keywords, like water and hi, she did know a little French. Renata was always chatty. And they wanted to know all about my scarless implant job. I wasn't a "joiner" with new girls and would typically scoff at her friendliness. But there was something extra sweet about her. When I told them I had to fly to Alberta to get this kind of surgery, they lost interest, saying they'd never be able to do that. None of these three girls had any dance experience, and they hung around like club hustlers, focusing on their looks because they couldn't really talk to the patrons.

Then I noticed that every night big, sunglasses-wearing, bodyguard-looking guys came to pick them up. The more I watched them, coming and going, having hush-hush conversations with the club owners, I started to wonder if these girls had been *trafficked into this work*. Any time I asked Renata how she ended up in Canada, she shut down the conversation and changed the subject. It was like equal parts shame, equal part fear to talk about it. I was really young myself and didn't know much about it, but I gave Renata my phone number and address, just in case she needed it. She often looked at me like she wanted to tell me something, but she never did.

During this time, I also got to know Tessa, the girl who walked on her hands during her stage performances. Her performances were like Cirque du Soleil shows, and she could do handstands on the small tableside stages in the VIP rooms, which made her very popular. Her husband, who often brought her food at work, was an Indigenous man. They were older than me—Tessa was probably thirty and her husband looked closer to forty. He was always "in-between" jobs and she obviously paid all the bills. He seemed like the kind of man who hid his controlling nature behind seemingly kind gestures, like lunch on a long day at work. And Tessa worked hard. She'd be icing her joints, barely able to walk, by the end of the night. Even though I wasn't sure about him, I liked Tessa. She was blonde-haired and blue-eyed, always wrapping and unwrapping some injury. She'd been performing like that for years. And while I sat and talked with her, she told me about how some of her friends were working in clubs down in Texas.

"It's amazing there," she said. "The money is completely American currency, so we're going down to meet some of my friends and check it out."

While she was telling me all of this, Texas started to sound like such a great idea, even better than the Twilight. And I couldn't stop myself from thinking about how much closer Texas would be to Tom. So I really felt like I needed to work on my friendship with Tessa, and make sure that she liked me so she'd come back and tell me the inside scoop on working in Texas.

Tom and I continued to talk on the phone regularly, and he asked a million questions about my new breasts. I was nervous and excited to show him. He'd already told me that he liked the way I looked before and didn't care how big my breasts were. I flew down to Fort Lauderdale to spend a few weeks with him while I couldn't work, and as soon as he saw me, I could tell from the look on his face that he was excited. The bruising had faded to yellow and purple shadows by then, and the doctor encouraged me to wear a tight-fitting sports bra with a front closure, but the heavy-duty tension bandages were gone. And as long as I wasn't moving around too much, I was fine.

The first night Tom saw them, it was an extremely elevated sexual experience for him. I started to feel like I was excited about that. I wanted to please Tom. I wanted him to like me. I wanted him to like me a lot. I had always thought of the breast implants as a tool to make more money, and I didn't realize that my personal life and relationship could change as well. So his excitement about my breasts was an extra bonus, and he showed me off to all his friends. He told me how much he missed me, and it seemed like we were falling in love.

We bought roller blades and skated around the beaches. And he took me to a Miami Dolphins game so I could learn about American football. I loved American football explained to me and soon picked my favourite quarterback—Brett Favre—after deciding that Dan Marino was getting too old to bring a Lombardi trophy home to Florida. It felt great to be back in Florida. I fell in love with the Cuban food—the plantains, and rice and beans. I loved the pastel-coloured houses and the Spanish-inspired architecture. At night, I could go out dressed in the skimpiest dresses with my platform heels and no bra on my fresh, firm breasts. They were so tight and big that they didn't move or bounce at all. And we'd drink until four or five in the morning. I thought Canadian boys drank a lot, but Tom and his cop friends drank a lot too.

Most of the time it was Tom and me and a few of his work friends. They sometimes brought a girl along, but they were plain, girl-next-door types who didn't know what to think of me. I was a Canadian girl with big boobs who dressed like it was night in Miami all the time. Forming relationships with normal women was difficult when I looked like that. They were always skeptical that I would steal their man, even though I wasn't even remotely interested in doing that. But I started to see what happens when you change your outer shell. It changed the way men looked at me, and it changed the way women looked at me. Sometimes I liked it, but other times I didn't know if I liked it at all.

On the weekend, Tom and I were invited to hang out with his friend Knoll and his fiancé, Julie. Tom had told me all about Julie and her house on the water and her Hatteras yacht, so I was anxious to meet her and spend more time with Tom's closest friends. So, we drove to her house in Miami, a beautiful place on a canal that led to the ocean. All her neighbours, up and down the water, had boats docked in the back. It was an amazing place to live, and Tom told me he was saving his money to buy even a shack on the water so he could have a boat too.

Julie was warm and beautiful, with very short, soft blonde hair and a deep tan. She worked as a registered nurse and scuba instructor and had a two-year-old daughter named Katie, who didn't seem to be around. The four of us had a little barbecue and then went out on the mini-yacht. The boat, gleaming in the setting sunlight, had a tall fishing tower and living quarters underneath. As we motored down the canal, past waterfront house after waterfront house, I started to see what Miami life was really like and why Tom loved it so much. They all worked for the weekends, when they could get out on the water, scuba dive and fish for mahi-mahi and other ocean treasures. Knoll, Julie, and Tom were all scuba certified, and if they could be on the water, they were on the water.

Later that night I said to Tom, "Julie seems pretty wealthy for a nurse. What's her backstory?"

"Yeah," he said. "She's Knoll's sugar mama." This was apparently the inside joke among his friends. Julie's husband had died suddenly and she was left with a windfall of money that she was forbidden to speak about. However, I gleaned that she had just given birth to their daughter when this occurred.

During the week, Tom went to work and I hung around his place or went to the gym where I used the stair-climber or treadmill and slowly worked on regaining my full mobility. He let me use his five-speed Camaro and was impressed that I knew how to drive a standard transmission. Then we went out to eat supper in the evenings. And whenever I could persuade Tom to put the rollerblades on and go for an evening stroll down the beaches, we would do that as well. We went fishing on different docks around the area, and Tom told me all about the different types of sea life and how much he loved scuba diving. He had all his own equipment and went as often as possible. He showed me pictures of the lobsters he caught on diving trips. The more he talked about it, the more interested I was in trying it, even though I could encounter a shark. Florida waters had plenty of tiger sharks, nurse sharks, bull sharks, but also barracuda, fire coral, sting rays, and other potentially dangerous creatures.

"What about great whites?" I asked. As a land-locked Canadian, nothing scared me more than sharks.

Tom laughed and said he'd never encountered a great white. But there were plenty of other things to watch out for. Tom said they carried bang sticks in case they encountered any aggressive sea animals. The water on the Atlantic side of Florida was deeper and clearer than the water on the Gulf side, so the water was warmer and murkier, a completely different diving experience. He explained how all the equipment worked and how to get certified. He talked about it so much that I said I wanted to try it too. I was there for a few weeks and had plenty of time while he was at work to take the certification course. I could easily rent everything I needed, and then we could pull up to the beach and go diving out of his trunk or go out with Knoll and Julie. And it was lobster season.

The very next day he took me to the scuba school where he'd been trained. Tom was a PADI Advanced Open Water Diver, which meant he could do nighttime dives and use different blends of oxygen and nitrogen in his tanks for deeper dives. I could get an open water certification, which was level one with PADI, in a few classes. So I committed to learning, and when Tom went to work, I went to scuba class.

We started off in pools, learning how to manage our equipment and feel comfortable under water. We practiced different scenarios, like having your mask ripped off, feeling around for it with our respirators on, getting the mask back on, and blowing air up through it to clear out the water. We had to learn how not to panic. New divers who aren't as comfortable under water tend to suck up all their tank-air because they're breathing heavy. Learning how to relax and breathe under water not only conserved the air supply, it allowed you to look around and fully experience the dive. It was scary at first, but slipping under the water in the pool felt lovely. And every day it got a little easier.

At the end of the class, we had to complete three dives with the instructor, Piper. My classmates and instructor took a boat out to a shipwreck in the Atlantic Ocean for our open water dives. Piper tied a tagline that we used to descend down forty feet to the site. As a group, we'd congregate around the tag line so she could count us and keep track of us. We could hang out by the tag line, or if we felt comfortable, we could explore the wreck. At this point, I'd taken the class, I knew my equipment, I knew my hand signals, and so into the water I went.

The first ten feet or so, the water was cloudy and I couldn't see beyond a few feet in front of me. Then we descended into a cold, expansive, blur of deep blue. I started to panic a little bit, thinking there could literally be great white sharks circling around me and I wouldn't even know it. I was in their habitat. I couldn't see past two feet in front of me.

I looked at my oxygen gauge and saw my supply dwindling fast and knew I needed to calm down. Piper swam up to me and used hand signals to ask if I was okay.

I nodded yes and gave the okay signal, but I showed her my oxygen, which was already over a quarter of the way down.

She signaled again, "Are you okay?"

I nodded again, confirming that I didn't want to quit, and consciously tried to slow my breathing. We descended together, and she stuck close to me for the rest of the dive. When we reached the bottom, a man-made shipwreck spread out across the sand. The government sunk the boat there to promote reef building activity and make new habitats for all the types of fish that would inhabit coral reefs. The hull was covered in barnacles, and I saw pufferfish and needlefish. And lurking all around were barracuda. We were surrounded by aggressive fish, and all I could think about was one swooping in and taking a bite of me.

Freaking out about the barracuda didn't help my oxygen supply. I signaled to Piper that I was low on air and needed to go back up, and she helped me with the controlled ascent. We had to stop and take a break about halfway up to avoid decompression sickness, which can happen if you rise to the surface too fast. When we emerged, I ripped off my mask and regulator and was smiling from ear to ear.

"Are you okay?" Piper asked. "You were sucking up so much oxygen. Were you panicking?"

"Yes, I was totally panicking," I said, treading water. "But it was the most fascinating, wonderful, scary thing. It was so sensory. I loved it." Another scary and thrilling task learned, for me.

Scuba diving was one of the most incredible experiences I'd ever had. After those dives with Piper, I was certified. And Tom was thrilled to hear I had so much fun because now we could dive together.

The following weekend, we went out on Julie's boat to dive and fish for lobsters. After hearing all their diving adventure stories, I was excited to be part of the club. And I was excited about being in Florida with Tom. I had new friends, I was healing and still staying active, and every day I got stronger and could move my arms more. I felt like myself again.

We set out on the boat, the *Katie Bug*, named for Julie's daughter, although her daughter was with her nanny. Julie was a beautiful, young, and wealthy widow, and Knoll played the alpha-male role, driving the boat and taking care of her. He was a proficient sea captain. He was a type-A kind of guy who seemed like he could be a little bit of a control freak cop, while she was more passive and timid. And they seemed to balance each other well and really be in love. But Knoll could have also been taking advantage of his sugar mama. When you're an exotic entertainer, working in all these clubs, you start to see men for what they are. And you can recognize someone being opportunistic because you're opportunistic yourself.

Tom and I secretly joked that Knoll maybe wouldn't really have it so great without Julie and her money. But I never asked Tom how much he made. He seemed to have enough, and never hesitated to pay for dinner. I assumed I had more money than him, but he seemed to have plenty. And he spent it like a gentleman.

We cruised through the canal and out onto the bay. Knoll was the captain and Tom was the first mate. I had new bikinis that the costumers at Twilight made for me, and I was excited to get some sun on my new breasts. The boat had an area on the deck where we could sunbathe, and I was really surprised to find Julie there sunbathing topless. She'd had her breasts done too, but she had the procedure where they cut underneath and moved the nipple to get the implant in. She said getting sun helped the scars fade, and she admired my scarless operation results. So there we were, a couple of big-booby girls on this beautiful boat, cruising around the Florida waters in classic Florida sunshine. All of it was an eat-your-heart-out postcard.

Because hunting and fishing were so big in Canada, I was excited to go lobster fishing with my new scuba license. The water was only about twenty feet deep, so we didn't need to worry about decompression or tag lines. And the water was warmer and not as blue and expansive as it had been out on the Atlantic.

I planned on doing more observing than actual catching, but Tom explained how to find the lobsters hanging out in small pods under rocks and caves under the coral.

"Never put your hand under the rocks because nurse sharks like to hang out under there too," Tom said. Each of us would have a spring-loaded snare stick, which we could use to scare off any sharks and catch the lobsters.

Down we went into the water, and I explored alongside Tom and watched as he used his stick to poke around under rock structures to clear any sharks. He obviously knew what he was doing. When he found lobsters, he positioned his snare and tried to grab them before they swam away backwards and disappeared. When he caught one, he tucked it into a mesh bag hanging from his belt.

Even though I was mostly watching and practicing being under the water, this was my second dive ever in the ocean, and I didn't panic or use up my oxygen like crazy. Being with Tom and seeing how proficient he was, I felt so safe and comfortable. I checked out the wildlife, found a pufferfish that blew up into a ball when I scared it. I was wearing gloves so I reached out and touched the spiky fish, ecstatic to get to interact with nature like this. A few times Tom pointed out fire coral and motioned for me not to touch it, and I marvelled at all the different creatures and experiences from our conversations spread out before me.

When we came up, we had three lobsters and Knoll and Julie had two. We cracked them open and grilled them in the galley of the boat. With the music turned up, we started boozing and chillin' out. Julie and I walked around topless, the hot sun beating down on our bare breasts, just having so many laughs. When the sun started to set, we put on our pretty coverups and ate lobster.

The following weekend was the Columbus Day Regatta, which was a sailboat race and whole weekend of partying on the water around Elliott Key. Again, we met up with Knoll and Julie and took the boat out. It took almost a full day to get all the way across the Florida Keys. But by sunset, we could hear the loud music and some of the biggest boats I've ever seen in my life came into view. Big, beautiful millionaire yachts, and giant catamarans as well as boats of all shapes and sizes, clustered together out on the water. We cruised around until we found their friends and a place to drop anchor, and we started partying.

The friends' boat was like Julie's only much bigger, so we hopped on their little dinghy and joined them on their yacht. The music blasted, and we jumped in and out of the water, swam and partied with some players from the Florida Panthers—a new NHL team in Florida. All girls in sight were completely topless, and everybody was drunk. Late at night, we went back to Julie and Knoll's boat and passed out in the sleeping quarters. When we woke up the next morning, we made breakfast and started boozing again. Lots of people had clothes on, lots of people didn't, even men, just walking around nude on their boats. It was a fun, hedonistic weekend on the water. There were gorgeous bodies and ugly bodies; I loved it all. When the party was over, everyone packed up and chugged back home. This was so different from the farm back in Canada, but so much fun. And I wanted more of this life with Tom.

After having such a great time, I told him about Tessa going to Texas and that I was thinking about joining her, feeling out what he would say about me moving closer. Texas would still be a plane ride away, and I liked having the separation between work life and play. With Tom, I was a regular person in a regular world with a regular boyfriend. At work, I was a savage profiteer. I wanted to spend more time together, but I wasn't ready for my two worlds to meet.

"Hey, you come and go here as you please," Tom said just before I left. "I would love it if you spent more time here."

Then I flew home just days before Hurricane Irene was about to crash on Florida shores. Tanned and healed with a full range of motion, I went back to work in Niagara Falls.

When I got back, Annika was already enrolled in school in St. Catharines. As a student, she was up early studying and going to class, and she no longer appreciated my lifestyle of late nights and all-day sleep. And the hour-long commute each way to school was wearing on her. She worked only two nights a week at the Twilight, so she decided to give up the Niagara Falls apartment and move closer to school. She offered to let me take over the lease, but it was too much apartment for me. Within walking distance from work, I found a one-room bachelor suite for $400 a month—with a living area/kitchen and tiny bathroom—and put my air mattress there. I worked all the time, so I didn't bother getting furniture or a television. I ate my cereal at the counter. And if I wasn't at work, I was reading on my mattress or rollerblading around the city.

As soon as Tessa returned, I beelined right to her and asked, "So, how was Texas?"

"Carmen, it's wonderful," she said. "The clubs in Texas are what they call 'titty bars,' so it's not fully nude. They're just *topless* clubs. Can you believe it?!"

Not being fully nude was a huge step up in decency for people like us, and she said the money was *phenomenal*. Because her husband was Indigenous North American, he could easily get citizenship, making relocation to the US easy for her. They'd already found a place and were packing their moving van. Of course, I wanted in and implored her to call me when they got settled.

"Sure," she said. "We're leaving in four days."

With Annika gone most of the time, and Tessa leaving, I tried to talk with Renata more. I was torn about what to do about her. Should I get to the bottom of her "scene" to see if she needed help? But Renata started retreating away from me. She wasn't nearly as chatty as she used to be, and when I asked her in French how she was doing, she shied away. It was like she didn't want to be rude, but was avoiding me.

One night in the dressing room, I asked her if she'd walk downstairs with me and hit the club. We walked down together, and then she disappeared. And then one day, I came in, and she had moved her station to the far end of the change room, as far away from me as she could get. I got the impression that she wasn't allowed to talk to me. I rarely saw the other two European girls who came to work with her. The whole thing was very bizarre. These bodyguard guys, whoever they were, had these girls in some kind of human trafficking or cultish situation.

When I told Tom about it, he said I'd have to call the police and tell them I suspected she was being trafficked.

"That's probably not going to be the best thing for you if you want to continue to work there," he said. "And it sounds like you're going to Texas anyway."

So I shifted my focus toward leaving town, Renata still on my mind. Sure enough, as soon as Tessa called me from Texas and said, "We're all settled into my new house here, come on down and meet up with me," I was on the next flight to Bush International. It was 1999, so I could spend six months on a visitor visa to the United States before having to go back to Canada. After that six months, I could cross the border, get my passport stamped, and then turn around and go back to the States for another six months. The six-month time limit reset every time I crossed the border, so I could spend as much time down there as I wanted as long as I visited home every once in a while.

Tessa helped me get a room at the Extended Stay America, which had a queen bed and kitchenette like my first place at the Howard Johnson in Markham. And it was only about two blocks away from the club, Treasures, where Tessa had been working. That night, she introduced me to the manager, who was thrilled to have me.

"If you can put on a show like Tessa," he said enthusiastically, "you're hired."

Treasures was a palatial, Roman-inspired topless club that had stages and a plush, luxurious champagne room like Whiskey A Go-Go. The girls wore sleek gowns. Big companies like Pepsi and 3M and Budweiser came in to entertain elite clients and associates, and if we got picked to go in the champagne room, we got paid from their expense accounts. These fellas' expense accounts seemed limitless!

The girls in Texas were all lazy; they weren't dancers and most of them avoided the stage altogether, instead trying to make money on the floor and in the champagne room. They came from all walks of life—many were Mexican immigrants, some were college girls trying to make money.

And about 150 girls worked every night. Even in the few weeks before I left Niagara Falls, I noticed how much more money I made with my new breasts, so I couldn't wait to flex them in this decadent, high-end gentlemen's club in the great state of Texas. The club manager wasn't so crazy about the rules. He let me work a few nights without a license, but then I had to register as a sex-trade worker with the Houston Department of Alcohol, Tobacco, and Firearms. This was different from other cities, where I had to register with the police. ATF sounded scary and very serious, but since clubs in the US deal with liquor, ATF is their ultimate governing authority. I hated getting licensed, in any country. I learned that my conscience needed to take the rest of the day off to shake off the process and reality.

Even when I was getting my license, my breasts did all the talking. The police officers were extra nice, falling all over themselves to fingerprint me. Men, no matter how professional the situation, can be so easily disarmed with breasts. I never really experienced that as a small-chested person. I had relied on athletic skill and my dancing ability, witty banter, but now I didn't have to worry about that anymore.

Seeing how easy it was to manipulate people with my body, I started to feel pretty untouchable. I was making three to four to five thousand dollars a night in USD at Treasures, and when I went on stage, I brought down the house because I was newly twenty-one and actually performing. Tessa had a little more trouble because she was older, so she started working at other less picky clubs in the area.

One girl I got to know in Houston was named Carla. She was from Seattle, Washington, and Carla had had every plastic surgery operation imaginable. She'd had a nose job, a chin job, a boob job, even injections in her buttocks to make it more plump and round. And Carla's main goal was finding a sugar daddy or many of them. She had told her parents she was going to university, but instead she was working in the club, trying to pick up rich men who would support her and take her out on dates and buy her expensive gifts. She didn't care about being an exotic entertainer, she only cared about meeting men tableside who she could hustle. I chalked it up to laziness. Carla didn't want to work that hard. She was really pretty with shoulder-bobbed jet black hair and she was two years older than me.

I, on the other hand, worked seventy-two days in a row. I showed up first thing in the morning so I could be there when the club opened at 11:00 a.m. for the lunch crowd. And I stayed through the afternoon when the big account executives started coming in to entertain clients. And I didn't cash out and leave until two or three in the morning. I felt like I could make my own money, just fine on my own. I didn't have to be like Carla. I didn't judge her too harshly, but when she needed another girl to entertain her sugar daddies' friends, I always declined. It just felt like that was one fancy step away from being a prostitute. Whereas at least as an entertainer, I could control how much money I made, who I was with, where I was at, and still leave and go home by myself every night, *in control of my own life.* Being at some lonely sap's beck and call mortified me.

Before long, the safe in my room at the Extended Stay America was so full of hundred-dollar bills that I couldn't fit anymore in it. I had so much USD money, I didn't know what to do with all those Benjamins. Although I worried about getting a bank account because I wasn't a citizen, Tessa assured me that yes, I could.

"Just go to Bank of America and open an account," she said. "But you'll want to keep the majority of your cash in a safe deposit box. Don't tell anyone about that money. They're not allowed to ask about what you keep in the safe deposit box."

I didn't know anything about money laundering or anything like that. In fact, I didn't even know that I was doing it at all. Our business was pure cash, and none of us had an accountant. But I did know that I didn't want to attract unwanted attention or get in trouble. So I took a bag full of cash to the bank, opened an account with $10,000 and put the rest in the safe deposit box. I was shocked when the banker led me to the safe deposit room, helped me open my box, and then left me alone to put whatever I wanted in there. No one was watching me. Then every two weeks, I emptied out the cash from my room safe, went to the bank, and put it in my box. The next problem was getting that money back to Canada.

I learned from Tessa that I could travel with $10,000 in cash on my person; any more than that, I would have to declare the asset and likely answer questions about where I got the money. For this exact reason, she said she always stopped in Vegas when she had *a lot of cash* to move because if she got questioned about it, she could say it was prize winnings and her travel itinerary would back that up. She said I could wire back home smaller amounts, like ten or fifteen thousand here and there to my bank account in Canada without it really popping any red flags. But if I were transferring twenty thousand or more, frequently at the same bank, someone might ask questions about where the money was coming from and whether or not I paid taxes on it. I didn't want to do that.

After working a few months in Texas, I called my dad and told him I wanted to come home for a visit. He and his wife Doris were getting ready for a trip to Vegas, so I said, "Great, I'll meet you there." I had never stopped to celebrate my birthday since turning seventeen. I found myself in the club every birthday night since then and once and awhile the club girls of that night would get a cupcake with a candle on it for me. I was excited to roll into Vegas with tons of cash and treat my parents to any shows that they wanted to see with the best seats in the house. Since my devil-may-care attitude lay down with Dad after Bolivia, he backed off of me. And we both just didn't talk about "it." My life, my choices, or any of it. This strange coping mechanism space that we resolved to occupy allowed him and us to accept each other.

By this time, I had turned twenty-one, and although everyone in my family knew my profession, no one had seen me since my operation. So we met up in Vegas, and I got a room next to theirs at the casino. My dad loved gambling, and we had a good time. Then on the flight back to Canada, I gave my Dad $10,000 to carry, I gave Doris $10,000, and I carried $10,000 myself. I deposited the cash in my account in Canada and figured out how to set up electronic funds transfers from my US bank so I could start moving my money from my safe deposit box to Canada.

Back in Bonnyville for Thanksgiving and the start of the holiday season, I wanted to see my family, but I didn't want my mom or any of my grandparents or anybody else to really know about my breast implants. So I bought big, heavy, fuzzy sweater vests to wear. If someone asked, I was forthcoming; my Auntie Brenda asked. But most people didn't. My brother was kind of creeped out by the whole thing, and my grandparents didn't ask either.

While I was home, I decided I wanted to get a new vehicle. I had my eye on a fancy Chevy short box 4x4 pickup truck with a high-performance engine and stereo system that I'd seen at the dealership in town, so I asked my dad to come with me. Debbie, the lady who owned the dealership with her father, was my dad's grad escort back in the day, so I could tell he wanted to impress her. I told her which truck I wanted and asked her to add a better stereo, bigger tires, and a few other extras with it. Debbie nodded and smiled, and then she asked if I wanted to lease it or get financing.

"No, I'm paying cash," I said. And I plopped $35,000 cash down on the counter when it was time to pay.

My dad changed his tone after that. I think he realized that not only was I wealthy, but I wasn't a huge drinker, I wasn't strung out on drugs, and my job wasn't really all that scary. Yes, I had to escape South America, but that was in the past. I told him about my boyfriend, Tom, who had a respectable career as a drug enforcement agent. I had plenty of time to come home and spend with family and help out on the farm or in Grandma Betty's kitchen and huge garden. He started to see that I was *truly okay*. And he loosened up and started treating me like a regular person, with respect. Our relationship actually became stronger.

§

A few weeks after my new vehicle purchase, I received a tin of luxury cookies in the mail from Tercier Motors and a lovely thank-you card expressing appreciation for my patronage. I mused that they were $35,000 cookies and shared them all with Porky at Grandma's kitchen table. Never experiencing anything that was remotely elegant in his entire life, Porky thought these were the most glorious shortbread cookies that he'd ever tasted.

Being back on the farm was amazing. At dinner time, I helped Grandma Betty cook and clean up, and I made her sit still and drink her tea while I washed all the dishes by hand. And Porky was so proud of me.

"Look at Dolly Girl," he whistled when he saw me. "She's so rich now."

And I replied, "Remember, Porky, when you used to tell me that you were going to sell me to a rich man in Bangladesh and be so wealthy? Now I'm the rich man from Bangladesh and you will never be poor again."

He laughed and laughed. And even my grandparents were happy for me. We didn't talk about my job or my lifestyle, but they could tell that I was happy and healthy. And they were thrilled I was spending time with them.

Even my aunts and uncles were totally fine with me hanging out with my little Kissel cousins, who were growing like weeds now. My cousin, Brett, who'd practically been a toddler the last time I saw him, was learning to play guitar. He played songs for us all and said he was going to be a country singer. I was in awe of how he and all my cousins were developing into kind, caring, and intelligent individuals.

Even though it was just Thanksgiving, I wanted to do something for Christmas because I was going to be with Tom in Florida for the holidays and the year 2000 turnover. So I bought seven gingerbread house kits, one for each of my Kissel cousins, and we spent two days building them and decorating them. I also bought two hundred dollars' worth of candy and adornments. We mixed the kits together and created not only gingerbread houses, but gingerbread castles. My grandma couldn't keep up making icing for all the candy decorations. We filled the kitchen table and had a wonderful time. And I felt so fortunate that I could come and go as I pleased, that I had my family's love and acceptance, and that I was still welcome at their table. I was fiercely proud of this new crop of little Kissels and felt blessed to spend time with them.

I didn't see my mom's side of the family much, which was okay. The Kissels accepted me. However, I wasn't so sure about the community at large. All my high school friends were in town for the holiday weekend, so they started calling and asking me to go out. But being seen and talking to people would mean confirming whatever rumours were floating around about me. Especially if they saw my new body. Although I could get on a plane and leave, my dad would have to bear the brunt of public scorn. So, I felt like I needed to talk to him before making any public appearances. I cared to help manage his lingering guilt and shame.

"Okay, so does everybody know what I do now?" I asked him.

"Yeah," he said, looking at the ground, "everybody knows." Talking about it was difficult for him, and he didn't want me to know how hard it was for him to wear that badge of shame—having a daughter who was a stripper—in our small town. But now that I was there, he could see it wasn't a big deal, and I was making all that money. So perhaps I had a glimmer of hope that if he could see I was still a decent person, that the rest of the community might see that too.

I put on my tightest top and winter coat and met up with some high school friends to hit both clubs in Bonnyville. Carla had taken me shopping in Houston to spend some of my "moldy money" as she called it, and I'd bought a Louis Vuitton handbag, Cartier bracelets, and a Rolex Lady Datejust, but generally I wasn't overly interested in luxury goods. Still, I stood out in Bonnyville, especially with my new body and my new ride. All of my girlfriends that I went to high school with said, "*Oh, my God, you look amazing!*"

I was the biggest thing to rock our little town in a while. Which wasn't saying much or hard to do. Everyone, all of a sudden, knew what I was doing, and everyone was completely fine with it. They were all so interested to hear about my life. No one rejected me; I was very much accepted and, oddly, became a source of fascination.

And as we hung out, some of my girlfriends started telling me how they really wanted breast implants, too. They opened their hearts and souls, telling me their deepest, darkest fantasies, and it seemed like I was the only one actually living the fantasy. They assumed that I was some sort of badass and proceeded to volunteer their most "badass" experiences since we'd seen each other last. I listened quietly. Nothing they shared was as wild and crazy as my stories, and I didn't want to correct them. I wanted to freeze them in my mind just the way they were, the way we all were at twenty-one years old. I knew then that their stories might end up being all they had coming up on their long, working stiff lives after their degrees were settled. I was definitely living in a real fantasy world. But it wasn't because I sought it out. When I looked back on it, it felt like a strange set of circumstances, one to the next, to the next, to the next, rolled into each other, *and there I was*. None of it was scripted or planned. I didn't know how to launder money; I didn't really want to get breast implants. I never planned on moving to Texas or meeting the Hells Angels or weird biker chicks or sugar babies or girls who were trafficked or athletes or account executives. I would've never asked for any of it in my wildest dreams. But it was happening to me, and moment to moment I was just learning how to navigate the situations I found myself in, like a chameleon.

14

CURTAIN CALL

"How much of my mother has my mother left in me?
How much of my love will be insane to some degree?
And what about this feeling that I'm never good enough?
Will it wash out in the water, or is it always in the blood?"
—John Mayer

ALTHOUGH THE EXTENDED STAY AMERICA had everything I needed, I started to feel like all I did was work and sleep and like I could use some company. Carla, who'd take me to all her favourite shopping destinations downtown and was always filling my pockets with concert tickets and other gifts from her sugar daddies, said I could move into her condo, which would be cheaper than the hotel and would give me someone to talk to when I wasn't at work. These perks were enough to overcome my hesitation about being so close to Carla's sugar baby lifestyle choices.

Carla was only working two nights a week at the club. On the other nights, while I was getting ready for work, she was waiting for a car to come pick her up and take her to whatever special friend she was seeing for the evening. Much of what she had been gifted was in exchange for her company. Her luxury condo, her jewelry collection, her designer clothing and accessories were all paid for by men who had enough money to keep a girl. She even had a Range Rover that a man let her drive as long as she went on three or four dates a month with him. She never thought of shoring up a savings account or investing, which was all I cared about. I didn't understand why she didn't want to make her own money and not have to worry about men and the provisions they doled out to her, whenever they felt like it. When I asked her if she'd ever marry any of her special friends, she said she'd consider it if it ever came up. But I think deep down we both knew that our kind of girls were *not the kind you married.*

Making friends at work, for me, was a completely different endeavour. Some of the patrons of the club in the VIP sections where we worked at Treasures were younger executive account salesmen for Coors, Budweiser, and Miller, and they became my friends. These guys came in to entertain clients, and I helped them achieve that. I'd pick all my favourite club girls to join my lucrative accounts. Then we'd all hang out at various hip-hop clubs on our off time in the vibrant city of Houston when they weren't being greasy salesman and I wasn't being an entertainer. "No—SLEEP—'til Brooklyn" blared in our favourite clubs and we'd dance for hours and hours. They loved having me as their braless, tight-T-shirt-and-apple-bottom-jeans-wearing friend. I helped them score all sorts of girls and I usually drove them home when they were too drunk and struck out. The best part was that, unlike Carla, I got to go home to my own bed every night. I felt very much in control of my own life.

One night, Carla had floor tickets to the Family Values Tour featuring all sorts of artists like Method Man and Limp Bizkit. She'd acquired them through one of her wealthy and well-connected special friends. And Carla was desperate to get backstage to hang out and party with all the artists.

"Why don't we flash our big boobs at the crowd," I volunteered. She loved the idea. So we found two really tall guys who looked like they weren't around any women, sidled up to them and smiled.

"Hey, can you lift us up on our shoulders?"

They—two brawny, Texas boys—took one look at us, and up on the shoulders we went. Then up went our shirts. The crowd around us went wild. God bless Texas. Then the Jumbotron started broadcasting us, and the whole stadium laughed and cheered. About five minutes later, bouncers were tapping on our shoulders and inviting us backstage. Everyone in the arena had seen us in our glory.

Carla pleaded for me to go with her. Although I had been happy to help her get the invitation, I didn't want to be caught up in the kind of whoring that I was pretty sure was going on backstage. We had just bared our breasts for an entire arena to see, and that was why they'd tapped us on the shoulder. What would they expect next? I was afraid of what I'd get myself into. Riding the line between wild fun and totally square felt okay, but I wanted to keep it at a distance. I really liked where my relationship with Tom was going. He seemed different—a normal guy in a normal job. I wasn't looking for anything I could find backstage at the Family Values Tour—Fred Durst or not. And I was a bit of a voyeur who preferred to watch rather than take part. So, I decided to stay with the two farm boys who'd lifted us up on their shoulders and party with them instead. I told Carla I'd see her in the morning. I reminded her that the club had marked us both down to work the prestigious and world-famous Houston Oil Show starting that week, and if she wanted to make astronomical money on the golf course with the oilmen, and snag her dream husband, then she'd better get back home on time.

Not long after I moved in with Carla, I was talking to Mack, one of the cooks at Treasures, about how he was signing up for a GED prep course at San Jacinto College. He'd never finished high school, but if he could take the class and pass the test, he could then start at a community college and maybe move up to a university after a couple years. The class was two nights a week for five weeks. Finishing high school had been in the back of my mind, and the class sounded manageable, so I asked him to get me an enrollment form when he picked his up.

I was surprised at how easy it was to enroll as a Canadian on a visitor visa. It was so easy that I started dreaming about how it could be my first step toward something better. On the San Jacinto campus, with its manicured gardens and quaint courtyard, the world felt full of possibility. I could maybe even enroll in the University of Miami and wear a Hurricanes sweater and live with Tom. I certainly had more than enough money to pay my tuition. Carla had told me about her aunt who married a Mexican man who'd been living in the United States undocumented for thirty-five years. He had children and worked, but never became an American citizen. Carla made living under the radar sound so easy and common that I started imagining myself in the American dream. And I kind of already was living it. I had lots of money. I didn't have to claim it. I even got a Texas identification card and driver's license. Still, I wanted to become a legitimate American citizen. I loved their food, their diversity, their people, their patriotic pride for their amazing country. We didn't have a lot of that in Canada. No flags on our front porches. Nothing but wheat fields, oil, and endless racism for our Indigenous populations, it seemed. Canada was boring and bland compared to the grandeur of the United States of America!

Our GED classes were easy. Lots of my fellow students struggled with literacy and English as a second language, but being bilingual and because French and Spanish are similar, I was able to pick up their Spanish and help them with their English. And it made me feel like I was capable of more than what I was doing.

But my fear of getting caught didn't fully subside. I didn't want Carla to find out about my GED program because, helpful as she was, I didn't feel I could fully trust her. I had trouble trusting anyone, always kept that guarded distance and didn't divulge too much. I didn't want her to have any leverage over me because she could report me to any number of organizations that I didn't even know existed. If she reported me to authorities who came after illegal aliens or tax evaders, then what would I do? Call Tom and beg him to use his position to get me out of trouble? That would be the ultimate mortification. So I kept Carla, and other people, at a distance. We were like ships passing in the night anyway. I was often up and out of our apartment, heading to work while she was still sleeping off the night before. Many days I didn't see her at all. And I gave San Jacinto Mack's address to mail my GED test results.

A few days after the test, I came into work and found Mack with two envelopes in his hand.

"Look," he said. "I got our results back." Anxious to see the results, we opened our envelopes together. And, of course, we both passed.

I was so excited to have my general education diploma from the great state of Texas or as I called it: my "good enough diploma"—GED. And I started envisioning what avenues I could pursue and what shape my life could take in the future. I could get mature student status, go to school in Miami, and spend the summer working in Texas while school was out of session. This would put me closer to Tom, which I was sure he would want, too. I had always been fascinated by people, so I could study anthropology or sociology or journalism and apply that fascination. During this time, nearby Texas A&M University suffered a giant loss when their annual Aggie Bonfire construction collapsed, killing twelve students. My heart grieved for them and all of Houston was immensely saddened.

§

I couldn't wait to go see Tom and tell him all about my GED. Since moving to Texas, I'd been visiting him once a month or every six weeks and staying for a week or so. This would prove to him that I wasn't just a big-breasted airhead; I had dreams and funny and smart things to say. And with his help, I was sure I could upgrade my visitor visa to a student visa.

When I flew to Florida and told him about all of this, he was excited for me. But at the same time, I could see in his eyes a flicker of the same hesitation I saw in Ryan's eyes every time I tried to pay for his dinner. At this time, Tom and I had known each other for about two years, and we had gone on so many adventures. We'd had endless and steamy Miami nights in the clubs. We'd talked about everything under the sun and bonded at extreme levels. So, I wasn't quite sure what his hesitation was about. He was happy for me, and I could tell he cared for me, but maybe I was moving way too fast for him.

We went down to one of Tom's cop friend's places in Key Largo, where we all sat down with cocktails in his living room. While the men talked and smoked their cigars, I picked up and thumbed through one of several books he had sitting on his coffee table. There was a stack of classic coffee table books highlighting all the underwater world treasures and some by India Hicks, a famous Caribbean designer that I liked. I immediately chose the textbook on money laundering, which stood out to me among the lifestyle and sailing magazines. Jared, the cop friend, said in all the years and parties he'd had, no one had ever picked up that book before. They laughed because they knew what I did for a living and suspected that I made a lot of money, even though it was never talked about. Mostly they found it funny that out of all the reading material on the table—books about beautiful beaches, yachts, and tropical fish—why would anyone want to look at the money laundering textbook? It was funny and a bit of a dig all at the same time. We all laughed, and they seem to find hilarity in me. I was always the youngest in Tom's crowds. I know they liked this about me because it put them in a position of power. Cops liked power and control, just like the Hells Angels did. I could see that all—day—long. The discerning element, of course, was who fought on the good side and who fought on the bad side, but they *both* enjoyed power and control. While I regarded Tom as very accomplished, with his master's in criminology and career rising up the ranks with US Customs, I started to see a different side of him. *He liked me fun.* He liked me crazy. He liked my big breasts—couldn't stop touching them. This was the same guy who also said to me that I didn't need them. I was perfect the way I was—until I got them. My gut sensed that maybe Tom didn't like the part of me that was starting to reach for more intellectual topics and exploration and development of my own character.

I became desperate to prove to Tom that I wasn't just a party girl, or a just a good time. I started to really think no man was ever sincere. None of them, no matter what they said, no matter what went on, their visceral, primal, biological, visual selves dominated almost everything else. I had seen the smartest high-ranking executives be rendered completely childish when a really beautiful woman was in front of them. It seemed like it just tampered with their cognitive ability to focus on anything else of substance or worthy of merit.

I didn't want to see this line of thought, though. I didn't want to think that Tom was perhaps the same as Ryan or any man I'd met. I idolized Tom. I thought his elite government position and strong moral compass to live by pure truth was always so inspiring. So, I dropped it and spent the rest of the visit partying.

Tom and I continued to have wild adventures all over the gator-ridden state of Florida. Once while attending a Jimmy Buffet concert in West Palm Beach, I saw another example of his moral compass made of steel. As we sat on the sprawling lawns waiting for Buffet to come on, the nice older couple seated next to us fired up a stick of devil's lettuce. As we chatted with them and the skunky smoke wafted towards us on our blanket, I wondered how Tom would react to this situation. Would he bust out his badge and arrest them? They were so kind and sweet, simple concert fans. Then the woman offered me a pull from her joint by passing it to me. Eager to fit in and relax on the hot lawn, I grabbed it. But I instantly froze as I looked at Tom for an indication of "yay" or "nay." He looked away slightly embarrassed and whispered in my ear.

"You can have some if you like, but I can't be near you if you do. I can't be a witness to this, or I could lose my job," he stated kindly and without judgement.

"Really, Tom, who's going to know? I'm certainly not going to tell anyone and neither are these people that we don't even know," I implored, growing annoyed. He looked away, and I handed back the weed. I immediately felt like I should remain on his team and support his lifestyle and job commitments.

But I sure loved Florida's restaurants on the causeways and channel boat life and Friday nights in Coconut Grove or Key West. We rang in the year 2000 on South Beach and partied to Silverchair and Will Smith's "Miami": "Party in the city where the heat is on, all night on the street till the break of dawn. Welcome to Miami, Bienvenidos a Miami." Nothing beats Miami nights when you're twenty-one with a size-two body with double D breasts. Nothing.

But I couldn't help feeling like I was being used all over the place for the idea of what I was, not who I actually was or desired to become. Tom didn't really care that I said smart things. Or did he? Maybe he, too, just really liked that I was really good-looking and nice arm candy to show to guys in the club or out on the beach. Tom liked my looks best, just like the guys in the strip club. He was an Alpha male, proficient and visual. I never counted on Tom being like regular guys. Regular guys to me were my work life—the ones I loved to use and exploit, to fake laugh at their jokes and take all their money. I started looking for that authenticity, and I thought I found it with Tom.

I started to notice a new, unsettled feeling though. It deeply rattled me. I'd always been good at being on my own. I'd always been good at sleeping in an apartment with literally just a mattress on the floor, a sink, and a toilet. I never needed anything more than that. I loved my oodles and oodles of alone time. But one morning I woke up at 5:00 a.m. to catch a flight from Fort Lauderdale Airport, connected in Minnesota, and then landed in Edmonton a few hours later. That night, I was tucked into my bed at the farm. I'd gone from one world to another all on the same day. I noticed as soon as I closed my eyes that I wished to be back in Florida, and I had literally just gotten home.

Then the same phenomena happened in reverse. I'd leave the farm early in the morning, drive to Edmonton, catch a flight, connect in Minnesota or New Jersey, and arrive in Florida that evening. And I don't know if it was the amount of travel, or going from snow on the farm to beach and sunshine and palm trees. But as soon as I would get back to Tom's place, I felt instantly unsettled too, like I couldn't wait to go back to the farm. I'd never experienced this before in my life. And I couldn't figure out why it was happening. Suddenly, I hated being all alone. I couldn't turn off my mind and anxiety started to creep in anytime it was quiet and I was alone.

The only place I didn't feel that way was in Houston, Texas, because there life was all about work, work, work. Texas also reminded me of home on the prairie lands of Alberta—cattle ranches, oil wells with big personalities everywhere. But when I was either in my personal life at home in Canada or in my personal life with Tom in Florida, something felt severely disconnected. It was like looking out a window and expecting to see something else. I started to realize it was because I didn't have a plan. I didn't know what I was doing with my life.

I knew Tom cared for me, but I suspected that I was getting all I would ever get from him. He wouldn't say, "Yes, move to Florida, get your own place, go to school, let's be together." But he always wanted to doll me up and take me out for a night with his friends. Sometimes it felt no different from a night working at Treasures in Houston, where I was an important prop in a life they wanted to live. No matter what, I was the young, dumb, hot girl. This unsettled feeling of going back and forth without any real direction lasted for months. But I started to feel, at twenty-one years old, that I needed to make a plan for my life because I couldn't do this forever. And I didn't want to do this forever. And I would never appreciate being this dumb prop like Carla. I couldn't tell just yet, but I felt it was going to be curtain call for Alexa sometime soon.

Everything started to feel so false. The most honest interactions I had were at the club, where everyone knew what I did. I was an entertainer of the topless variety. That's why I was there, and boys came into the club looking for *just that*. It was incredibly straightforward. There were no lies, no deception. It was all laid out, easy and straightforward.

Those guys went there to entertain clients with naked girls, and they paid for it. It was very simple. I found it so ironic that that was where I felt the most honest and sincere with my own character. I only felt used and like I wasn't in control of the situation when I was with Tom and his friends. Older men with young girlfriends have a visceral desire to be "the man." They don't love being challenged. Sometimes it comes from liking being wanted and needed, but most often it's because *young girls are not challenging*. They're not as experienced and easier to manipulate; they're less likely to throw out alternative opinions. Tom was a cop who possibly got used to total control, and maybe I had been unwilling or too blind to see this before. I don't think that was Tom's intention or his friends' intention. Maybe it wasn't about control, maybe he just wanted to have fun forever? But I started to see how regular guys were just not that impressive. They could be easily disarmed and dismantled with a safe, dumb laugh at their jokes or breasts in their face. It was so simple it was nauseating. Who needs that? I concluded that Tom was likely going to break a few more hearts in his lifetime. I decided firmly that I wanted to do me; but first I had to figure out what that was.

I came to understand that my innards never really matched my exterior shell. Outside I had curves and a pretty face. Inside, I was coursing with too much unchecked *male energy*. Fight or flight energy, reptilian brain always on overdrive. I typically thought like a boy; like an *opportunist, and a mercenary*. I even looked like a boy until I was twelve. On the farm, growing up, my family didn't care much to entertain gender-assigned roles. If I wanted to help with farm work, it was always just as welcome as sewing or gardening with Grandma Betty or Mémère Anita. But the root of my androgyny was laid down with my mother and all those years spent in her charge. Françoise taught me how to survive without a man, and the importance of making your own money. She was my dad, she was my teacher, she was brazened, and she could be extremely violent and volatile.

Unfortunately, that was about all the value that I would understand from years spent with her.

Maybe there was much more to her and maybe I was onto something about my burgeoning thoughts about androgyny? I loved the disarming shell I had going, it was a *good tool*. A real door-opener. It was also good to fool any boy or any man. And on the inside, if I was just like them, I could understand them best. I would never be that hapless, gooey, crying mess of a woman who'd just gotten dumped. I didn't even know what that felt like. I never wanted to either. It looked painful and confusing and stuck on *defense* rather than the *offense*. That just always looked like weakness taking over. *Girl* feelings and energy were always too much for me. But, I learned young and from Françoise, that having lots of money afforded choice, and if you had choice, you had freedom—and it seemed that no part of that was fed by female energies.

§

I started thinking about repairing my relationship with my mother, and started to see that maybe I'd been blaming her when really she was trapped in a system of power and control herself, where she was being used too. Maybe I had lots of masculine energy, just like her, always trying hard to impress a man and only sometimes they'd notice. My grandfather needed her to be a good little soldier and make that money for the family. And *she was human*. She got a divorce when she was very, very young. I started to think of my mother in a totally different light. I stopped feeling sympathy for myself and I felt sympathy for her, living her whole life under some man's thumb. She never escaped. She never went her own way. She had another person's version laid out for her to step in and exist. Did she ever even want what she was doing? Did she ever feel regret, like I felt? I knew that I still had a long way to go before I could ever understand why *she didn't want me*. Or why we failed to bond properly as mother and baby. Maybe it came at the expense of her having to be both Mom and Dad to us? My mother was the patriarch in our immediate family, for my brother and me. She was so much male energy with only a smattering of female energy. I adopted that somewhere along the way and saw the incredible power that this could bear over men. Weak men, I learned, were looking for strong partners or "mamas," usually because their own male energy was vibrationally low. Or, adversely, they were Alpha males, exploding with male energy and merely looking to partner with more of it for the addiction of extremism. Both of those reasonings about men read as "dumb" or "weak" to me.

§

I know that *something broke inside of me* at the butcher shop. I traced my inability to form real relationships back to there. That's where all my excess male energy was sprouted. Back to standing up to my mom, battling my inner-self voice (her voice) that screamed at me to do better, be better. Maybe while I was peeling back hides from fat layers or ripping muscle tissue from bone is where I somehow *detached?* Humans are animals too. Just at the top of the cognitive capability of the food chain. Our human brains are wild, beasty, competitive, and primal. Humans will typically be hunter or prey too. My primal instinct to provide for myself was always my constant companion. I knew I needed to think and be this way to survive. I liked being the *hunter*. I certainly was not going to be Tom's doe-eyed prey.

I realized I had a choice. I didn't have to succumb to that relationship dynamic, with my family or my romantic relationships. I could take care of myself. And there was no way I could have a normal life if I continued to be an exotic entertainer. No man or future partner was ever going to see me for more than that. I knew, because males are too primal, often ruled by their reptilian brain. I'd seen it enough times to know that this was fact. I could take all of my money and use it to feed my mind, to grow my character, live the cliché of the stripper putting herself through school. Except in my cliché, I'd saved on the upfront.

That's when I decided to have the talk with Tom. I certainly loved him, and I felt that he loved me, despite his hesitation. So, one night after dinner, I told him that I was feeling incredibly unsettled. I told him that when I was at home on the farm in Canada, I couldn't wait to be in Florida, with him. And when I was with him, I couldn't wait to be back on the farm in Canada. I told him I needed to figure out my life. I needed roots or something to grab onto that was more than just another good time.

"You have a career. You have good friends. You have a house. You have your life all settled. I don't have any of that," I mustered. "And I want to do that with you. I want to go to school and be here with you, or I'm going back to Canada to go to school there."

I told him everything that had been in my heart for so many months and asked him to throw down on a relationship with me. Tom didn't really know what to say. I think he was completely taken aback, and the thought of fun time ending for half of a second and having a serious talk was maybe a little too much for him. We talked about it, didn't get anywhere, and the next morning he got up and went to work.

Then that evening when he came home, I said, "So what do you think about everything we talked about last night?"

"Yeah," he said. "I think it's important that if you continue to stay in the United States that you do it the right way. It's time to upgrade your visa. You should go to school, get your own place here in Florida."

Basically, he repeated back to me all the things I told him I wanted to do. He stopped short of making any promises or offering to be a part of my life while I did it. So I heard him out, and thought, Okay, sounds good, heard you loud and clear, Mister Forever Bachelor.

His half-hearted response woke me up. Why was I investing so much of myself in him when he just wanted to be a playboy forever? As long as I was willing to be a part of that narrative, he was fine with it. I, too, was still in that party phase. After all, I was the one who was twenty-one and he was approaching his mid-thirties. I suddenly felt sad for him. I still wanted to adventure and scuba dive and check out all of the Florida and naked yacht parties on the water for Columbus Day and all of that type of hype. I wanted to do all of that too. Until I started to realize that there was no way that my delusional ideas of maybe getting married to him and continuing this fun, adventurous journey in a real relationship was what he was after. He didn't even have to come out and say it. He loved the fantasy. He loved the beauty on display and endless nights of fun. And it alarmed me. It felt like he was no different from any of the men who went into strip clubs. If I wanted to grow as a person, I had to count on myself. And I started to make that plan.

Later that night I booked my tickets back home to Canada, and when I got into Edmonton, I found an apartment in the city, straightaway. I didn't want to reach out to Shay or Jolene or anyone from my start-up stripper life anymore. I felt like nothing would have changed with them and they'd likely stay the same forever. I wanted to use my money to start constructing some sort of a life and leave my last few years behind me forever. Because if I didn't, a stripper is all I'd ever be to anyone else I loved. Men would always want to be with me, touch me, date me, sleep with me, but they'd never want to marry me or build a life with me. I wasn't ready to get married, but I was ready for more depth. And if I ever wanted to have a long, stable relationship and maybe have children someday, it wouldn't happen if I was a stripper.

I cast a net over some of the people that I had gone to high school with to see who was still living in Edmonton and maybe still going to university. By this time, they were working on their master's or finishing up their four-year degrees. Elaine, one of my close friends from when we were little, heard I was looking for a roommate and contacted me. I still needed to go back to Texas to close out my life down there, so I gave her the key to the apartment and told her I'd see her in a month or so. I reassured her that I'd furnish our entire place with new furniture and decor upon return.

I flew back to Houston and worked for a few more weeks while I closed out my life in America. I packed my stuff into suitcases and got out of Carla's. And I said goodbye to everybody I knew—Carla, all of the people I got to know in the clubs, Mack and the DJs, even my favourite grocery store people and banking clerks. They had all become like a family to me. And many of the girls at work joined together, got me a great big card and a sheet cake. Everyone gave me their phone numbers and insisted I keep in touch. It was wonderful and bittersweet because I knew that I'd never look them up.

§

I recognized that the demand for live nude entertainment was dying and about to be replaced by online pornography which was newly exploding. There would be reduced capacity to pull *this kind* of money out of the trade soon. I felt it. I was about to get out while the timing was ripe. I lived through the last "belle époque" of the burlesque movement. It started out by showing a tiny bit of ankle in the mid 1880s and was collapsing in a cesspool of dissolved fantasy by the year 2000. There is a definite and *cautionary warning* to all human exploration. Nudity was no exception. The peak was about to pass and too much had been revealed and nothing was sexy anymore. There's an old saying in the theatre community: *"Don't sit too close to the ballet, it spoils the show."* Now that the mystique of what came slightly above the ankle was revealed, raped by human zealousness and society's push to explore and demand more from our sexualities . . . the subtle art of seduction was subsequently and forever ruined.

Getting on the plane home to Canada felt different. I was flying back to my new life, to my new Edmonton apartment, to my new school at NorQuest College. After settling into my seat and performing my lengthy OCD flight safety ritual, I looked out the window with my head on the thick plastic glass and for the first time started to process the events of the past four years. All of it. Ryan, Tom, Shay, Carla, Annika—would I ever see these people again? I didn't think so. At twenty-one, my life was technically just starting. But those years felt like I'd just simply *pressed pause* on real life. Leaving the farm, the oilfield. Leaving Ryan, Shay, Annika, Tom. Leaving everyone right where they would stay forever in my mind and right at our last words spoken.

I worried that Shay would get gobbled up by the Hells Angels forever and never get to be a real mother. I wanted Ryan to find a good girl who was stable and easy to love. I prayed that Annika would become a psychologist like she so strongly desired. Carla, I hoped, would find her own two feet someday. And Tom—I wished for him to stay safe, out of bullets' way, and to rise up high with the mighty United States government as the champion I knew him to be: a forever good guy. I was so excited to say goodbye to Tom, bittersweet as it was. But he taught me a lot. He helped me grow up. He helped me see a different life, and I'll always be thankful for that, for him and the time that we had together. I would say he was the first time that I ever felt like I was deeply in love.

I decided that I liked the pause button. It allows you to never fully deal with anything and to just keep going on some other track. What a snappy feature on life's great big mixed media stereo. I had hit pause, cut, and run every chance I got for as long as I could remember. Detachment followed every time. Was I ever fully attached to these people? Probably not, as I never had any trouble leaving them. I certainly loved them. I loved every one of them immensely, but I don't think they could really tell. This made me feel incredibly sad. I still didn't know how to make authentic connections. I still had a long way to go on that front. I hoped that they could tell how much I loved them, how I deeply appreciated them, and how each of them helped me grow. They were all weird too, like me. Each with their own respective, glorious weird. If we are in fact the sum of who we've spent time with, then my final balance of the equation was *incalculable*.

There's a consequence to using the pause button too much, though. You never get resolve. You won't make it to the end of the song with some people or lifestyles. And maybe that was okay.

But what did I want for me? I knew that I ached for my aunties and everyone in my giant family—my little cousins who were older now, my grandparents, and Porky. I was ready to overcompensate for lack of protection for Maurice, too. I'd spoil him every chance I got, and I left him when he may have needed me most. I would never leave him again. That was a good start, I decided.

The past four years made little sense. Trying to map it felt like trying to follow a honeybee home. Swirly twirly paths leading to psychedelic gardens to explore but only for a few nips at each bud. The pause button could be another word for sabbatical. Maybe that's all this was? A giant, unplanned, unscripted sabbatical. However, my sabbatical happened to hit at the prime of my coming of age journey. I laughed at the word—sabbatical! That was what forty-year-olds did, wasn't it? When they had enough of their heavy, adult lives and screwed it all to recharge, re-center, reconnect, *or get to know themselves*. I could identify with this. I was young, but my body felt used and tired. Intense dance routines performed several times a day, long hours talking, talking, talking in clubs, jumping off yachts into the ocean, in and out of airports, needles in the lips and major surgery—I needed a break. A long one. I needed a break from my sabbatical. A break from my body and a tune-in to my mind. I was so ready for it. I came, I saw, and I lived through a peculiar period, with even more peculiar types of people.

§

It became clear to me with eyes closed, head resting on that thick plexiglass airplane window. Every trauma-filled moment of my little girl life flashed before my mind's big screen TV. The traumatic disconnect of family at five years old. The toxic detachment of the Mother-Child bond. Animal flesh. Escaping South America. Good guys. Bad guys. Good things and bad things. I ran fearlessly down the gullet of all of it. For the first time, stopping to digest it all, I truly surprised myself with the journey. Detachment somehow makes you immune to fear. It allows you to mobilize into waters where others dare not swim. And I was glad for the dip. I felt little shame or remorse for the journey behind me.

Now I needed a stable home, and I was going to make one for myself. One that felt endlessly comfortable, a place for my worn-out soul. A home that could give me my kind of solid roots required. Weird sparkly and sequined roots. I had spent my young life wishing to be normal, not spent with an abusive mother and from a broken home, in a butcher shop while taking care of my brother. I spent my coming of age in seedy strip clubs, from Canada to South America. And I learned that there was no such thing as normal. And why would you want it anyway? Normal was a sham. Normal was bullshit to begin with. There is little sunshine to be found in Normal Land. Even normal people seek out weird—boy, do they ever! That's where the fun is. I was creative and financially free; I hoped Virginia Woolf would be proud of me.

As American Airlines touched down in YEG International Airport, I was confident that I was a weirdo. There was nothing ever normal about me—who I was born and assigned to, what I'd ever done. I was going to be a weirdo, possibly forever. And for the first time in my life, I was okay with that. I was intensely excited to be a weirdo in disguise at my new college and in my new life. Would anyone be able to tell? Always a chameleon, I would certainly put on a show.

ABOUT THE AUTHOR

Carmen Kissel-Verrier was born in rural Alberta, Canada. These days, she is a technical writer and a graduate of Mount Royal University. Carmen still loves a wild time spent with peculiar people and appreciates a good ribeye steak. She remains fascinated by the diversity of the human spirit. Carmen lives with her husband and their two children on the shoreline of Moose Lake, Alberta. *The Butcher Shop Girl* is her first book.

TheButcherShopGirl.com